A Declaration by the Representatives of the UNITED STATES OF AMERICA, in General Congress assembled.

When in the course of human events it becomes necessary for one people to dissolve the political bands which have connected them with another, and to assume among the powers of the earth the separate and equal station to which the laws of nature & of nature's god entitle them, a decent respect to the opinions of mankind requires that they should declare the causes which impel them to the separation.

We hold these truths to be self-evident; that all men are created equal & independent, that from that equal creation they derive rights inherent & inalienable, among which are the preservation of life, & liberty, & the pursuit of happiness; that to secure these ends, governments are instituted among men, deriving their just powers from the consent of the governed; that whenever any form of government becomes destructive of these ends, it is the right of the people to alter or to abolish it, & to institute new government, laying it's foundation on such principles & organising it's powers in such form, as to them shall seem most likely to effect their safety & happiness. prudence indeed will dictate that governments long established should not be changed for light & transient causes: and accordingly all experience hath shewn that mankind are more disposed to suffer while evils are sufferable, than to right themselves by abolishing the forms to which they are accustomed. but when a long train of abuses & usurpations [begun at a distinguished period, &] pursuing invariably the same object, evinces a design to reduce them under absolute Despotism, it is their right, it is their duty, to throw off such & it to provide new guards for their future security. such has

Die „Geburtsurkunde" der USA: Thomas Jeffersons Unabhängigkeitserklärung im handschriftlichen Entwurf, mit Ergänzungen von Benjamin Franklin und (nicht auf der Abbildung) John Adams. Dies ist das erste politische Dokument, in dem die Menschenrechte und das Recht auf Widerstand gegen die Regierung formuliert sind.

The Declaration of Independence – shown here in Thomas Jefferson's first draft along with Franklin's emendations – was the product of the authors' remarkable political imagination and their thoroughgoing knowledge of the philosophies of Europe's Age of Enlightenment.

Zweihundert Jahre deutsch-amerikanische Beziehungen
Two Hundred Years of German-American Relations

1776-1976

Eine Dokumentation mit 391 Abbildungen im Text und auf Tafeln
A documentary with 391 illustrations and plates

Herausgegeben von Thomas Piltz
General Editor Thomas Piltz

Heinz Moos Verlag München

Mitarbeiter/Contributors:

Donald Arthur   Lothar Bähren   Liselotte
Barth-Flacke   Jeffrey van Davis   Angela
Djuren   Anita Eichholz   Helmut Färber
Louisa Fleischman   Wolfgang J. Fuchs
Uschi Gnade   Peter Hahn   Armin Herrmann
Hans H. Hofstätter   Hans Jaeger   Maddalena
Kerrh   Michael Köhler   Till Leberecht
Lahusen   Julius Lengert   Bernhard Matt
Reinhard Paesler   Christoph Peters   Thomas
Piltz   Gert Raeithel   Wolfram von Raven
Patricia Reber   Ursel Richter   Leibl
Rosenberg   Bernd Rüster   Dieter Seelmann
Traudl Seifert   Alfons Schulze-Dieckhoff
Adelheid Schwark   Ulrike Stadler   Sigfred
Taubert   Horst Ueberhorst   Birgit Wagner-
Gelberg   Bernhard Wittek   Rüdiger Wersich

Übersetzung/Translation:

Deutsche Originalbeiträge wurden übersetzt von:
Louise Fontaine, Renata Lenart.
Louis Bloom: Editor.

Englische Originalbeiträge wurden übersetzt von:
German translations:
Uschi Gnade

Redaktion/Editorial Staff:

Wolfgang J. Fuchs   Michael Köhler
Till Leberecht Lahusen   Thomas Piltz
Elke von Schulz

Printed in the Federal Republic of Germany

Die Satzarbeiten besorgte das Typostudio
Schumacher-Gebler, München, unter
Verwendung der Baskerville. Reproduktionen:
Repro Center Färber & Co., München.
Gedruckt auf holzfrei weiß Samt-Offset durch
Gebrüder Bremberger, München. Einband:
Conzella Verlagsbuchbinderei Urban Meister,
München

ISBN: 3-7879-0092-6

IN CONGRESS, JULY 4, 1776.

The unanimous Declaration of the thirteen united States of America.

When in the Course of human events, it becomes necessary for one people to dissolve the political bands which have connected them with another, and to assume among the powers of the earth, the separate and equal station to which the Laws of Nature and of Nature's God entitle them, a decent respect to the opinions of mankind requires that they should declare the causes which impel them to the separation.

We hold these truths to be self-evident, that all men are created equal, that they are endowed by their Creator with certain unalienable Rights, that among these are Life, Liberty and the pursuit of Happiness.—That to secure these rights, Governments are instituted among Men, deriving their just powers from the consent of the governed,—That whenever any Form of Government becomes destructive of these ends, it is the Right of the People to alter or to abolish it, and to institute new Government, laying its foundation on such principles and organizing its powers in such form, as to them shall seem most likely to effect their Safety and Happiness. Prudence, indeed, will dictate that Governments long established should not be changed for light and transient causes; and accordingly all experience hath shewn, that mankind are more disposed to suffer, while evils are sufferable, than to right themselves by abolishing the forms to which they are accustomed. But when a long train of abuses and usurpations, pursuing invariably the same Object evinces a design to reduce them under absolute Despotism, it is their right, it is their duty, to throw off such Government, and to provide new Guards for their future security.—Such has been the patient sufferance of these Colonies; and such is now the necessity which constrains them to alter their former Systems of Government. The history of the present King of Great Britain is a history of repeated injuries and usurpations, all having in direct object the establishment of an absolute Tyranny over these States. To prove this, let Facts be submitted to a candid world.

He has refused his Assent to Laws, the most wholesome and necessary for the public good.

He has forbidden his Governors to pass Laws of immediate and pressing importance, unless suspended in their operation till his Assent should be obtained; and when so suspended, he has utterly neglected to attend to them.

He has refused to pass other Laws for the accommodation of large districts of people, unless those people would relinquish the right of Representation in the Legislature, a right inestimable to them and formidable to tyrants only.

He has called together legislative bodies at places unusual, uncomfortable, and distant from the depository of their public Records, for the sole purpose of fatiguing them into compliance with his measures.

He has dissolved Representative Houses repeatedly, for opposing with manly firmness his invasions on the rights of the people.

He has refused for a long time, after such dissolutions, to cause others to be elected; whereby the Legislative powers, incapable of Annihilation, have returned to the People at large for their exercise; the State remaining in the mean time exposed to all the dangers of invasion from without, and convulsions within.

He has endeavoured to prevent the population of these States; for that purpose obstructing the Laws for Naturalization of Foreigners; refusing to pass others to encourage their migrations hither, and raising the conditions of new Appropriations of Lands.

He has obstructed the Administration of Justice, by refusing his Assent to Laws for establishing Judiciary powers.

He has made Judges dependent on his Will alone, for the tenure of their offices, and the amount and payment of their salaries.

He has erected a multitude of New Offices, and sent hither swarms of Officers to harrass our people, and eat out their substance.

He has kept among us, in times of peace, Standing Armies without the Consent of our legislatures.

He has affected to render the Military independent of and superior to the Civil power.

He has combined with others to subject us to a jurisdiction foreign to our constitution, and unacknowledged by our laws; giving his Assent to their Acts of pretended Legislation:

For Quartering large bodies of armed troops among us:

For protecting them, by a mock Trial, from punishment for any Murders which they should commit on the Inhabitants of these States:

For cutting off our Trade with all parts of the world:

For imposing Taxes on us without our Consent:

For depriving us in many cases, of the benefits of Trial by jury:

For transporting us beyond Seas to be tried for pretended offences:

For abolishing the free System of English Laws in a neighbouring Province, establishing therein an Arbitrary government, and enlarging its Boundaries so as to render it at once an example and fit instrument for introducing the same absolute rule into these Colonies:

For taking away our Charters, abolishing our most valuable Laws, and altering fundamentally the Forms of our Governments:

For suspending our own Legislatures, and declaring themselves invested with power to legislate for us in all cases whatsoever.

He has abdicated Government here, by declaring us out of his Protection and waging War against us.

He has plundered our seas, ravaged our Coasts, burnt our towns, and destroyed the lives of our people.

He is at this time transporting large Armies of foreign Mercenaries to compleat the works of death, desolation and tyranny, already begun with circumstances of Cruelty & perfidy scarcely paralleled in the most barbarous ages, and totally unworthy the Head of a civilized nation.

He has constrained our fellow Citizens taken Captive on the high Seas to bear Arms against their Country, to become the executioners of their friends and Brethren, or to fall themselves by their Hands.

He has excited domestic insurrections amongst us, and has endeavoured to bring on the inhabitants of our frontiers, the merciless Indian Savages, whose known rule of warfare, is an undistinguished destruction of all ages, sexes and conditions.

In every stage of these Oppressions We have Petitioned for Redress in the most humble terms: Our repeated Petitions have been answered only by repeated injury. A Prince, whose character is thus marked by every act which may define a Tyrant, is unfit to be the ruler of a free people.

Nor have We been wanting in attentions to our Brittish brethren. We have warned them from time to time of attempts by their legislature to extend an unwarrantable jurisdiction over us. We have reminded them of the circumstances of our emigration and settlement here. We have appealed to their native justice and magnanimity, and we have conjured them by the ties of our common kindred to disavow these usurpations, which, would inevitably interrupt our connections and correspondence. They too have been deaf to the voice of justice and of consanguinity. We must, therefore, acquiesce in the necessity, which denounces our Separation, and hold them, as we hold the rest of mankind, Enemies in War, in Peace Friends.

We, therefore, the Representatives of the united States of America, in General Congress, Assembled, appealing to the Supreme Judge of the world for the rectitude of our intentions, do, in the Name, and by Authority of the good People of these Colonies, solemnly publish and declare, That these United Colonies are, and of Right ought to be Free and Independent States; that they are Absolved from all Allegiance to the British Crown, and that all political connection between them and the State of Great Britain, is and ought to be totally dissolved; and that as Free and Independent States, they have full Power to levy War, conclude Peace, contract Alliances, establish Commerce, and to do all other Acts and Things which Independent States may of right do.—And for the support of this Declaration, with a firm reliance on the protection of divine Providence, we mutually pledge to each other our Lives, our Fortunes and our sacred Honor.

John Hancock

Button Gwinnett
Lyman Hall
Geo Walton.

Wm Hooper
Joseph Hewes,
John Penn

Edward Rutledge.

Thos Heyward Junr.
Thomas Lynch Junr.
Arthur Middleton

Samuel Chase,
Wm Paca
Thos Stone
Charles Carroll of Carrollton

George Wythe
Richard Henry Lee
Th Jefferson
Benja Harrison
Thos Nelson jr.
Francis Lightfoot Lee
Carter Braxton

Robt Morris
Benjamin Rush
Benja Franklin
John Morton
Geo Clymer
Jas Smith.
Geo Taylor
James Wilson
Geo. Ross
Caesar Rodney
Geo Read
Tho M:Kean

Wm Floyd
Phil. Livingston
Frans Lewis
Lewis Morris

Richd Stockton
Jno Witherspoon
Fras Hopkinson
John Hart
Abra Clark

Josiah Bartlett
Wm Whipple
Saml Adams
John Adams
Robt Treat Paine
Elbridge Gerry
Step Hopkins
William Ellery
Roger Sherman
Sam el Huntington
Wm Williams
Oliver Wolcott
Matthew Thornton

4. Juli 1776: Die Unterzeichnung der Unabhängig-
keitserklärung vor dem Kongreß der 13 Staaten in Phila-
delphia. Thomas Jefferson, damals 33 Jahre alt, später
der dritte Präsident der USA, legt das Dokument John
Hancock zur Unterzeichnung vor. Rechts neben ihm
Benjamin Franklin, ganz links in der Gruppe John
Adams, später zweiter Präsident der USA. Gemälde von
John Trumbull (1756–1843).

July 4, 1776 – the signing of the Declaration of Independence. John Trumbull's famous painting shows the
president of the congress and first signatory, John Hancock, seated facing the author of the Declaration, Thomas
Jefferson, fourth from left in the central group, with his
collaborators John Adams and Benjamin Franklin in the
extreme left and right of the group.

Inhalt

Contents

Die früheste Darstellung der Landung von Christoph Kolumbus im vermeintlichen Indien: König Ferdinand blickt wohlgefällig über den Atlantik, während der Entdecker die „Indianer" begrüßt. Florentinisches Flugblatt aus dem Jahr 1493.

The earliest known illustration of Columbus' landing in America. It shows King Ferdinand glancing benevolently across the Atlantic, while the explorer and his three ships prepare to greet the supposed "Indians". Leaflet, Florence 1493.

Die Abenteuer des Kolumbus auf einem Bronzeportal des Capitol in Washington. Die zehn Tonnen schwere Tür wurde 1858 von dem amerikanischen Bildhauer Randolph Rogers in Rom entworfen und bei Ferdinand von Miller in München gegossen. Aus derselben Gießerei stammt die Bavaria (unten), ein Wahrzeichen Münchens und des Oktoberfestes.
Gegenüber drei Details: Die Abreise aus Palos am 3. August 1492; Kolumbus nimmt Eingeborene an Bord, um sie bei Hofe vorzuführen; triumphaler Einzug in Barcelona im März 1493.

The bronze door of the Capitol Building in Washington illustrates Columbus' journey. Designed in 1858 by the American sculptor Randolph Rogers, the ten – ton door was cast in the foundries of Ferdinand von Miller in Munich. The same foundry also cast the monumental statue of "Bavaria" (below), which stands on the hill overlooking Munich's popular Oktoberfest.
Facing page: Details from the bronze door – Columbus' departure, August 3, 1492; Columbus takes natives on board for later display of his discoveries to his Spanish patrons; triumphant entry into Barcelona on his return to Spain, March 1493.

1492: Kolumbus entdeckt Amerika, auch für die Deutschen

Wer nun wirklich als Erster den Atlantik überquerte – Ägypter, Etrusker, Phönizier, Griechen, oder später, im 10. Jahrhundert, Normannen, Schweden oder Dänen – darüber sind sich die Gelehrten bis heute nicht einig. Ob es Papyrusflöße, Trieren oder Wikingerboote waren, die Amerikas Küsten zuerst erreichten – diese Frage ist letztlich auch nur für die Gelehrten von Interesse. Denn keines der Völker, die vor den Spaniern drüben gewesen sein sollen, ist auf die Idee gekommen, auch drüben zu bleiben.

Gold und Gott waren die Leitmotive, unter denen sich der Genueser Christoph Kolumbus am 3. August 1492 im Auftrag der spanischen Krone auf das „Meer der Finsternis" wagte, um der Sonne nachzusegeln. „Wir schicken diesen edlen Mann durch die ozeanischen Meere nach Indien", hieß es in dem „Reisepaß", den Ferdinand und Isabella ausgestellt hatten, „zur Verbreitung des göttlichen Wortes, als auch zum Nutzen und Vorteil unserer selbst".

Indien, oder gar „Cathay" (China) und „Cipango" (Japan) waren Zauberworte, seit Marco Polo im 13. Jahrhundert von den sagenhaften Reichtümern im Lande des Großkhans berichtet hatte. Ein irdisches Paradies malte sich Europa aus, wo unter Dächern von purem Gold im Überfluß vorhanden war, was man so dringend brauchte. Zum Beispiel auch Gewürze: Die Länder, in denen der Pfeffer wächst, waren von höchst praktischer Bedeutung für eine Zeit, die vom Kühlschrank noch nicht zu träumen wagte und mancherlei Verdorbenes auf den Tisch bringen mußte.

Der Landweg, seit der türkischen Eroberung Konstantinopels 1453 ohnehin gefährdet, war lang und teuer – der Seeweg um das Kap der Guten Hoffnung noch nicht erforscht. Aber behaupten die Geographen nicht, „daß der Anfang des bewohnten Ostens der Erde dem Ende des bewohnbaren Westens sehr nahe liegt"? Kolumbus, Besitzer einer Landkartenfirma in Genua, hatte an dieser Theorie von der Kugelgestalt der Erde keine Zweifel. Realist und religiöser Schwärmer zugleich empfand er es als Auftrag, den Heiden das Christentum zu bringen – übersah aber keineswegs die Chancen, die ihm eine Expedition in den goldenen Westen wirtschaftlich bot. Von seiner Idee besessen, suchte er 7 Jahre lang vergeblich Geldgeber. Erst durch die Fürsprache Königin Isabellas von Kastilien stimmte König Ferdinand schließlich dem verwegenen Plan zu, das ferne, reiche Indien westwärts zu suchen.

Nach über 2 Monaten Fahrt, gerade als die Mannschaften der drei Schiffe „Santa Maria", „Pinta" und „Nina" zu meutern begannen, sichtete der Matrose Rodrigo da Triana am Morgen des 12. Oktober 1492 Land! An der Küste von San Salvador, dem heutigen Watling Island der Bahamas, hatten Kolumbus und seine Leute zum ersten Mal wieder festen Boden unter den Füßen. Begrüßt wurden sie von staunenden und friedlichen Eingeborenen, die nicht ahnten, daß sie von nun an als „Indianer" in die Weltgeschichte aufgenommen waren.

Kolumbus selbst hat nie erfahren, daß er nicht den Wasserweg nach Indien, sondern einen neuen Kontinent entdeckt hatte. „Niemals", so urteilte der deutsche Historiker Leopold von Ranke, „hat ein großartiger Irrtum eine großartigere Entdeckung hervorgebracht."

1492: Columbus Discovers America — for Germans too!

Scholars still disagree today on the question of who first crossed the Atlantic. Was it the Egyptians, the Etruscans, the Phoenicians, or the Greeks? Or perhaps the Normans, the Swedes, or the Danes in the 10th century? Whether the American coast was first touched by a papyrus raft, a trireme, or a Viking ship is only of academic interest. For none of the peoples who may have been there before the Spanish arrived ever thought of remaining there.

God and gold were the motives which led Christopher Columbus of Genoa, on behalf of the Spanish Crown, to set sail on August 3, 1492, across the "Sea of Darkness" to follow the sun. In the "passport" issued by Ferdinand and Isabella, it stated: "We are sending this noble gentleman across the vast seas to India to spread the Word of God, as well as to promote the interests and advantages of Ourselves".

India, "Cathay" (China), and "Cipango" (Japan) had been words with a magic aura ever since the 13th century, when Marco Polo returned from his travels to describe the unbelievable riches in the land of Kublai Khan. Europe imagined a paradise on earth, an endless abundance of all things needed by man, housed under roofs of pure gold. One of these things was spices. Any land where pepper grew had great practical importance for an era without refrigerators – sitting down to a well-balanced meal of rotten food was nothing unusual.

The route by land was long and expensive, and, since the Turkish conquest of Constantinople in 1453, also dangerous. The sea route around the Cape of Good Hope had not yet been discovered. But weren't the geographers saying that "The beginning of the inhabited East is very close to the end of the uninhabited West"? Columbus, owner of a map-making firm in Genoa, firmly believed this theory – that the world was round. Being of strong religious convictions, he felt the need to bring Christianity to the heathen. But he was just as much a realist, and very aware of the lucrative possibilities offered by an expedition to the golden West. The idea gave him no peace, and for seven years he searched in vain for a patron. It took the intercession of Queen Isabella of Castile finally to persuade King Ferdinand to agree to the daring scheme of attempting to reach the distant and rich land of India from the west.

After a voyage of more than two months, just as the crews of the three ships, the "Nina", the "Pinta", and the "Santa Maria" began to mutiny, the seaman Rodrigo da Triana sighted land – on October 12, 1492. It was on the coast of San Salvador (today Watling Island in the Bahamas) that Columbus and his crew again set foot on land. They were greeted by astonished and peaceful natives, who had no idea that from now on they would be referred to as "Indians".

Columbus himself never learned that he had discovered a new continent rather than a sea route to India. "Never", in the opinion of the German historian Leopold von Ranke, "has a great mistake given birth to a greater discovery".

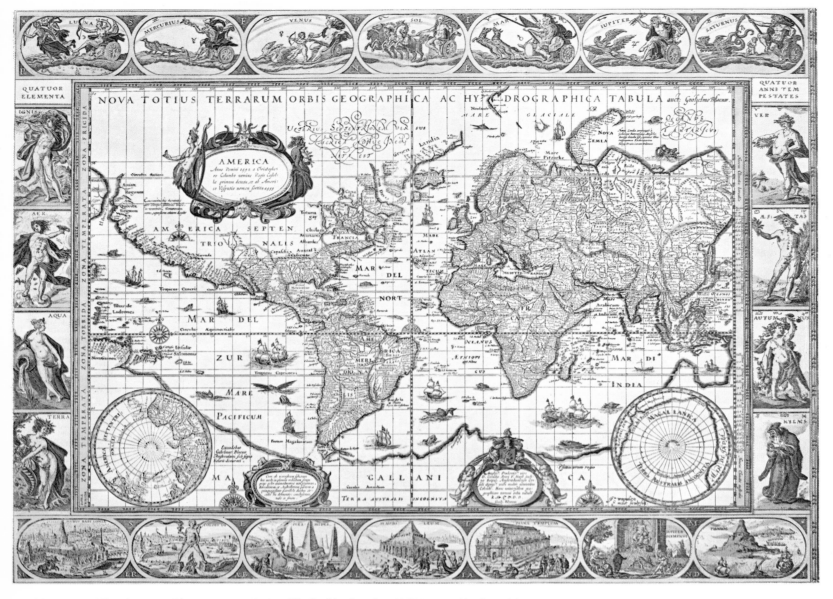

Weltkarte von Willem Janszoon Blaeu, 1630, prunkvoll eingerahmt von den sieben Weltwundern (unten) und allegorischen Darstellungen der Planeten (oben), der vier Elemente (links) und der Jahreszeiten (rechts).

W. J. Blaeu's atlas (1630), superbly framed by the Seven Wonders of the World, and allegories of the Planets (above), the Four Elements (left), and the Seasons of the Year (right).

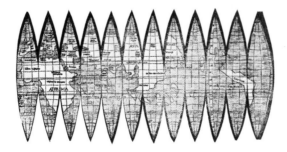

Martin Waldseemüllers Karte von 1513 bildet die Karibischen Inseln bereits erstaunlich exakt ab.

Martin Waldseemüller's map of 1513 shows the Caribbean islands in remarkable detail.

Peter Appians Weltkarte von 1520, die in zukunftsweisender Unkenntnis den Panamakanal vorwegzunehmen scheint.

Peter Appian's world map from 1520 shows a remarkable prophetic gift by digging the Panama Canal 400 years early.

Seinen Namen erhielt Amerika in Deutschland: Hier die Segmente des Globus von Martin Waldseemüller aus dem Jahr 1507, auf dem Amerigo Vespuccis falscher Ruhm erstmals verewigt ist.

America actually received its name in Germany. Martin Waldseemüller indicated this geographic designation on his globe, dated 1507.

Das frühe Bild der Neuen Welt

„Nun ist aber ein vierter Weltteil durch Amerigo Vespucci entdeckt worden", teilte der Kartograph Martin Waldseemüller in der *Cosmographiae Introductio* 1507 seinen – sicherlich erstaunten – Lesern mit und machte den Vorschlag: „Ich sehe deshalb keinen Grund, warum man ihn nicht mit vollem Recht nach seinem Entdecker Amerigo, einem Mann von großem Scharfsinn, America nennen sollte". Waldseemüller war dann auch der erste, der den Namen auf eine Karte eintrug. Er entwarf nämlich gerade einen Globus, und auf dessen Kugelsegmenten ist eine Landmasse zwischen den Küsten Europas und Asiens durch das Wort „Amerika" bezeichnet. Wie konnte es zu dieser „falschen" Namensgebung kommen?

Gegen Ende des 15. Jahrhunderts hatte der lothringische Herzog René eine Reihe von deutschen Gelehrten, unter ihnen Waldseemüller, in dem Städtchen St. Dié um sich gesammelt. Es sollte ihre Aufgabe sein, alle Nachrichten von Entdeckungsfahrten, die in jenen Tagen so zahlreich unternommen wurden, zu sammeln und wissenschaftlich auszuwerten. Eine Schrift erregte besonderes Aufsehen. Sie enthielt den Bericht eines italienischen Kaufmanns, Amerigo Vespucci, über seine vier Reisen in eine Gegend, von der er behauptete, sie sei eine „Neue Welt" – so der Titel seines Werkes. René ließ es sofort ins Lateinische übersetzen und durch Waldseemüller mit einem Vorwort – eben der *Einleitung in die Kosmographie* von 1507 – versehen. Da von Kolumbus nur die Beschreibung seiner ersten Reise vorlag, mußten die Gelehrten annehmen, er habe lediglich „die indischen Inseln hinter dem Ganges" gefunden, während Vespucci die Entdeckung eines ganzen noch unbekannten Erdteils gelungen sei. Schon bald bemerkte Waldseemüller seinen Irrtum. Auf der Amerikakarte der Straßburger Ptolemäus Ausgabe (1513) suchte er sich zu verbessern. Dort trägt das Festland die Bezeichnung „unerforschtes Gebiet" mit dem Zusatz: „Dieses Land nebst den anliegenden Inseln ist auf Befehl

Epiſtola Chriſtofori Colom: cui etas noſtra multũ debet: de Inſulis Indie ſupra Gangem nuper inuẽtis. Ad quas perqreñ das octauo antea menſe auſpiciis τ ere inuictiſſimoɣ Fernãdi τ Heliſabet Hiſpaniaɣ Regũ miſſus fuerat: ad magnificum dñm Gabrielem Sanchis eoɣundẽ ſereniſſimoɣ Regum Theſaurariũ miſſa: quã nobilis ac litteratus vir Leander de Coſco ab Hiſpano idiomate in latinum cõuertit tertio kal's Maii. M.cccc.xciii Pontificatus Alexandri Sexti Anno primo.

Kolumbus' erster Bericht über seine Entdeckungsreise; das Faksimile zeigt den Anfang einer lateinischen Übersetzung, die der Katalane Leandro da Cosco anfertigte.

Columbus' first report on his discoveries. The facsimile shows the beginning of a Latin translation, made by the Catalonian Leandro da Cosco.

Sebastian Brant; sein Narrenschiff (1494) ist das erste literarische Werk, in dem der neuentdeckte Kontinent erwähnt wird.

Sebastian Brant's Ship of Fools (1494) was the first literary work to mention America.

The New World's Early Image

"Now, however, a fourth Continent has been discovered by Amerigo Vespucci", the cartographer Martin Waldseemüller informed his – undoubtedly surprised – readers in the *Cosmographiae Introductio* of 1507, adding: "And I therefore can see no reason why it should not rightfully be named America for its discoverer Amerigo, a man of great perspicacity". And so Waldseemüller actually became the first to enter the name on a map. On the globe he was designing at the time, we find a land mass identified as "America" between the coasts of Europe and Asia. How could it happen that such a "wrong" name was selected?

Toward the end of the 15th century, Duke René of Lorraine had gathered together a number of German scientists, among them Waldseemüller, in the little town of St. Dié. It was to be their task to collect and scientifically evaluate all the news coming in from the many voyages of discovery being undertaken at the time. One manuscript proved to be of particular interest. It dealt with the report of an Italian merchant, Amerigo Vespucci, on his four voyages to a country which he described as a "New World" – which was also the title of his report. René immediately had it translated into Latin, and had Waldseemüller write an introduction – the *Introduction to Cosmography* of 1507 mentioned above. Since they knew no more about Columbus than the description of his first voyage, the scientists had to assume that he had merely found "the Indian islands beyond the Ganges", while Vespucci had succeeded in discovering a whole new continent. Waldseemüller soon realized his mistake. On the Strasbourg Ptolemaeus edition of the map of America (1513), he attempts to correct his error by adding: "This country as well as the adjoining islands was discovered by the Genoese Columbus at the order of the King of Castile". But by now it was too late. The name "America" stuck – strange as the ways of history sometimes are.

The news of a New World on the other side of the ocean rapidly spread throughout Germany by

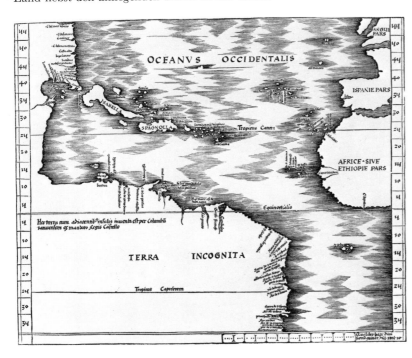

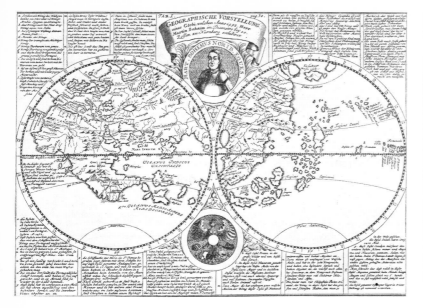

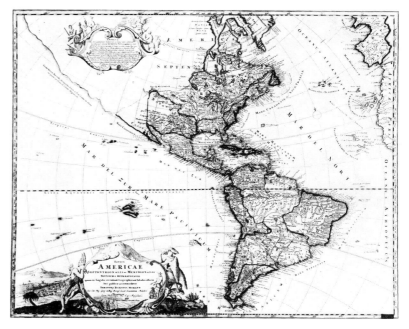

„Geographische Vorstellung" des Globus von Martin Behaim aus dem Jahr 1492, auf dem noch keine der Entdeckungen des Kolumbus vermerkt ist; gezeichnet von Johann Gabriel Doppelmayr, Nürnberg 1730.

This map drawn by Johann Gabriel Doppelmayr in 1730 in Nürnberg is a reconstruction of Martin Behaim's globe of 1492 in which none of Columbus' discoveries are noted.

Auf Gerhard Mercators Karte von 1587 sind nur Arktis und Antarktis noch unerforscht.

Gerhard Mercator's map (1587) is a much more accurate description of the western hemisphere in every way.

Sebastian Münsters Karte aus dem Jahr 1540, auf der die Insel Zipangi (Japan) der Westküste Amerikas vorgelagert ist.

The right hand side of the American continent is fairly accurately drawn in Sebastian Münster's map published in 1540. We are however led to believe that Japan (Zipangi on the map) is only a short sea journey from the "West coast" of Texas.

Mit Johann Baptist Homanns Karte von 1720 ist die geographische Aufnahme Amerikas fast abgeschlossen. Nur zwischen Kalifornien und Alaska bleibt noch Spielraum für die Phantasie des Kartographen.

Johann Baptist Homann's map of 1720 is remarkably accurate on the eastern coast but indicates the northwestern half of the continent with a simple line suggesting where Homann's imagination placed the coastline.

des Königs von Kastilien durch den Genuesen Kolumbus entdeckt worden". Aber das änderte schon nichts mehr. Bei dem Namen „Amerika" ist es, so seltsame Wege geht die Geschichte bisweilen, geblieben.

Die Kunde von einer Neuen Welt jenseits des Ozeans verbreitete sich in Deutschland rasch durch die noch junge Kunst des Buchdrucks. Bereits 1494 reimte Sebastian Brant in seinem *Narrenschiff:* „Ouch hat man sidt in Portigal / Und in Hispanien uberall / Golt, inseln funden und nacket lüt, / Von den man vor wußt sagen nüt." In der Folgezeit erschien eine Flut von Flugblättern und Broschüren, für die sich der neuartige Begriff „Zeitung" einbürgerte. Die erste volkstümliche Sammlung solcher Zeitungen gab 1508 der „wirdige und hochgelahrte" Doktor Jobst Ruchamer heraus. *Newe unbekannte landte Und newe weldte in kurz vergangener Zeythe erfunden* lautete der Titel seiner Schrift, in der er als Entdecker Amerikas einen gewissen „Christoffel Dauber" vorstellte; denn neben den Texten hatte Ruchamer auch die Eigennamen der handelnden Personen eingedeutscht.

Wie lange sich der falsche Ruhm Vespuccis halten konnte, zeigt das Beispiel des verdienstvollen Kosmographen Sebastian Münster, der ihm noch 1532 die Entdeckung der Neuen Welt zuspricht. Ansonsten zeigen seine Amerikakarten einen deutlichen Fortschritt im geographischen Wissen der Zeit. Gegenüber Peter Appians herzförmiger Projektion aus dem Jahr 1520 zeigt Münster die zwei Teile des Kontinents wieder als zusammenhängende Landmasse, ohne die Durchfahrt nach Westen, die zu finden so viele vergebliche Anstrengungen unternommen wurden. Auch über die Westküste der südlichen Hälfte hatte man inzwischen genauere Nachrichten zur Verfügung. Nur der Norden des Kontinents war nach wie vor unerforscht und die Umrisse, die Münster ihm gab, beruhten mehr auf Spekulation als auf Information. Besser hat diesen Teil auf seiner Weltkarte von 1587 Gerhard Mercator getroffen, der wohl wichtigste deutsche Kosmograph der Renaissance. Er zeigt, daß Amerika weder eine Landverbindung zu Asien noch eine mit Grönland besitzt, eine Ansicht, die nicht allgemeine Zustimmung fand: So benutzte Johann Baptist Homann, der führende deutsche Kartograph seiner Zeit, zwar 1720 schon eine begriffliche Unterscheidung der beiden Teile des Kontinents in ‚Amerika septentrionalis' (für den Norden) und ‚Amerika meredionalis' (für den Süden); den Westen des nördlichen Subkontinents läßt er aber immer noch in eine weiße Zone der Ungewißheit auslaufen. Und das zu einer Zeit, als sich schon die ersten deutschen Auswanderer in den Kolonien an der Ostküste niedergelassen hatten, von denen Gottlieb Mittelberger 1756 in seiner *Reise nach Pennsylvanien* zu berichten wußte.

means of the recent invention of printing. As early as 1494, Sebastian Brant wrote these rhymes in his *Ship of Fools:*

> Lately in Portugal were found
> As were in Spain and all around
> Islands of gold and naked men
> That no one knew about till then.

Shortly after, Germany was flooded with pamphlets and booklets which soon became known under the new name of "newspapers". The first popular collection of newspapers of that kind was published in 1508 by the "most honorable and learned" Doctor Jobst Ruchamer. *New, Unknown Countries and New Worlds Discovered Recently* was the title of this publication, in which he declared the discoverer of America to be a certain "Christoffel Dauber". Ruchamer, as it happens, had "translated" not only the text but also the proper names of the persons mentioned.

How long the undeserved fame of Vespucci persisted may be seen by the example of the able cosmographer Sebastian Münster, who credited him with the discovery of the New World as late as 1532. In other respects, his maps of America show definite progress in the geographic knowledge of the times. In contrast to the heart-shaped projection drawn by Peter Appian in 1520, Münster shows the two parts of the continent as a continuous land mass, without the Northwest Passage which was searched for in vain for so long. He also had more exact information at his disposal as to the conformation of the West Coast of the Southern half. Only the North of the Continent still remained unexplored, and the outlines it was given by Münster owed more to guesswork than to actual information. Mercator, probably the most prominent German cosmographer of the Renaissance, came closer to the facts in regard to this section on his world map of 1587. It shows that there is no land bridge between America and Asia or America and Greenland; an opinion which was not undisputed. Thus, although Johann Baptist Homann, the leading German cartographer of his time, in his work of 1720 already makes a clear distinction between North and South America ("Amerika septentrionalis" and "Amerika meredionalis"), he still has the boundary lines of the Pacific Northwest melt into a white zone of uncertainty. And that at a time when the first German immigrants to the colonies had already established themselves on the East Coast, a report on which is found in Gottlieb Mittelberger's *Journey to Pennsylvania* (1756).

The title page of an early German book describing a journey to Pennsylvania, the state with the best-known and one of the earliest German colonies.

Deutsche Siedler vor 1776

Gut hundert Jahre vergingen nach Kolumbus Entdeckung, ehe auch der Teil der Neuen Welt kolonialisiert wurde, den die Spanier wegen der – von ihnen so empfundenen – Unwirtlichkeit des Klimas gemieden hatten. Die Initiative dazu ging von den Engländern und Franzosen aus; Holländer und Schweden folgten. Deutschland war zu dieser Zeit durch den 30jährigen Krieg so sehr mit seinen eigenen Problemen beschäftigt, daß Deutsche im 17. Jahrhundert nur vereinzelt und im Dienst fremder Mächte nach Nordamerika kamen.

Die ersten dürften drei Zimmerleute gewesen sein, Unger, Keffer und Volday mit Namen. Sie gehörten zur Mannschaft jenes Captain Smith, der 1607 Jamestown gründete und damit die englische Besiedlung der Ostküste einleitete. Bereits in Amt und Würde überquerte Peter Minuit (Minnewit) aus Wesel den Atlantik. Als Generaldirektor der holländischen Besitzungen in Nordamerika landete er 1626 auf Manhattan. Für ganze 60 Gulden kaufte er den Indianern die Insel ab, auf der heute die Wolkenkratzer New Yorks stehen. Diesen Namen erhielt Minuits Siedlung allerdings erst, nachdem die Engländer Neu-Holland 1664 in ihren Besitz gebracht hatten. Später, im Verlauf der „Glorreichen Revolution", die im englischen Mutterland ganz unblutig verlief, kam es auch in New York zu Unruhen. Die Bevölkerung vertrieb den Gouverneur Thomas Dongan und beauftragte den Kommandeur der Bürgermiliz, den aus Frankfurt gebürtigen Kaufmann Jacob Leisler, mit der kommissarischen Verwaltung der Kolonie. Zweieinhalb Jahre lang versah dieser das Amt mit Umsicht und Tatkraft. Als der vom neuen König ernannte Nachfolger eintraf, erreichten Leislers Gegner, daß er unter der Beschuldigung des Hochverrats festgenommen,

German Settlers before 1776

It was a good hundred years after Columbus' discovery before colonization took place in that part of the New World which the Spaniards had avoided – they did not care for the "inhospitable" climate. The British and the French were the ones to take the initiative in this direction, followed by the Dutch and the Swedes. Germany had so many problems of her own at that time, such as the ravages of the Thirty Years War, that very few Germans even thought of making the trip to North America, and when they did, it was in the service of a foreign power.

The first of these Germans were probably three shipwrights – Unger, Keffer, and Volday by name. They belonged to the crew of the Captain Smith who founded Jamestown in 1607, opening the way for English settlement of the east coast. Peter Minuit (Minnewit) of Wesel had been appointed governor of the Dutch colonies in North America before crossing the Atlantic. He landed on Manhattan in 1626, and proceeded to buy the island from the Indians for the sum of twenty-four dollars – the same island on which the skyscrapers of New York stand today. However, Minuit's settlement did not receive this name until after the English king, Charles II, had taken possession of New Netherland in 1664. Later, following uprisings in New York, the colonial governor was driven out, and the provisional administration of the colony was entrusted to the commander of the civilian militia, the Frankfort-born merchant, Jacob Leisler, who conscientiously performed the duties of this office for two and a half years. When the governor appointed by the new English king arrived, Leisler's opponents conspired to have him arrested on a charge of high treason. Within the same year, he was falsely convicted and publicly

Denkmal Peter Minuits in seiner Geburtsstadt Wesel am Rhein.

This modern statue is a monument to Peter Minuit. It stands in the city of his birth – Wesel on the Rhine.

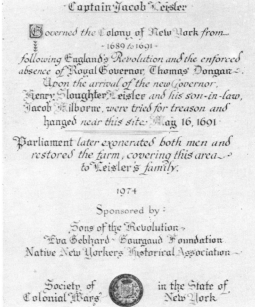

Der legendäre Tauschhandel von 1626, bei dem Minuit den Indianern Manhattan für Glasperlen und Ketten im Wert von 60 Gulden abkaufte.

The legendary transaction in which Minuit purchased Manhattan island from the Indians in 1626 for $24.00 worth of beads and trinkets.

Amerika gedenkt seiner Vergangenheit: 1965 wurde in New York ein Denkmal für den deutschstämmigen Jacob Leisler, Gouverneur der Stadt von 1689 bis 1691, errichtet. Einer seiner Nachfahren, Walter Leisler Kiep (im Bild rechts), ist heute Mitglied des Bundestages.

Captain Jacob Leisler from Frankfurt governed New York between 1689 and 1691. His descendant, Walter Leisler Kiep (here shown at right), is currently a member of the German Bundestag.

Der Rathausplatz von Neu-Amsterdam, dem heutigen New York, um die Mitte des 17. Jahrhunderts.

An early engraving of a street in the village of New Amsterdam. The city hall of the time is shown in the center.

ungerechterweise verurteilt und noch im selben Jahr (1691) öffentlich hingerichtet wurde. Doch schon vier Jahre später rehabilitierte das englische Parlament den Patrioten, der zwar für mehr Eigenständigkeit der Kolonie gekämpft hatte, bei alledem aber königstreu geblieben war.

Zog es die ersten deutschen Einwanderer zunächst nach New York, Maryland oder Virginia, so änderte sich das mit der Gründung Pennsylvaniens 1681. Dort errichtete der englische Edelmann William Penn eine Kolonie, in der absolute religiöse Toleranz herrschte. Wer, wie die Quäker, zu denen sich Penn bekannte, in der Alten Welt aus Glaubensgründen verfolgt wurde, der sollte in diesem Staat die Freiheit finden, das ersehnte „ruhige, ehrliche und gottgefällige Leben" zu führen. Gern folgten die Mitglieder der zahlreichen pietistischen Sekten Deutschlands, darunter Mennoniten, Schwenckfelder, Tunker und Lambadisten dieser Einladung. Den Exodus begannen 13 Krefelder Mennoniten-Familien. Der Tag, an dem ihr Schiff 1683 im Hafen von Philadelphia anlegte, der 6. Oktober, wird noch heute in weiten Teilen der USA als German Day begangen. Vor den Toren der Stadt erwarben die Krefelder ein großes Stück Land und legten darauf ihre eigene Siedlung an: Germantown. Zum Bürgermeister

executed (1691). But after only four years, Parliament rehabilitated this patriot, who, although he fought for more independence for the colony, had always remained loyal to the Crown.

The first German immigrants tended to settle in New York, Maryland, or Virginia, until the founding of Pennsylvania in 1681. It was there that the English nobleman William Penn, a Quaker, established a colony dedicated to the ideal of absolute religious tolerance. The Quakers were one of the many sects which had suffered persecution in the Old World for religious reasons. They and all others would find in his state the freedom to pursue a "quiet, honest, and God-fearing life" without interference. This thought appealed greatly to the numerous pietistic sects in Germany, among them the Mennonites, the Schwenkfeldians (Confessors of the Glory of Christ), the "Dunkers", and the Lambadists. The exodus was begun by thirteen Mennonite families from Krefeld. The day on which their ship docked in Philadelphia (October 6, 1683), is still celebrated in many parts of the United States as "German Day". The immigrants from Krefeld acquired a large piece of land outside the city limits and founded a settlement. The man who had organized the ocean crossing, Franz

Die Gründung Pennsylvaniens: William Penn schließt am 5. März 1681 seinen Vertrag mit den Indianern ab.

William Penn's treaty with the Indians on March 5, 1681, opened up a huge territory to settlement, including the largest German concentration in the colonies.

Germantown, die erste deutsche Siedlung, bewahrte lange ihren kleinstädtischen Charakter. Heute ein Stadtteil Philadelphias.

Germantown was the earliest German settlement, founded by Mennonites escaping religious persecution in Westphalia. Today it is a part of Philadelphia.

wählten sie Franz Daniel Pastorius (1651–1720), der schon die Überfahrt organisiert hatte. Dieser tatkräftige junge Gelehrte war von Haus aus Jurist und Theologe, besaß daneben aber auch umfangreiches praktisches Wissen, das es ihm ermöglichte, sich erfolgreich an der Lösung öffentlicher Aufgaben zu beteiligen. Schnell wurde er ein enger Freund und Berater William Penns. Sein besonderes Interesse galt dem Aufbau eines Schulsystems, das auch Abendklassen für Erwachsene umfaßte. Bereits 1688 verfaßte er das erste Manifest gegen die Sklaverei.

In der Regel blieben die Mitglieder pietistischer Gruppen auch nach der Überfahrt zusammen und erschlossen ein gemeinsames Siedlungsgebiet. Als Gemeinschaft weiterexistieren zu können war meistens ein ausschlaggebendes Motiv für die Auswanderung gewesen. Der Zusammenhalt sollte sich als so stark erweisen, daß noch viele Nachkommen dieser Einwanderer bis auf den heutigen Tag im Siedlungsgebiet ihrer Vorväter zuhause sind. Auch die religiös motivierten Vorschriften, die oft genug Anlaß zu Verfolgungen gewesen waren, haben sich durch die Jahrhunderte kaum merklich gelockert. So bleibt es den Mitgliedern mancher Sekten nach wie vor verboten, Ehen zu schließen, Kinder zu taufen, Eide abzulegen, Gewalt anzuwenden oder Kriegsdienst zu leisten. Oft regeln diese Vorschriften noch weitere Bereiche des täglichen Lebens, bis hin zu Kleidung und Haartracht. So entwickelte sich ein vielfältiges, bisweilen auch exzentrisches, aber eigenständiges Brauchtum, das die deutschstämmigen Einwohner Pennsylvaniens, die „Pennsylvania Dutch", von Anfang an von ihren Nachbarn abhob.

Traditionen ganz anderer Art kennen die Herrnhuter oder „Moravians", wie sie in Amerika ihrer Herkunft aus Mähren wegen genannt werden. Sie hatten sich die Bekehrung der Indianer zur Aufgabe gemacht, wobei sie große Erfolge erzielen konnten. Noch heute helfen sie, vor allem in städtischen Ballungsräumen, rassische und nationale Barrieren zu überwinden.

Seit Anfang des 18. Jahrhunderts folgten den pietistischen Sekten auch Angehörige der protestantischen Konfessionen. Dabei kam es zu den ersten Massenauswanderungen, als das obere Rheintal im Verlauf des Spanischen Erbfolgekrieges völlig verwüstet wurde und die katholischen Herrscher der Pfalz damit begannen, ihre Untertanen lutherischen und reformierten Bekenntnisses zu verfolgen. 1708 brachte Josua von Kocherthal 60 mittellose Pfälzer nach London, deren Überfahrt die ebenfalls protestantische Königin Maria aus ihrer eigenen Schatulle bezahlte. Im folgenden Jahr waren es gleich 13000 Auswanderungswillige, die sich in der Hoffnung auf eine freie Überfahrt in London einfanden. Eine Gruppe wurde nach Nord-Carolina geschifft, die andere nach New York. Dort war schon im Jahr zuvor Kocherthal an Land gegangen und hatte im Tal des Hudson, der ihn an den heimatlichen Rhein erinnerte, eine Siedlung, Newburgh, angelegt. Doch die Gegend erwies sich als wenig fruchtbar. Er faßte deshalb den Entschluß, mit den Neuankömmlingen weiter flußaufwärts zu ziehen. Aber auch dort fanden die Pfälzer keine Ruhe. Streitigkeiten mit den holländischen Großgrundbesitzern veranlaßten sie nach wenigen Jahren, entweder nach Nordwesten ins Mohawktal vorzudringen oder sich – wie die Mehrzahl – nach Süden zu wenden, wo man ihnen in Pennsylvanien bereitwillig Aufnahme gewährte.

Daniel Pastorius (1651–1720), was elected mayor. This energetic young scholar was a lawyer and theologian by profession, but he also possessed practical knowledge and common sense, which enabled him to deal successfully with the problems of governing a community. He soon became a close friend and adviser to William Penn. He was particularly interested in establishing a school system which would include evening classes for adults. As early as 1688, he composed the first manifesto condemning the institution of slavery.

As a rule, members of the different pietistic sects stayed together even after the sea voyage and founded their own settlements. The thought of being able to exist as a community was usually what had made them decide to emigrate. This feeling of close solidarity is still so strong that many of the descendants of these groups are satisfied to live in the same way and in the same area as their forefathers. Certain religious customs, which in the past had often led to persecution, continue to be almost as strictly observed today as they were centuries ago. Members of certain sects are still forbidden to marry, to baptize children, to swear an oath, to resort to violence, or to serve in the armed forces. These customs often carry over into other areas of daily life, up to and including the type of clothing worn and hair styles. So over the years, that varied, sometimes eccentric, but stubbornly self-reliant culture developed, which continues to set Pennsylvanians of German extraction – the "Pennsylvania Dutch" – apart from their neighbors.

The Moravians – so called because they came from the Habsburg province of Moravia – were heirs to totally different traditions. They set themselves the task of converting the Indians to Christianity, and in this they were very successful. Their descendants are still active today in the struggle to overcome national and racial prejudice, especially in overcrowded urban areas.

In the 18th century many other Protestants followed pietistic sects to America. The first mass emigrations took place after the upper Rhine valley was completely devastated during the course of the War of the Spanish Succession, and the Catholic rulers of the Rhenish Palatinate began the religious persecution of Lutherans and Calvinists in their territories. In 1708, Josua von Kochertal brought sixty penniless religious refugees from this region to London. Their passage to the New World was paid by Queen Mary, who was also a Protestant. The following year, nearly 13,000 people had gathered in London, hoping for a free crossing. One group was shipped to North Carolina, the other to New York, where Kochertal had landed the year before. He had founded Newburgh, a settlement in the Hudson Valley, which reminded him of his native Rhineland. But the area proved to be rather barren, so he and the others decided to move further upriver. But this did not help matters much. After a few years, constant conflict with the Dutch landowners drove them to move either northwest to the Mohawk Valley, or to the south, which is what the majority of them did. In Pennsylvania, they finally found peace and acceptance.

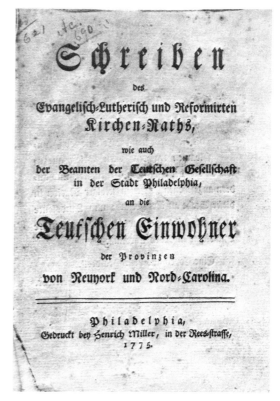

Pennsylvania wurde zum Zentrum der religiös motivierten deutschen Einwanderung. Sendschreiben des Kirchenrats von Philadelphia an deutsche Einwanderer in anderen Kolonien.

An open letter from the Lutheran Church Council of Philadelphia and the German society of the same city to the German residents of New York and North Carolina.

Eine weitere Gruppe von Reformierten, diesmal aus der Gegend um Braunschweig, war schon 1707 in Richtung New York gesegelt, durch widrige Winde aber in den Hafen von Philadelphia getrieben worden. Sie ließen sich schließlich im benachbarten New Jersey nieder, wohin 1733 auch der Urahn einer der heute reichsten Familien der Welt, Johann Peter Rockefeller, auswanderte.

Die Berichte der Auswanderer an die in der Heimat Zurückgebliebenen malten die Zustände in den Kolonien in derart glühenden Farben, daß der Strom der Einwanderer ständig anschwoll. So lebten bei Ausbruch des Unabhängigkeitskrieges schon 250 000 Deutsche zwischen Maine und Georgia. Unter ihnen befanden sich außergewöhnlich viele Handwerker, an denen es damals noch allenthalben mangelte. Sie trugen entscheidend dazu bei, daß die deutschen Siedlungsgebiete sich im jungen Amerika schnell zu wichtigen Zentren von Industrie und Handel entwickelten.

Another Protestant group, from the area of Braunschweig, had set sail for New York in 1707, but unfavorable winds forced them to dock in Philadelphia. They eventually settled in nearby New Jersey, which in 1733 became the home of the immigrant Johann Peter Rockefeller, founder of what became one of the world's wealthiest families.

Reports from the "New World" to the "Old World" painted such as rosy picture of life in the colonies that more and more people decided to emigrate. When the War of Independence broke out, there were already 250,000 Germans living between Maine and Georgia. Among them were many skilled craftsmen, who were in great demand everywhere. They made a significant contribution to the rapid development of these early German settlements into important centers of trade and industry.

Der harmonische Stadtplan von Harmony, 1805 von den Rappisten gegründet.

The first map of Harmony, Pennsylvania, founded in 1805 by the Rappist sect.

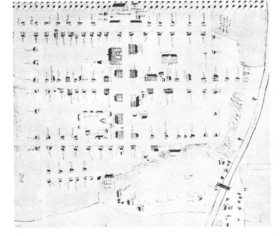

Eine typische Szene, mitten aus dem 20. Jahrhundert: In den Siedlungen der „Amish-People" ist die Zeit stehengeblieben.

The "plain people", as the Amish call themselves, enjoy a little Saturday afternoon social among the local teenagers. This is a recent photograph.

Neun Generationen – eine deutsche Einwandererfamilie in Pennsylvanien:

1738 verließ Johan(nes) Bernhard Reber Langenselbold in Hessen, um in Pennsylvanien eine neue Existenz aufzubauen. Die Urkunde von 1761 dokumentiert, daß sein Enkel Valentin(e) Land kaufte, das Thomas und Richard Penn, Sohn und Enkel des 1718 verstorbenen William Penn, parzelliert hatten. Der größte Teil der für 675 Pfund erworbenen 200 Morgen ist bis heute in Familienbesitz, ebenso die Urkunde, die eine Mitarbeiterin dieses Buches, eine Reber der neunten Generation, aus dem Familienarchiv holte. Valentin(e) Reber, ein Veteran des amerikanischen Revolutionskrieges, starb 1818 – sein Grabstein (rechts) trägt eine deutsche Inschrift. Wie viele deutschstämmige Familien, halten auch die Rebers Teile ihres deutschen Erbes lebendig, wie etwa Mitgliedschaft in der „Gemeinde der Brüderlichkeit", einer einst aus Hessen geflohenen Anabaptistensekte.

Nine Generations – A German Immigrant Family in Pennsylvania:

In 1738, Johan(nes) Bernhard Reber left the village of Langenselbold in Hesse to start a new life in Berks County, Pennsylvania. His grandson, Valentin(e) (1742–1818), purchased land parcelled out by Thomas and Richard Penn, son and grandson of William Penn. The deed, dated 1761 (above), as well as the other pictures and information from the family archives, were made available by ninth-generation Patricia Reber. Most of the original 200 acres (bought for 675 Pounds) are still held by the Reber family today. Valentine Reber fought in the Revolutionary War and lived into the administration of the fifth President of the United States. His tombstone (left) in Bernville, Pa., is in German. Many Rebers today can still speak the "Pennsylvania Dutch" German of the region, and many are still members of the Church of the Brethren, an Anabaptist sect which fled from early 18th century persecution in Hesse.

Ein „Reber Wagon" um 1900. Diese einst wegen ihrer Haltbarkeit beliebten Wägen erzielen heute auf Antiquitätenauktionen stolze Preise. Nach Erfindung des Verbrennungsmotors bauten die Rebers Lastwagenchassis aus Holz.

A Reber Wagon, around 1900. These wagons, once popular because of their sturdiness, still fetch a good price at antique sales. Today, Lewis Reber, at the age of 88, still builds small model Reber Wagons.

Rückkehr in die alte Heimat: Norman Reber bei einer von der Bundesrepublik ausgerichteten Informationsreise für amerikanische Landwirtschaftsredakteure auf einem Rheindampfer, umgeben von deutschen Kindern.

Return to origins: Norman Reber and German children on a Rhine boat cruise in 1971, when members of the American Agricultural Editors' Association were guests of the Federal Republic.

Deutschamerikanische Familien wie die Rebers haben einen kleinen, aber dauerhaften Beitrag zur amerikanischen Lebensart geleistet. Oben: Der bärtige Jonathan Reber (7. Generation) mit Söhnen und Angestellten vor seiner Wagenfabrik (1907). Später förderte er Kohle, was ihm, auf Pennsylvania-Deutsch, den Beinamen „der Kola Pitty" (der Kohlengrübler) einbrachte. Unten: Die Familie um 1920: Drei Söhne tragen nicht das für die „Gemeinde der Brüderlichkeit" typische „schlichte Gewand", weil sie dieser noch nicht beigetreten waren, und belegen so die feste Überzeugung der Eltern, daß Kleidung ein Glaubenssymbol ist. Einige Kinder wurden Handwerker oder Selbständige, andere studierten, als die Familie wirtschaftliche Stabilität erarbeitet hatte. Die Kinder des Jüngsten, Norman, sind inzwischen Chemotechniker, Hausfrau und Journalistin.

The photo at the top, taken around 1907, shows Jonathan Reber of the seventh generation (far left), with seven sons (front row) and employees of his Centerport, Pa., wagon works. He later invested in coal dredging on the Schuylkill River, where his dusty beard earned him the nickname "der Kola Pitty" (coal punk). The second photo shows the family around 1920. All but three sons are already members of the Brethren, and are shown wearing the "plain suits" customary then. The women wear "prayer coverings", testimony to the family's conviction that dress is a symbol of faith. Some of the sons went to college, and others became craftsmen or small businessmen. The youngest son, Norman Reber, became editor of *The Pennsylvania Farmer*. Today his son is a chemical engineer; one daughter is a journalist, and the other, a housewife.

Das „Bostoner Massaker" vom 5. März 1770 auf einer zeitgenössischen populären Druckgraphik, die mehr Propaganda als Berichterstattung im Sinn hat: Das Zollamt, vor dem sich das angebliche Gemetzel abspielt, wird hier als Schlachthaus („Butcher's Hall", rechts im Hintergrund) ausgegeben. Am Rande bemerkt: Crispus Attucks, der hier das erste Opfer des Unabhängigkeitskampfes wurde, war ein Schwarzer!

This contemporary illustration of the so-called "Boston Massacre", March 5, 1770; an early example of the use of printing as propaganda. Crispus Attucks was shot dead in the mêlée and has gone down in history as the first American to be felled by a British bullet in what later developed into the Revolutionary War. Incidentally, Attucks was a black man.

Von der Revolution zur Unabhängigkeit 1776 - 1784

Die amerikanische Revolution war die erste Auflehnung einer Kolonie gegen ihr Mutterland: so wurde sie richtungweisend für andere Kolonialvölker. Weltweite Bedeutung erlangte diese erste Revolution der Neuzeit vor allem auch, weil sie auf den Prinzipien der Selbstbestimmung begründet war und auf Schutz der bürgerlichen Freiheiten zielte.

Der Revolutionskrieg war äußerst komplex: teils Kampf für die nationale Unabhängigkeit, teils Bürgerkrieg, und nicht zuletzt eine weltweite Auseinandersetzung Englands mit Frankreich, Spanien und den Kolonien. Bemerkenswert ist, daß dieser erste koloniale Aufstand der Neuzeit gerade gegen England, die aufgeklärteste Monarchie Europas, gerichtet war. Die englischen Kolonien erfreuten sich weit größerer Unabhängigkeit und Freiheit als die Besitzungen aller anderen Kolonialstaaten: Die französischen und spanischen Kolonien beispielsweise waren strengster diktatorischer Kontrolle unterworfen. Dagegen hatten die englischen Kolonien in Amerika seit mehr als einem Jahrhundert weitgehende Freiheiten genossen und sich im Verlauf dieser Zeit Geschick und Erfahrung in der Selbstbestimmung erworben.

England – von innenpolitischen Problemen und Streitigkeiten belastet – war in seinem Verhalten den Kolonien gegenüber unschlüssig, seine Politik nie eindeutig. Sein Versuch, die Geldnot der Krone auf Kosten der nordamerikanischen Besitzungen zu beheben, rief eine ernsthafte Krise hervor. Sondersteuern auf Zucker (1764), Drucksachen (1765), das Zollgesetz von 1767 und die „Zwangsakten" von 1774 forderten den Kolonien schwere Opfer ab. Ihr Handel wurde zwangsweise auf das Mutterland beschränkt. So mußte ihnen die britische Regierung als Regierung der britischen Kaufleute und Fabrikanten erscheinen, deren Interessen sie rücksichtslos verfolgte. 1764 wurde in allen Kolonien das Papiergeld sowie der Gold- und Silberimport verboten: nach 1764 herrschte ernsthafte Geldknappheit. Der Mangel an Tauschwaren, verbunden mit der gleichzeitigen Androhung hoher Steuern, trug dazu bei, radikale Gesinnungen bei den Kolonisten aufkeimen zu lassen. Daß die Situation der Kolonisten, die praktisch aller Zahlungsmittel beraubt waren, untragbar war, wurde bald auch in England erkannt: Es mußte der Eindruck aufkommen, daß Eigeninitiativen der Kolonien dem britischen Parlament nur in der grauen Theorie willkommen waren, im politischen Alltag jedoch besser unterdrückt wurden. Ursprünglich wurden die englischen Gesetze recht leger gehandhabt. 1765 begann England mit der „Stempel-Akte" sein

From Revolution to Independence 1776—1784

The American Revolution was the first revolution in modern history to be fought for the right of self-government and the guarantee of civil liberties. It was also the first revolution of a colony against the mother country in modern history. Thus the American Revolution was an event of worldwide significance, which set an example for other colonial peoples.

The Revolutionary War was many-faceted. To begin with, it was a war for national independence; but it was also a civil war, and a factor in a world conflict which saw Britain pitted against France and Spain as well as against her own colonies. We must bear in mind that this first rebellion against a motherland was directed against the most enlightened imperial power in Europe. British colonies enjoyed more independence and freedom than any of the many other colonies in the world. French and Spanish colonial policies were brutally severe and repressive.

This liberalism on the part of the British meant that the American colonies entered the war with more than a century of relative autonomy behind them. Had certain other matters not prompted the British to tighten their hold on the American colonies, it is likely that the present United States would have remained a British dominion to this day.

Plagued by internal problems and power struggles, Britain was unable to maintain a consistent colonial policy. A series of special enactments, intended to establish a greater degree of order in the colonies, only resulted in provoking resentment and causing a crisis within the empire. The imposition of the Sugar Act of 1765; the Townshend Duties, which went into effect in 1767, and the Coercive Acts of 1774 exacted painful sacrifices from the colonies. Their freedom to trade anywhere in the world was restricted, and they were forced to deal exclusively with the markets of their mother country. The American colonists soon began to realize that the government of Britain existed largely to serve the interests of Britain's merchants and manufacturers, even when these interests were inimical to those of the colonies. In 1764, paper money was forbidden in all the colonies, resulting in a severe money shortage. This lack of ready capital, combined with a threat of high taxes, helped to bring about the kind of conditions which nurture radicalism in any society. America was no exception here. Whenever an American business posed a threat to a British competitor, the American was weakened by an Act of Parliament. At the beginning, these enactments were more honored in the breach than in the observance as far as enforcement was concerned, but by the time of the

Die „Boston Tea Party" vom 16. Dezember 1773: Als Indianer verkleidete Kolonisten werfen den aus England kommenden Tee ins Meer, um gegen die Sondersteuer zu protestieren.

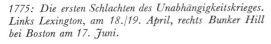

The Boston Tea Party on the 16th of December, 1773, was one of the first acts of revolution in the colonies.

1775: Die ersten Schlachten des Unabhängigkeitskrieges. Links Lexington, am 18./19. April, rechts Bunker Hill bei Boston am 17. Juni.

1775: The first battles of the War of Independence, at Lexington on April 18/19 (left), and at Bunker Hill on June 17 (right).

Durchsetzungsvermögen unter Beweis zu stellen. Dies und die darauf folgenden Gesetze stellten jedoch einen Angriff auf das Selbstbewußtsein der Kolonisten dar und gossen reichlich Wasser auf die Mühlen patriotischer Propaganda.

Mit dem Ende des Englisch-Französischen Krieges 1763 war die Neue Welt der französischen Gefahr enthoben: dennoch blieben viele englische Truppen in den Kolonien zurück und wurden dort dauerhaft einquartiert. Da die Amerikaner keinerlei Nutzen in deren Anwesenheit sahen, entstanden Unstimmigkeiten zwischen den Truppen und den Kolonisten, die besonders in New York und Boston, den größten Garnisonen, die ohnehin angespannte Lage verschärften. Vor dem „Beherbergungsgesetz" von 1765 waren die Kolonisten keinesfalls gewohnt, Soldaten bei sich aufnehmen zu müssen, und dementsprechend verbittert war auch ihre Reaktion auf die ihnen neuerlich auferlegten Einschränkungen. Die feindseligen Gefühle gegen die englischen Soldaten, zusammen mit weiteren Steuererhöhungen für die Kolonien, ließen einen Zusammenstoß unvermeidlich werden. Am 5. März 1770 bewarf eine Gruppe von Kolonisten die englischen „Redcoats" mit Schneebällen und Steinen: im anschließenden Gefecht gab es 3 Tote und 8 Verletzte, darunter den Neger Crispus Attucks, der als erster bei den Feindseligkeiten mit den Engländern sein Leben ließ. Zum „Massaker von Boston" aufgebauscht ging dieser Vorfall in die Geschichte ein.

Durch Erlaß der „Tee-Akte" vom Mai 1773 wollten die Engländer überschüssigen Tee in den Kolonien absetzen und der British East India Company ein Monopol auf dem amerikanischen Markt sichern. Am 16. Dezember 1773 brannten in Boston die Sicherungen durch: Empörte Kolonisten, die sich als Indianer verkleidet hatten, verhinderten das Löschen einer Teeladung, indem sie von Bord ins Hafenbecken kippten. Englands Rache für die „Boston Tea Party" bestand im Erlaß dreier „Zwangsakten" im Mai 1774: der Hafen von Boston wurde geschlossen und der Modus der Gouverneurswahl verschärft. Dies löste eine Kette von Ereignissen aus, die schließlich zur Unabhängigkeitserklärung führten.

Im September 1774 wurde in Philadelphia der „Erste Kontinentalkongreß" einberufen. Die Kongreßmitglieder beschlossen, daß die Kolonisten keine Zugeständnisse machen würden, ehe England nicht die „Zwangsakte" aufgehoben habe, und einigten sich auf ein weiteres Treffen im Frühling 1775. Währenddessen verschlechterten sich die Verhältnisse: die „Minutemen", Rebellen in Massachussetts, bereiteten sich auf die Bekämpfung aller Aktionen der in Boston stationierten „Redcoats" vor und trugen in Concord Gewehre und Schießpulver zusammen. Als der britische Militärgouverneur am 18. April 1775 700 Soldaten aussandte, um die Magazine in Concord zu zerstören, kam es in Lexington und Concord zu Zusammenstößen mit den „Minutemen", wobei die Engländer durch den Verlust von 300 Männern eine Niederlage zu verzeichnen hatten. Der „Zweite Kontinentalkongreß" im Mai 1775 ernannte den Landjunker George Washington aus Virginia zum Oberbefehlshaber der regionalen Truppeneinheiten. Am 6. Juli 1775 nahm der Kongreß die „Declaration of the Causes and Necessity of taking up Arms" an, in der die Amerikaner ihrem Mutterland gegenüber zum Ausdruck brachten, daß sie nicht gewillt seien, von ihren Überzeugungen abzuweichen. „Unsere Sache ist

Stamp Act in 1765, Britain began to exert heavy pressure for strict enforcement of these laws: a heavy blow to the self-confidence of the colonists and a rich source of grist for the propaganda mills of the patriots.

By the end of the French and Indian War (1763), the French no longer posed a threat to the North American continent; nevertheless, thousands of British troops continued to be maintained in the colonies. The colonists could not understand what further purpose this large military aggregation was supposed to serve. Bad feelings between the troops and the colonists led to sharp tension, especially in New York and Boston, where most of the troops were stationed. The Quartering Act of 1765, requiring New York colonists to house British troops in their homes, was understandably bitterly resented. With feelings against the British soldiers running high, and the levying of further taxes, the outbreak of actual hostility could only be a question of time. On March 5, 1770, it happened. A group of Boston colonists began taunting a group of Redcoats and pelting them with rocks and snowballs. Their commander ordered the men to fire, killing five men and wounding six others, two of them mortally. The commander was subsequently brought to trial and acquitted of the charge of murder, but the incident, rather grandly exaggerated by the propagandists with the title "The Boston Massacre", did bring about the repeal of the Townshend Duties, and thus proved to the colonists that violence was clearly a language the British understood. It is an ironic footnote to this event that the first person to be felled by a British bullet happened to be a Black sailor by the name of Crispus Attucks. To a large degree, the American Revolution was fought by slaveholders, and the issue of Black slavery was hotly debated at the Congress of 1776 which led to the signing of the Declaration of Independence. The threat of a Southern walkout prompted Jefferson reluctantly to remove an anti-slavery clause from the document. It would be another hundred years before the Black American even began to achieve his independence.

With the passage of the Tea Act in May 1773, the British attempted to force the Americans to purchase all surplus tea from the British East India Company, which was also granted a monopoly on all commerce in this commodity in the colonies. When a ship loaded with tea landed in Boston harbor on December 16, 1773, a band of men disguised as Indians dumped the tea in the harbor. In response to this "Boston Tea Party", the British passed three Coercive or "Intolerable Acts" in March and May of 1774. These Acts closed the port of Boston, changed the manner of selection of the colonial governor and set in motion a series of events which would culminate in armed rebellion.

The first Continental Congress was called together in Philadelphia in September, 1774. The members adopted resolutions asserting that the colonies would make no concessions unless the Coercive Acts were repealed. When this first Congress adjourned, its members agreed to meet again in the spring of 1775, should concessions from Britain not be immediately forthcoming, but this was not to be the case. Conditions actually worsened. In Massachusetts, a citizens' militia, called the "minute men" because of their ability to be combat ready at "a minute's notice", went into training. They began storing munitions and ammunition in Concord. On April 18, 1775, the

Detail aus Trumbulls „Unterzeichnung der Unabhängigkeitserklärung".

Detail from Trumbull's "Signing of the Declaration of Independence."

General Washington führt seine Truppen in die Schlacht gegen hessische Söldner bei Trenton, am 26. Dezember 1776.

General Washington leads his Troops into battle against Hessian mercenaries at Trenton on December 26, 1776.

gerecht. Unsere Gemeinschaft vollkommen. Unsere eigenen Mittel sind bedeutend, und Hilfe von außen ist zweifellos erhältlich, wenn die Notwendigkeit besteht." Daraufhin erklärte der englische König im August 1775 seine Untertanen zu Aufständischen und begann, fremde Söldner anzuheuern und Truppen aufzustellen. Im Januar 1776, nach dem Erscheinen von Thomas Paines *Common Sense*, flutete der Wille zur Unabhängigkeit unaufhaltsam durch alle Kolonien, bis schließlich am 4. Juli 1776 der Kongreß die Unabhängigkeitserklärung verabschiedete. Sie tat weltweit kund, daß „diese Vereinigten Kolonien rechtmäßig freie und unabhängige Staaten sind".

Diese Erklärung war auf John Lockes Philosophie vom Naturrecht begründet und machte die Gleichheit aller Menschen sowie die Unveräußerlichkeit bestimmter Rechte geltend: auf Leben, Freiheit und das Streben nach Glück. Auch Überzeugungen, die die Amerikaner längst praktizierten, wurden nachträglich postuliert und theoretisch untermauert: daß Regierungen auf der Zustimmung der Regierten begründet und zum Schutz der Rechte des Volkes eingesetzt sind.

Die amerikanische Revolution war kein Aufstand der Verzweifelten oder der Gesetzlosen; ganz im Gegenteil, es saßen einige der hervorragendsten Amerikaner im Kongreß: John Hancock, George Washington, Thomas Jefferson, John Adams und Benjamin Franklin. Aufgrund ihrer hohen Stellung und ihrer Achtung vor dem Gesetz fühlten sich diese Männer einer neugierigen Welt gegenüber verpflichtet, ihr drastisches Vorgehen zu rechtfertigen. John Hancocks berühmte Unterschrift fiel so groß und deutlich aus, „daß der englische König sie ohne Brille lesen kann".

Der Unabhängigkeitskrieg sollte bis Vietnam Amerikas längster Krieg bleiben; aber er spielte sich in wesentlich kleinerem Rahmen ab. Washingtons Armee umfaßte im allgemeinen zwischen 5000 und 9000 Mann und überschritt 20000 nie. Die meisten seiner Soldaten verpflichteten sich für kurze Zeit, manchmal nur 3 Monate, und entsprechend niedrig war auch die Kampfmoral. Die hohe Desertionsquote machte es fast unmöglich, Disziplin aufrechtzuerhalten. So kam es oft zu verfrühten Angriffsbefehlen, weil die Befehlshaber befürchten mußten, ihre Soldaten von einem Tag auf den anderen zu verlieren, sobald ihre Verpflichtung abgelaufen war. Als der Krieg für die amerikanische Seite den Tiefpunkt erreicht hatte – Washingtons Truppen waren halb verhungert und erfroren in Valley Forge umzingelt – kam unerwartete Hilfe aus Deutschland: Baron von Steuben, ein ehemaliger Rittmeister im preußischen Heer, bot der Kontinentalarmee als begeisterter Verfechter der amerikanischen Ideale seine Unterstützung an. Washington erkannte Steubens hervorragendes Organisationstalent sofort und ernannte ihn zum Generalinspektor der gesamten Armee. Die wachsende Disziplin, Organisation und der Zusammenhalt des amerikanischen Heeres gehen auf Steubens Bemühungen zurück. In der Schlacht von Yorktown war er der Oberbefehlshaber, der als erster das Kapitulationsangebot von Lord Cornwallis erhielt. Amerika zeigte sich Steuben durch Landschenkungen im Norden New Yorks erkenntlich, wo er seinen Lebensabend verbrachte.

Aber auch die britischen Truppen befanden sich in keinem allzu guten Zustand. Sowohl die königliche Flotte als auch die Landstreitkräfte waren bei Kriegsbeginn weit unter ihre übliche Zahlenstärke gesunken. England behalf sich mit dem

British military governor sent 700 regulars out from Boston to destroy the Concord storehouses. They were met by companies of minute men who inflicted 300 casualties on them. The Redcoat company was almost completely annihilated in this battle – the "shot heard 'round the world'", in Emerson's words, had been fired.

During the second Continental Congress in May of 1775, a gentleman planter from Virginia by the name of George Washington was appointed commander in chief of the provincial forces surrounding Boston. On July 6, 1775, Congress adopted a "Declaration of the Causes and Necessity of Taking up Arms" making it clear to the British that the colonists meant business. "Our cause," the Declaration stated, "is just. Our union perfect. Our internal resources are great, and, if necessary, foreign assistance is undoubtedly attainable." In August, 1775, the King of England declared his subjects to be in rebellion, and he began recruiting foreign mercenaries and preparing British regulars.

In January, 1776, Thomas Paine published *Common Sense*, which more than anything else written at the time served to unite public opinion behind the cause of independence. On July 4, 1776, Congress made its Declaration of Independence, proclaiming to the world that "these United Colonies are, and of right ought to be Free and Independent States."

The philosophy upon which the Declaration was based was John Locke's philosophy of natural law. The Declaration stated that all men are created equal, and that each person was endowed with certain unalienable rights. Locke had defined these rights as "Life, Liberty and Property". Jefferson and his collaborators changed it to "Life, Liberty and the Pursuit of Happiness". The document reaffirmed what Americans had long recognized in actual practice: that governments are based upon the consent of the governed, and are established to secure these fundamental rights for the people. The American Revolution was not a social revolution of desparate, lawless individuals. On the contrary, the leadership of the Continental Congress included some of the most prominent men in America – John Hancock, George Washington, Thomas Jefferson, John Adams, and Benjamin Franklin. Their high positions and high regard for the rule of law obligated them, they felt, to explain this drastic step to an interested world in unmistakable terms. John Hancock's signature was written large and clear; "so fat George in London can read it without his glasses." The War for Independence was to prove the longest war in America's history, except for Vietnam. Unlike Vietnam, it was fought on a much smaller scale. George Washington's army never exceeded 20,000 men, and there were seldom more than from 5,000 to 9,000 under his command at any one time. He was also constantly plagued by low morale and a high desertion rate. It was difficult to establish and maintain discipline among troops, many of whom had only enlisted for short periods of time, sometimes as little as three months. Often a commander in the field would give a premature order to attack, knowing that if he waited another day, his men's enlistments would expire, and they would desert him. At America's lowest point of the war, when Washington and a few thousand troops were starving and freezing in the terrible winter at Valley Forge, the American cause was given an

Molly Pitcher, die populäre amerikanische Revolutionsheldin, bedient hier anstelle ihres wegen der Hitze ohnmächtigen Mannes dessen Kanone. Sie entstammte einer deutschen Familie aus Pennsylvanien.

Molly Pitcher was the nickname of Mary Ludwig Hays McCauley, née Hass (or Has), the descendant of German immigrants in Pennsylvania. The illustration shows the famous legend of the lady who carried pitchers of water to the soldiers taking over her artilleryman husband's cannon as he was prostrated by the heat on the extremely hot day of the battle of Monmouth.

REGULATIONS
FOR THE
ORDER AND DISCIPLINE
OF THE
TROOPS OF THE UNITED STATES.

BY BARON DE STUBEN,
TO WHICH ARE PREFIXED THE
LAWS AND REGULATIONS
FOR
GOVERNING AND DISCIPLINING
THE MILITIA OF THE UNITED STATES,
AND THE
LAWS FOR FORMING AND REGULATING
THE
MILITIA OF THE STATE OF NEW HAMPSHIRE.

PUBLISHED BY ORDER OF THE HON. GENERAL-COURT
OF THE STATE OF NEW-HAMPSHIRE.

PORTSMOUTH:
PRINTED BY J. MELCHER, PRINTER TO THE STATE OF

Friedrich Wilhelm von Steuben: Als mittelloser Rittmeister kam er 1777 nach Amerika und wurde ein Held der Revolution. In Valley Forge, Washingtons Winterquartier 1777/78, bildete er die zusammengewürfelten Truppen zu einer schlagkräftigen Armee aus. Seine „Regeln für die Ordnung und Disziplin der Truppen der Vereinigten Staaten" blieben jahrzehntelang Ausbildungsrichtlinien des amerikanischen Militärs.

Friedrich Wilhelm von Steuben was one of the great heroes of the Revolution. The Prussian soldier of fortune pounded military discipline into the farmers and yeomen encamped in Valley Forge, molding this rag-tag army into an effective military force. He has become the symbol of German-American relations, and von Steuben streets, halls and inns can be found in any German community in the United States.

Kauf von 30000 hessischen Söldnern, was in Deutschland zu lebhaften öffentlichen Auseinandersetzungen führte und in weiten Kreisen auf Widerspruch stieß. Kassel, im Herzen Hessens gelegen, wurde zu einem Zentrum des deutschen Engagements für die amerikanische Sache. Dagegen war Hannover mit seinen engen Verbindungen zum englischen Thron eher der britischen Sache gewogen. Die deutschen Soldaten, die in Amerika auf Seiten der englischen Einheiten kämpften, empfanden teils neutral, teils desertierten sie, um auf amerikanischer Seite weiterzukämpfen. Gneisenau, ein junger deutscher Offizier, erkannte den militärischen Wert einer patriotisch inspirierten Bürgerwehr und bemühte sich 30 Jahre später um die Demokratisierung der preußischen Armee. General von Riedesel, der deutsche Kommandeur des „Brunswick"-Kontingents, war so stark von Amerika beeindruckt, daß er seinen Soldaten nach Kriegsende empfahl, im Lande zu bleiben. Tatsächlich blieben auch mehr als 12000 der 30000 deutschen Soldaten in Amerika, um sich dort für immer niederzulassen.

Ein weiterer Vorteil, der zum Sieg der Kolonisten beitrug, war ihre Vertrautheit im Umgang mit Feuerwaffen. Waren die Europäer gewohnt, Kriege durch Berufssoldaten und Söldner austragen zu lassen, so war die amerikanische Revolution der Kampf eines gesamten Volkes, das mit Waffen umgehen konnte. Seit anderthalb Jahrhunderten die Verteidigung gegen die Franzosen und Indianer gewohnt, vertrauten sie auf ihre Gewehre, die ihnen im täglichen Leben zur Versorgung mit Fleisch und zum Schutz des Getreides unentbehrlich waren. Diese Vertrautheit mit Feuerwaffen fehlte dem zivilen Durchschnittseuropäer. Bei Concord und Bunker Hill, der blutigsten Schlacht, war dies von großer Bedeutung und räumte den Kolonisten beachtliche Vorteile ein. Frauen kämpften an der Seite ihrer Männer – unter ihnen auch die erste Heldin der Revolution, Molly Pitcher, die Tochter eines deutschen Immigranten. Während der Schlacht von Mon-

unexpected boost from Germany. Baron von Steuben, a retired cavalry officer from the Prussian Army, became an enthusiastic supporter of the American side, and offered his services to the Continental Army. George Washington was quick to recognize Steuben's remarkable disciplinary and organizational abilities, and appointed the German to be inspector general of the entire army. Steuben's ideas on the discipline of citizen-soldiers put into practice were a decisive factor in the American victory, a victory he was to witness as the field commander in Yorktown who received the first surrender overtures from the British commander, Lord Cornwallis. After the war, Steuben retired to a farm in upstate New York which had been awarded to him by a grateful nation in recognition of his service.

Much of the colonists' victory can be attributed to the sorry state of the British forces at the time of the war. The Royal Navy had been allowed to fall disastrously below its accustomed high standard, and the army was so far below strength that 30,000 German troops had to be enlisted from the Principality of Hesse. This stirred up considerable public controversy in Germany on both sides of the issue. Many Germans heartily disapproved of the dispatching of German troops to aid the British cause. The Hessian city of Cassel, right in the heart of the Principality, was a center of pro-American sentiment in Germany. With the head of the House of Hanover on the British throne, Hanover was obviously more sympathetic to the British. Most of the Germans serving the British in America can be said to have remained neutral in spirit. In fact, many deserted and went over to the American side. General von Riedesel, the German commander of the Brunswick contingent, was so impressed by America, that he encouraged his soldiers to remain there as civilians after the war.

A young officer named Gneisenau was so impressed by the enthusiasm of the citizen-soldiers that he later introduced democratic features into the

Washington und von Steuben in Valley Forge.

Washington and von Steuben inspecting the squalid conditions at Valley Forge.

Ende der Feindseligkeiten: Lord Cornwallis ergibt sich General Washington bei Yorktown am 19. Oktober 1781. Unter den 7200 Gefangenen befand sich auch der spätere preußische Generalfeldmarschall Gneisenau.

Lord Cornwallis surrenders to Washington at Yorktown, October 19, 1781. Among the 7,200 prisoners was the later Prussian Army General Gneisenau.

mouth am 28. Juni 1778 versorgte sie die Soldaten mit Wasser und Munition und nahm – laut Überlieferungen – den Platz ihres Mannes an der Kanone ein, als dieser von der Hitze überwältigt zusammenbrach.

Zu Kriegsanfang mußten die Amerikaner zahlreiche Rückschläge einstecken: So erlitt Washington in der Schlacht von Long Island eine Niederlage durch die britischen Truppen unter Howe, die New York bis Kriegsende besetzt hielten. Dagegen siegte Washington 1776 bei Trenton: in der Weihnachtsnacht überquerte er mit seinen Truppen den Delaware und nahm mehr als 1000 der auf englischer Seite kämpfenden Hessen gefangen. Der Wendepunkt zugunsten der Amerikaner kam aber erst im Sommer 1777, als Washingtons Armee in Saratoga, New York, auf die britischen Truppen unter General Sir John Burgoyne stieß. Dieser wollte das Hudsontal besetzen, um Neu-England von den südlichen Kolonien zu isolieren, büßte aber in der Schlacht am 17. Oktober 1777 nicht nur die verstreuten Überreste seines Heeres, sondern auch das Prestige der englischen Militärmacht ein.

Der Sieg bei Saratoga stellte die neuerworbenen taktischen Fähigkeiten der jungen amerikanischen Armee endgültig unter Beweis. Dieser Erfolg brachte den Amerikanern auch die erwünschte offizielle Unterstützung durch Frankreich, das 1778 in den Krieg eintrat und 1781 zum endgültigen Sieg über die englischen Truppen unter Lord Cornwallis beitrug. Bei seiner Kapitulation am 19. Oktober spielte eine Blaskapelle aus Washingtons Armee „Die Welt steht auf dem Kopf". Als diese Neuigkeiten England erreichten und offensichtlich wurde, daß der Krieg so gut wie verloren war, einigten sich die königlichen Minister auf einen Friedensschluß mit den rebellischen Kolonien.

So kam es 1783 zu den Pariser Friedensverhandlungen, und die Ratifizierung der Verträge durch den amerikanischen Kongreß setzte dem Krieg am 14. Januar 1784 ein Ende. Wichtigste Aufgabe Benjamin Franklins, John Jays und John Adams', der amerikanischen Unterhändler in Paris, war das Aushandeln der Grenzen für den neuen Staat. Man einigte sich darauf, daß sie im Süden durch den 31. Breitengrad und im Westen durch den Mississippi gebildet werden sollten; die nördliche Grenze, die damals festgelegt wurde, blieb bis heute unverändert. So besaßen die Amerikaner genug Raum, die Prinzipien, für die sie gestritten hatten, in die Tat umzusetzen.

Prussian Army. Of the 30,000 Germans who went to America as soldiers, 12,000 stayed on to settle the country they had been recruited to fight.

Another important factor in the American victory was the familiarity of the Americans with firearms, the long-barreled rifle in particular. Europeans were used to having their wars fought for them by armies of professionals and mercenaries. By contrast, the Americans could truly be called an army of the people. As citizens of a frontier society, they owned rifles and were proficient in the use of these accurate weapons, as they needed them every day to protect their fields or to go hunting. This played a significant role both at Concord and at Bunker Hill, the bloodiest battle of the war.

This was also a war which had its heroines as well as its heroes. The best-known of these brave women was "Molly Pitcher", the daughter of a German immigrant named Hass. She had picked up the nickname because she used to carry supplies and pitchers of water to the soldiers in the field. Legend has it that on one of these excursions, during the Battle of Monmouth on June 28, 1778, she saw her husband faint from the heat and scurried to take the place he had left vacant by his cannon.

The Americans suffered many setbacks in the early stages of the war. Washington was defeated by the British commander, Lord Howe, in the battle for New York, which kept New York City under British occupation throughout the course of the war. But Washington won an astonishing victory over the British on Christmas night of 1776. Crossing the Delaware from Pennsylvania, he attacked a garrison of Hessian troops at Trenton, capturing over a thousand men. The summer of 1777 marked the turning point of the war. At Saratoga, New York, Washington's army met the British, commanded by General Sir John Burgoyne. Burgoyne had hoped to capture the Hudson Valley in order to isolate New England from the southern colonies. Following a pitched battle on October 17, 1777, Burgoyne surrendered not only the tattered remnants of his forces, but also much of the prestige of British military strength. The victory at Saratoga proved once and for all that the young American Army could handle itself with distinction on the field of battle. It also served to convince the French to provide the assistance needed for the final victory. France entered the war in 1778, and in 1781 helped defeat Cornwallis at Yorktown. On October 19, 1781, Cornwallis' men marched out to lay down their arms while the band played "The World Turned Upside Down". When the news reached Britain, the King's ministers agreed that the war was all but lost, and that they should finally make peace with the rebellious colonies.

The Peace of Paris was negotiated in 1783 and ratified by Congress on January 14, 1784, bringing the war formally to an end. The American negotiators in Paris, Benjamin Franklin, John Jay and John Adams, won America a northern border which still exists, a western border at the Mississippi, and a southern border at the thirty-first parallel. The Americans now had plenty of room in which to realize their grand dream of freedom and democracy.

Der Freiheitskampf im Urteil deutscher Zeitgenossen

Die Neuigkeiten, die nach und nach aus dem Unabhängigkeitskrieg nach Europa drangen, wurden von den Gebildeten der Alten Welt mit großer Anteilnahme aufgenommen. Seiner historischen Bedeutung war man sich von Anfang an bewußt. „Ich will nicht weissagen, so verführerisch die apokalyptische Zahl 1777 auch dazu einladen mögte", schrieb schon bald nach Ausbruch der Kämpfe Johann Christian von Dohm im *Teutschen Merkur*, einem der meistgelesenen Journale jener Zeit. „Doch das größte politische Eräugniß des siebenten Decenniums unseres Jahrhunderts (und vielleicht bey der Nachwelt des ganzen Säkulums) ist ohne Zweifel der noch immer fortdauernde Prozeß zwischen Mutter und Tochter, Großbrittanien und seinen Kolonien; dessen Entscheidung vielleicht für einen großen Theil der Menschheit äußerst wichtig seyn kann . . . Eine interessante Abänderung des itzigen politischen Systems scheint eine fast unvermeidliche Folge . . . Dieser Ausgang kann dem Handel neue Wege bahnen, neue Verbindungen unter Nationen und Welttheilen knüpfen. Er kann der Aufklärung größern Kreis, der Denkart der Völker neue Kühnheit, neues Leben dem Freiheytsgeiste geben."

Man bewunderte die Fähigkeit der „Rebellen", mit der Feder ebenso erfolgreich umzugehen wie mit den Waffen. „Aus jeder dieser Zeilen spricht Patriotismus und Liebe zur Freiheyt, und sie verdienen würklich den schönsten Reden des Demosthenes und Cicero an die Seite gestellt zu werden", notierte der Herausgeber des *Teutschen Merkur*, Christoph Martin Wieland (1733–1813), einer der Wortführer der literarischen Aufklärung, bei der Lektüre offizieller Dokumente. Man feierte die Amerikaner als die „Hellenen unserer Tage", die dem feudalen Europa den Weg zu „süßer Gleichheit" gewiesen und der verhaßten „Adelsbrut" endgültig die Alleinherrschaft streitig gemacht hätten. Ihren Feldherrn, George Washington, rühmte man als neuen Herkules. „Die Namen Franklin und Washington fingen an, am politischen und kriegerischen Horizont zu glühen und zu funkeln. Man wünschte den Amerikanern Glück", charakterisierte Johann Wolfgang von Goethe (1749 bis 1832) die öffentliche Meinung jener Jahre in seinen Lebenserinnerungen *Dichtung und Wahrheit*. „Ein wundervolles Land", nannte er die junge Republik, „welches die Augen aller Welt auf sich zog."

Geradezu euphorische Begeisterung löste die Nachricht vom Ende der militärischen Aktionen und dem endgültigen Sieg der Patrioten bei jenen Deutschen aus, die Partei für die amerikanische Sache ergriffen hatten. Sie alle stimmten darin überein, daß mit der Unabhängigkeit der 13 Vereinigten Staaten eine neue weltgeschichtliche Epoche begonnen habe, das Zeitalter der Freiheit:

Frei bist du! (sag's in höherem Siegston),
Entzücktes Lied! frei, frei nun Amerika!
Erschöpft, gebeugt, bedeckt mit Schande
Weichet dein Feind, und du triumphierest.
Der edle Kampf für Freiheit und Vaterland,
Er ist gekämpfet, rühmlich gekämpfet. Nimm
Den Kranz am Ziel! Europens Jubel
Feire den heiligsten aller Siege.

The Fight for Freedom Through the Eyes of 18th Century Germans

The news gradually sifting through to Europe after the War of Independence was received with considerable interest by the educated classes of the Old World. From the first, there was no doubt as to the historical significance of the event. "I shall resist the temptation to prophesy, although the apocalyptic figure '1777' makes it almost impossible to do so" wrote Johann Christian von Dohm shortly after the start of hostilities in the *Teutsche Merkur*, one of the most popular periodicals of the day. "Nevertheless, the greatest event of the seventh decade of our century (and posterity may well decide, of the century as a whole) no doubt is this still-continuing conflict between Mother and Daughter, Great Britain and her colonies; its outcome may be of the utmost importance to a large portion of mankind . . . an interesting change of the present political system seems an almost inevitable result . . . this outcome may open up new avenues to trade, and create new ties between nations and continents. It can further enlightenment, encourage the nations to think more boldly, and infuse new life into the spirit of Liberty".

The ability of the "rebels" to handle the pen with the same dexterity as the sword was generally admired. "Every word breathes patriotism and love of Liberty, and they truly deserve to be compared with the most noble speeches of Cicero or Demosthenes" commented the publisher of the *Teutsche Merkur*, Christoph Martin Wieland (1733–1813), one of the spokesmen of Literary Enlightenment, when he read some of the official documents of the insurgents. The Americans were celebrated as the "Hellenes of our time" who had shown feudal Europe the way to "sweet equality", and had once and for all challenged the sole rulership of the hated "breed of the nobility". George Washington, their Commander-in-Chief, was praised as a new Hercules. "The names of Franklin and Washington started to glow and sparkle on the political and martial horizon. Our good wishes were with the Americans". Thus Johann Wolfgang von Goethe (1749–1832) describes public opinion of those years in his autobiographical work *Truth and Poetry*. "A magnificent country" he called the young Republic, "and a magnet for the eyes of the whole world".

The news of the end of hostilities and the final victory of the patriots resulted in delirious exultation and euphoria in the case of those Germans whose sympathies had been on the side of the Americans. They all agreed that the Independence of the 13 United States ushered in a new epoch of World History, the Age of Liberty.

You're free now – free! That is your Victory
Raise up your voice in song – America is free!
Humbled and bowed, your enemy's retreat
Proclaims your triumph, and his own defeat.
The fight for country and for Liberty
was fought – and won. Yours is the victor's
crown.
The nations of all Europe will resound
With echoes of this holy victory.

Thus an anonymous poet expressed popular feeling in the *Berlinische Monatsschrift* of 1783. As early as

In Deutschland fielen die Ereignisse der amerikanischen Revolution mit der literarischen Epoche des „Sturm und Drang" zusammen. Maximilian Klingers Stück gleichen Titels gab der Bewegung ihren Namen. Hier der Titelkupfer von J. Albrecht zu Klingers Trauerspiel „Die Zwillinge", das 1776, dem Jahr der amerikanischen Unabhängigkeitserklärung uraufgeführt wurde. Auf der folgenden Seite ein Aquarell von Victor Heideloff: Friedrich Schiller (am Baum lehnend) liest Mitstudenten aus „Die Räuber" vor, einem Drama, das ganz und gar vom revolutionären Geist jener Epoche durchdrungen war.

While the Americans declared their independence in Philadelphia, the revolutionary ideals of Sturm und Drang (Storm and Stress) were in full flower an ocean away in Germany. This etching is taken from the book edition of a play by Maximilian Klinger, "The Twins", first presented in Independence Year of 1776. On the opposite page we see Friedrich Schiller reading aloud to his fellow students from his play "Die Räuber" (The Robbers), one of the most ardent revolutionary plays of the period.

Mit diesen Worten gab ein anonymer Poet in der *Berlinischen Monatsschrift* von 1783 der allgemeinen Stimmung Ausdruck. Und schon zwei Jahre früher hatte Friedrich Klopstock (1724–1803) die neue Nation in *Der jetzige Krieg* hymnisch besungen:

> Du bist die Morgenröthe
> Eines nahenden großen Tags . . .
> Der Jahrhunderte strahlt.

Und ebenso hymnisch dichtet er an anderer Stelle: „In Amerikas Strömen / flammet schon eigenes Licht, / leuchtet den Völkern umher". Mit der Metapher von der Morgenröte schlug er den enthusiastischen Ton an, der die Haltung der Deutschen zu Amerika bis weit ins 19. Jahrhundert geprägt hat. Ihre klassische Formulierung fand sie in den fast sprichwörtlich gewordenen Verszeilen des alten Goethe: „Amerika, du hast es besser / Als unser Kontinent . . ."

Auch eher nüchterne und realpolitisch denkende Beobachter schlossen sich der überschwenglichen Beurteilung des erfolgreich verlaufenen Freiheitskampfes an. Mit Genugtuung stellten sie fest, wie die konservative Überzeugung, daß in der Demokratie „kein Menschenglück höherer Art" möglich sei – so der Göttinger Professor Schlözer – durch die Ereignisse in Amerika widerlegt wurde. Endlich waren die Ideen der Aufklärung vom natürlichen Recht der Bürger auf persönliche Freiheit und politische Selbstbestimmung, sowie die naturgegebene Gleichheit aller Menschen zur verbrieften Grundlage eines Gemeinwesens geworden und hatten sich in der rauhen Wirklichkeit eines turbulenten politischen Alltags glänzend bewährt.

Große Hoffnungen, daß nach amerikanischem Vorbild Veränderungen auch in Deutschland möglich seien, hegten vor allem die Vertreter der jungen Generation von Dichtern: neben Goethe vor allem Maximilian Klinger (1752–1831), Friedrich Daniel Schubart (1739–1791) und Friedrich Schiller (1759–1805), die „Stürmer und Dränger", wie sie die Literaturgeschichte genannt hat.

Schiller faßte sogar vorübergehend den Entschluß: „Wenn Amerika frei wird, so ist es ausgemacht, daß ich hingehe", und empörte sich im selben Jahr (1783) in seinem Stück *Kabale und Liebe* über den Verkauf hessischer Soldaten an die Briten. Und Klinger bestimmte als Schauplatz seines Dramas *Sturm und Drang* (1777), das der ganzen Bewegung den Namen gab: „Amerika – mitten im Krieg". Gleichermaßen begeistert verfolgte Schubart als Dichter und Publizist die amerikanischen Ereignisse. Als einer der ersten Deutschen hatte er schon 1775 mit dem *Freiheitslied eines Nordamerikanischen Kolonisten* für die Patrioten Partei ergriffen:

> Hinaus, hinaus ins Ehrenfeld
> Mit blinkendem Gewehr!
> Kolumbus, deine ganze Welt
> tritt mutig daher!
> Die Göttin Freiheit mit der Fahn!
> (Der Sklave sah sie nie)
> Geht, Brüder, seht: sie geht voran!
> O blutet für sie! . . .
> Auf, Brüder, ins Gewehr!

two years before, Friedrich Klopstock (1724 — 1803) had written a hymn to the new nation entitled "The Present War":

> You are the rosy dawn
> Of a great new day . . .
> That will last for centuries.

Just as lyrically he writes elsewhere: "The rivers of America/have a radiance of their own/lighting the way for other people". His metaphor of the rosy dawn set the enthusiastic tone which determined the German attitude toward America until far into the 19th century. It was given its definitive form by the aged Goethe: "America, your lot is fairer/than ours . . .".

Even fairly sober and politically realistic observers were carried away by the enthusiastic admiration which followed in the wake of the successful fight for Liberty. With some complacency, they noted that the conservative conviction that "no human happiness of a higher type" would be possible in a democracy – as Professor Schlözer of Göttingen put it – had been proved wrong by events in America. Finally, the ideas of Enlightenment as to the natural right of all citizens to personal liberty and political self-determination, as well as the natural equality of all men, had become the documented foundations of a society and proved themselves brilliantly in the midst of the rough reality of the turbulent everyday life of politics.

High hopes that changes along the lines of the American example might be possible in Germany too were cherished mostly by the generation of young poets. Besides Goethe, there was first of all Maximilian Klinger (1752–1831), Friedrich Daniel Schubart (1739–1791), and Friedrich Schiller (1759–1805); the generation of "Sturm und Drang" as it is known in the history of Literature. For a while, Schiller even came to the decision: "If America gains its Freedom, I'll go there. That is certain." And during the same year, (1783) in his play *Love and Intrigue* he bitterly denounced the sale of Hessian soldiers to the British. And Klinger set his drama *Sturm und Drang* (which gave its name to the entire movement) "in America – in the midst of the war". With similar enthusiasm, Schubart followed events in America both as a poet and as a journalist. One of the first Germans to take the part of the patriots, he had written his "Freedom Song of a North American Colonist" as early as 1775:

> Go forth, defend the sacred ground,
> Your musket bright with dew;
> Columbus, the whole world you found,
> Will bravely fight for you!
> High flies the flag of Liberty
> (no slave can ever see it)
> She leads you on – oh, can't you see?
> Freedom or Death – so be it!
> To Arms, my Brothers!

Die Americaner widersetzen sich der
Stempel Acte, und verbrennen das aus
England nach America gesandte Stempel-
Papier zu Boston, im August 1764.

Die Einwohner von Boston werfen den
englisch-ostindischen Thee ins Meer
am 18 December 1773.

Das erste Bürger Blut, zu Gründung
der Americanischen Freyheit, vergossen
bey Lexington am 19 ten April 1774.

Die erste förmliche Action zwischen
den Americanern und Engländern bey
Bunkers-Hill am 17 ten Junius 1774.

Der Congreß erklärt die 13 vereinigten
Staaten von Nord America für independent am 4 ten July 1776.

Die Hessen, vom General Washington
am 25 ten Dec 1776 zu Trenton überfal-
len, werden als Kriegsgefangne in Philadelphia eingebracht.

Die Americaner machen das Corps des
General Bourgoyne zu Gefangnen, bey
Saratoga, am 16 ten Octobr 1777.

Dr. Franklin erhält, als Gesandter des
Americanischen Frey Staats, seine
erste Audienz in Frankreich, zu Versailles, am 20 ten März 1778.

Landung einer Französischen Hülfs-
Armee in America, zu Rhode Island,
am 11 ten Julius 1780.

Major André, von drey Americanern angehalten zu Tarrytown
am 23 ten Septembr 1780.

Die Americaner machen den Lord Cornwallis mit seiner Armee zu Gefangnen,
bey Yorktown den 19 ten Octobr 1781.

Ende der Feindseeligkeiten. Die Engländer räumen den Americanern
Neu-Yorck ein. ——— 1783.

Durch seinen volkstümlichen Ton und die rückhaltlose Art, mit der er Kritik an Adel und Geistlichkeit übte und für die amerikanischen Freiheitsideen eintrat, machte er sich die Obrigkeit zum Feind. In seiner Zeitschrift *Teutsche Chronik* hielt er den eigenen Landsleuten vor, daß es „drüben" noch Menschen gebe, „die fühlen, daß ihre Bestimmung nicht Sclaverei sey; die mit edlem Unmuth das Joch eines herrschsüchtigen Ministeriums vom Nacken schütteln und diesen Volkspeinigern zeigen, daß man ohne sie leben kann". Nicht zuletzt wegen solcher Äußerungen wurde Schubart 1777 verhaftet und von seinem Landesherrn, Herzog Karl Eugen von Württemberg, einem der letzten absolutistischen Despoten, ohne rechtmäßige Verurteilung auf der Feste Hohenasperg gefangen gesetzt. Erst zehn Jahre später kam er durch Vermittlung des Preußischen Hofes wieder frei. Seine politischen Überzeugungen hatte er jedoch in der Haft nicht geändert. Die Vereinigten Staaten blieben sein politisches Ideal: „Man sieht augenscheinlich, daß Gott mit diesen Amerikanern ist. Das Land gedeiht allenthalben, der Handel blüht in allen Zweigen, alle Stände sind von Vaterlandsliebe begeistert, Religion wird als Hauptgrundpfeiler des Staates angesehen – Religion, diese Hüterin der Völker, die sie vor Lastern bewahrt und bei einfältiger Sitte erhält. Überdies werden alle Völker durch einen verborgenen Arm zurückgehalten, dies heilige Freiheitsland nicht anzutasten, bis es tief in die Erde gegründet ist, mit felsigten Wurzeln, und zu einem hohen Berge Gottes schwillt".

Das Echo, das der amerikanische Freiheitskampf in fast allen deutschen Kleinstaaten ausgelöst hatte, hallte noch lange über die unmittelbare Zeit der Ereignisse bis tief in das folgende Jahrhundert nach. Eine realistischere Beschäftigung mit den allgemeinen Grundsätzen der Politik verbreitete sich zusehends. In ihrem Gefolge regte sich bald eine freimütigere und kühnere Kritik der gegebenen Verfassungs- und Verwaltungszustände, die sich schließlich in ebenfalls revolutionären Aktionen Luft machte.

His popular style of writing, his blunt criticism of nobility and clergy, as well as the fact that he openly embraced the American ideas of Freedom, soon got him into trouble with the ruling classes. In his periodical *Teutsche Chronik* he told his own compatriots that "over there" there were still people "who feel that they are not meant to live in slavery, who with noble distaste throw off the yoke of a tyrannical government and prove to these oppressors of the people that it is possible to do without them." It was because of utterances such as this that Schubart was arrested in 1777 and imprisoned in the Fortress of Hohenasperg by the ruler of his homeland, Duke Karl Eugen von Württemberg, one of the last of the absolutist despots who did not bother with such formalities as a proper conviction or any kind of due process of law. He was not released until 10 years later, after the Prussian Court had interceded on his behalf. His political convictions had not changed during the period of his imprisonment. The United States remained his political ideal. "It is apparent that God is on the side of those Americans. The country prospers everywhere, all kinds of trade flourish, all classes are inspired by patriotism. Religion is looked upon as one of the pillars of the State – religion, that guardian of the people which keeps them pure at heart. And somehow all other nations are restrained, by some mysterious power, from threatening this holy land of Liberty until such time when it will have sunk deep roots into the rocky ground and will have grown to a lofty mountain of the Almighty."

The echo awakened by the American fight for Liberty in almost all of the small German states continued for a long time after the fight had been fought and won, far into the next century. A more realistic preoccupation with the basic precepts of politics spread rapidly all over the country. In its wake, a franker and more fearless criticism of the existing forms of constitution and administration grew up, which finally resulted in revolutionary uprisings in Germany itself.

Teutſche Chronik.

Fünfter Jahrgang.
Zweytes Stück.

Den 5. Jenner, 1778.

Von Amerika.

Wie lieb wär mir's, wenn ich die Chronik die„ſes Jahrs mit der Nachricht anfangen „könnte: In Amerika iſts Friede! Denn die Kla„gen, die jezt alle Ständ' in Engeland über die„ſen Krieg erheben, ſchneiden mir durchs Herz, „und ich möchte gar zu gerne mein liebes Enge„land beruhigt, und meine Brüder, die Teut„ſchen, wieder zu Hauſe ſehen."

So fieng voriges Jahr Schubart die Chronik an; und ich ſetze mich mit eben dieſem Wunſch an mein Schreibpult. Aber ſein Wunſch war eitel; wurde das ganze vergangene Jahr nicht erfüllt — und ſo wird auch der meinige eitel ſeyn, wird dieß ganze Jahr nicht in Erfüllung kommen.

Zwar ſoll an den Sire William Howe ein Paquetboot mit Depeſchen abgefertigt ſeyn, in welchen ihm aufgetragen ſey, dem Congreß den Frieden anzubiethen. Aber die Nachrichten aus Amerika geben wenig Hoffnung, daß friedliche Vorſchläge werden angenommen werden. Als die Capitulations-Artikel, auf welche ſich Bourgoyne ergeben, in Boſton angekommen, wurden ſie von dem Balcon des Hotels der Staaten öffentlich

Durch Schubarts „Teutsche Chronik" fanden die Nachrichten von den revolutionären Vorgängen in Amerika weite Verbreitung.

Schubart's journal "Teutsche Chronik" reported the Revolution to European readers.

Johann Wolfgang Goethe im Mannesalter: zu einem geflügelten Wort wurde der Anfang seines Gedichts „Amerika, du hast es besser . . ."

"America, your lot is fairer . . ." was the first line of a famous poem by Johann Wolfgang Goethe, shown in his forties in 1791.

Die Verhaftung Friedrich Daniel Schubarts 1777: Sein Eintreten für die Ideale der amerikanischen Revolution hatte ihn mit der Obrigkeit in Konflikt gebracht.

The imprisonment of Friedrich Daniel Schubart in 1777 was attributed to his revolutionary ideals and enthusiasm for the American War of Independence.

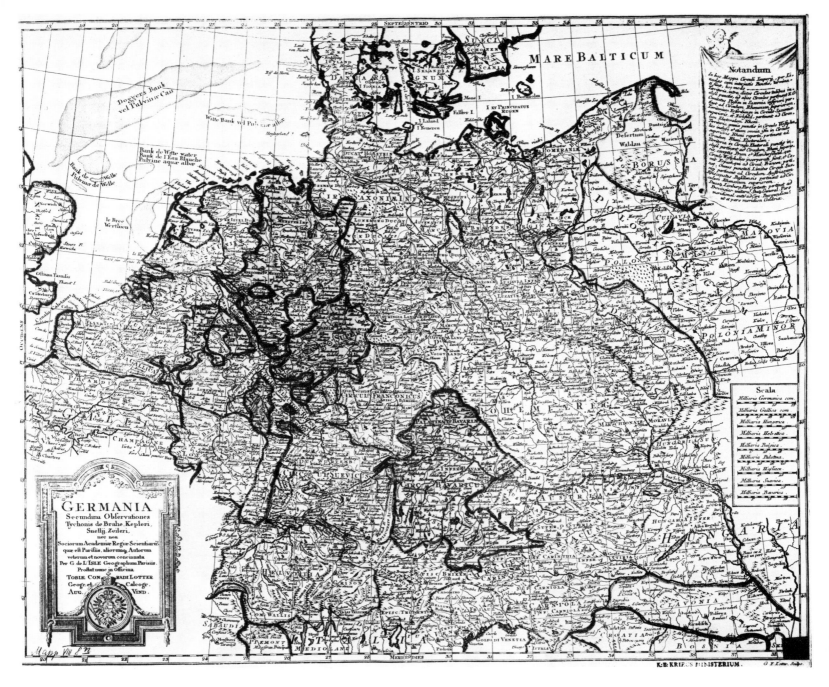

Zur Zeit der amerikanischen Revolution war ‚Deutschland‘ nur ein geographischer Begriff: Diese in Augsburg um 1770 gedruckte Karte zeigt das Mosaik absolutistisch regierter Kleinstaaten zwischen Nordsee und Alpen.

‘Germany’ was still a geographer’s figure of speech at the time of the American Revolution. This map, dating from about 1770, shows the many small, autonomous fiefdoms known then as Germany.

31

1777 wurde in London diese Karte der „Britischen Kolonien in Nordamerika" gedruckt. Offenbar hoffte England noch, daß die Unabhängigkeitserklärung von 1776 Episode bleiben würde.

This map of the British colonies was engraved by William Faden in 1777 in London. Obviously the British still nurtured the hope that the Declaration of Independence of the previous year would not be of any permanence.

Das Jahrhundert der großen Auswanderung

Amerika trat als Mythos in die Geschichte ein und wurde zur Legende seiner selbst: Ein Eldorado erwarteten sich die Spanier, ein ‚neues Kanaan‘ die religiösen Flüchtlinge des 17. und 18. Jahrhunderts; für die europäischen Zeitgenossen der amerikanischen Revolution schließlich war es die ‚Morgenröte der Demokratie‘, die im fernen Westen funkelte. Konkrete Unzufriedenheit mit den politischen und sozialen Zuständen im alten Europa spiegelt sich in solchen enthusiastischen Ansichten von Amerika wider – aber auch die irrationale und unauslöschliche Hoffnung, daß das Utopia der Philosophen oder das Schlaraffenland des Märchens irgendwo vielleicht doch existiert. Neben allen guten Gründen, die die Auswanderer hatten, ihre alte Heimat zu verlassen und gerade Nordamerika zu ihrer neuen Heimat zu wählen, werden immer auch diese unbewußten Träume mitgespielt haben: Nur sie können letztlich einen Entschluß erklären, der damals für die meisten unwiderruflich war und dessen persönliche Konsequenzen viel weiter reichten, als wir es heute noch nachempfinden können.

In nur hundert Jahren, zwischen 1820 und 1920, folgten über 6 Millionen deutsche Auswanderer dem Ruf der Neuen Welt. Verbesserte Verkehrsverhältnisse zu Land und auf See, mehr Informationen über Amerika, und nicht zuletzt die Tatsache, daß die USA nun ein unabhängiger Staat mit einer demokratischen Verfassung waren, trugen zu dieser rasanten Zunahme der Einwanderung gegenüber den vergangenen Jahrhunderten bei. Und die Vereinigten Staaten brauchten Menschen: Selbst ihre Ostküste war zu Beginn des 19. Jahrhunderts – verglichen mit Mitteleuropa – dünn besiedelt. Die Erschließung des Westens mit seinen unermeßlichen Weiten freien Landes wäre ohne die Einwanderer aus allen Ländern Europas kaum möglich gewesen.

Das Abenteuer begann, zunächst zaghaft, um 1820, nachdem die napoleonischen Kriege überstanden, die Grenzen und Häfen wieder frei waren. Nur vom amerikanischen Bürgerkrieg (1861–1865) unterbrochen, nahm die Emigration dann stetig zu, um in den Jahrzehnten um die Jahrhundertwende Ausmaße einer Völkerwanderung zu erreichen. Den Höhepunkt der Gesamteinwanderung in die USA bildet das Jahr 1907 mit über 1,3 Millionen Menschen – das sind fast 4000 an jedem Tag! Erst die amerikanische Isolationspolitik nach dem ersten Weltkrieg und die Wirtschaftskrise der 20er Jahre führten zu einer Beschränkung der Einwanderungserlaubnis und beendeten das ‚Jahrhundert der großen Auswanderung‘.

Im zeitlichen Ablauf der deutschen Auswanderung nach Amerika lassen sich drei große Wellen unterscheiden. Bis zur Mitte des 19. Jahrhunderts waren es vor allem Handwerker und Kleinbauern aus den südlichen und südwestlichen deutschen Staaten, die ihr Glück jenseits des Ozeans suchten. Gründe wird es so viele gegeben haben, wie es Auswanderer gab: Verallgemeinerungen sind gerade in dieser frühen Phase äußerst schwierig. Wirtschaftliche Schwierigkeiten mögen eine Rolle gespielt haben, vor allem bei den Handwerkern, die nach dem Ende der ‚Kontinentalsperre‘ nicht mit den englischen Industriewaren konkurrieren konnten, die nun auf den deutschen Markt kamen.

A Century of Immigration

America entered history as a myth and became its own legend; the Spaniards were looking for Eldorado, the 17th and 18th century refugees from religious persecution for a "New Canaan"; the European contemporaries of the American revolution, finally, hailed it as the "Dawn of Democracy" lighting up the far western sky. The very real discontent with the political and social conditions existing in "The Old Country" is reflected in those enthusiastic ideas about America. But there was also the possibly irrational and persistent hope that the philosophers' utopia of (from a more materialistic point of view) the "Land of Milk and Honey" did exist somewhere after all. Besides all the perfectly valid reasons which prompted the emigrants to leave the country of their birth and pick North America as their new home, these half-conscious dreams undoubtedly also played a part. Only these dreams can plausibly explain a decision which in most instances was irrevocable, and the personal consequences of which were more far-reaching than we can even imagine today.

Within no more than a hundred years, between 1820 and 1920, more than six million German immigrants followed the call of the New World. Improved transportation by land and by sea, more information about America, and of course the fact that the U. S. had now become an independent state with a democratic constitution, all contributed to this tremendous increase of immigration as compared to that of the preceding century. And the United States needed people: compared to Central Europe, even the east coast was only sparsely settled early in the 19th century. The winning of the West with its infinite stretches of free land would have been impossible without the immigrants from all the countries of Europe.

The adventure started – haltingly at first – about 1820, after the end of the Napoleonic wars, when frontiers and ports were once more thrown open to traffic. Interrupted only by the War between the States (1861–1865) immigration increased steadily, until, in the decades around the turn of the century, it had reached the scale of mass migration. The high tide of immigration was reached in 1907, with 1.3 million – almost 4,000 a day! Not until American isolationism after World War I and the economic crisis of the late Twenties had resulted in a sharp reduction of entry permits did the "century of immigration" come to an end.

Three major phases may be distinguished in the history of German emigration to America. Until the middle of the 19th century, it was mostly artisans and small farmers from the southern and southwestern German states who decided to try their luck on the other side of the Big Pond. As to reasons, there were almost as many as there were emigrants; generalizations, particularly during this early phase, are next to impossible. Economic problems may have played a part, especially in the case of artisans, who were unable to compete with the British industrial goods flooding the German market after the Continental Embargo had been lifted. Political unrest also played a part – all the more easily since America was just coming "into fashion" at the time. Travel reports such as those by Gottfried

Allegorische Darstellung Amerikas, Augsburg um 1760.

Allegorical depiction of the Americas published in Augsburg around 1760.

Auf einer deutschen Karikatur des 19. Jahrhunderts ist ein „Litzer" als reißender Wolf dargestellt.

A 19th Century German caricature showing a "runner" depicted as a ravenous wolf.

Die Szene zeigt einen skrupellosen Auswanderungsagenten, wie er einen jungen Mann ins sichere Verderben lockt, während dessen Mutter ihn anfleht, zuhause zu bleiben.

An illustration of an unscrupulous emigration agent luring a young man to certain ruin while his mother begs him to stay home.

Die beiden Vignetten auf dieser Urkunde der Ehrenmitgliedschaft im „Nationalverein für deutsche Auswanderung und Ansiedlung", die 1879 einem Mitglied des deutschen Reichstages ausgestellt wurde, zeigen die Emigranten beim bewegenden Abschied von der alten Heimat und ihrer freudigen Ankunft in der neuen.

This certificate of honorary membership in the "National Society of German Emigrants to America", issued to a member of the German Imperial Parliament in 1879, shows a romantic portrayal of Germans uprooting themselves from their native towns and seeking their fortunes in the New World.

Auch politische Unruhen spielten eine Rolle, die umso leichter war, als Amerika gerade zu dieser Zeit in Mode kam: Reiseberichte, wie jene Gottfried Dudens, malten den neuen Staat in verlockenden Farben, die an Buntheit aber noch von populären Drucken oder gar jenen großformatigen Bildtapeten übertroffen wurden, auf denen Amerika in der Tat ein Land war, das es, mit Goethe gesprochen, besser hatte. Noch heute sind in Deutschland Bauernhäuser aus dem 19. Jahrhundert erhalten, deren winkelige Stuben mit Darstellungen aus der amerikanischen Geschichte oder dem Indianerleben dekoriert sind. Ganze Dorfgemeinschaften aus Bayern oder Württemberg oder Baden verkauften damals Haus und Hof, luden das wenige, was transportabel war, auf ihre Karren und zogen, oft von ihrem Pfarrer angeführt, quer durch Frankreich nach Le Havre, wo sie sich nach Amerika einschifften. Die Zahl dieser Aussiedler betrug in dem Jahrzehnt von 1825 bis 1835 etwa 50000, von 1836 bis 1845 bereits 200000. Schon 1854 wurde diese Zahl jedoch in einem einzigen Jahr erreicht: Um die Jahrhundertmitte setzte die zweite Welle der deutschen Auswanderung nach Amerika ein.

Zeitlich fällt sie mit der großen irischen Hungersnot zusammen, und oft waren Mißernten und Verschuldung auch in Deutschland Auswanderungsmotiv. Die mißglückte deutsche Revolution von 1848 und der amerikanische Goldrausch von 1849 trugen dazu bei, den Auswandererstrom zu vergrößern, doch fallen die politischen Flüchtlinge und die goldsuchenden Abenteurer neben den großen Gruppen der Familienumsiedler kaum ins Gewicht. Der ganze deutschsprachige Raum war nun von der Auswanderungsbewegung erfaßt worden; neben Le Havre und Rotterdam wurden Hamburg und vor allem Bremen zu den wichtigsten Umschlagplätzen der Menschenfracht.

Die harte Formulierung trifft den Kern der Sache auch um die Mitte des 19. Jahrhunderts noch. Zwar war die Zeit der ‚Seelenverkäufer' lange vorbei: Das bis 1800 übliche Verfahren, mittellose Auswanderer die Reise am Ziel jahrelang abdienen zu lassen, war von der amerikanischen Regierung verboten worden. Doch die Fahrt selbst war immer noch ein strapaziöses Unternehmen – zumindest für die große Mehrheit, die sich den Luxus der ‚ersten Kajüte' nicht leisten konnte. Ihnen blieb das ‚Zwischendeck', ein luken- und lichtloser Raum zwischen Oberdeck und Fracht, der meist nur behelfsmäßig für die Aufnahme von Menschen eingerichtet war. Selten mehr als 1,70 Meter hoch, war er bis in den letzten Winkel mit mehrstöckigen Kojen verstellt, von deren Breite

Duden painted an alluring picture of the new state which, however, was even surpassed in splendor by the colorful popular prints or those "scenic wallpapers" which certainly depicted America as a country which, in the words of Goethe, was "better off". To this day there exist some 19th century farmhouses in Germany, the walls of which are adorned with scenes from the history of America or Indian life. Entire communities in Bavaria, Wurttemberg and Baden sold their homes and holdings, loaded their few remaining possessions on carts and, frequently led by the village parson, walked across France to Le Havre, where they went aboard a ship bound for the United States. From 1825 to 1835, there were about 50,000 of these emigrants – from 1836 to 1845, already 200,000. As early as 1854, however, this figure was achieved in a single year. About the middle of the century, the second wave of German emigration to America had begun.

This was also the time of the great Irish "potato famine", and frequently crop failures and indebtedness also were responsible for emigration from Germany. The abortive German revolution of 1848 and the California gold rush of 1849 helped to swell the stream of emigrants, although when it comes to numbers, the political refugees and would-be prospectors were only a drop in the bucket compared to the large-scale exodus of entire families. By now, all German-speaking areas had caught the fever: besides Le Havre and Rotterdam, Hamburg and especially Bremen became the most important way stations handling this human cargo.

Unfortunately, this bold way of putting it still hit the mark in the mid-19th century. It is true that the day of the "soul sellers" was long past; the method, customary till about 1800, of "indenturing" penniless immigrants and making them "work off" their passage with several years of virtual slavery, had been abolished by the U. S. Government. But the passage itself remained an ordeal – at least for the great majority, who could not afford cabin class. All that remained for them was steerage, a space without light or air between hold and upper deck, which had only been sketchily converted for the accommodation of human beings. Rarely higher than five and a half feet, it was crammed full of bunks stacked two and three high. An adult who had paid the minimum fare was entitled to 18 inches of a bunk – children had to make do with half of that! During the entire passage, which in the days of sail took about 6 weeks, this dungeon served as bedroom, dining hall and "living"-room, and the

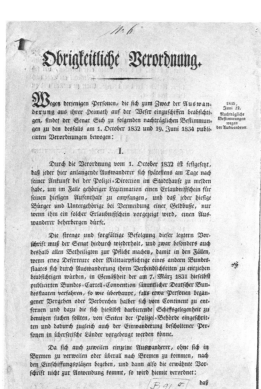

Dieser Schein zur Aufnahme ins Zwischendeck wurde 1854 ausgestellt. Er kostete 39 Thaler.

This ticket for passage in steerage was issued in 1854 for the price of 39 Thaler.

Die Emigranten durften alles an Bord bringen, was sie tragen konnten. Die Wochen auf offener See verbrachten sie naturgemäß auf allen Seiten eingeklemmt von eigenem und fremdem Hab und Gut.

Emigrants were allowed to take anything they could carry. The result was weeks on the open sea, crammed between other passengers and their belongings.

1853 veröffentlichte die Bremer Obrigkeit eine Reihe von Bestimmungen und Verordnungen, um des Emigrantenstroms, der durch ihre Stadt floß, Herr zu werden.

In 1853 the city fathers of Bremen published a series of rules and regulations governing the conduct of emigrants passing through the city.

Hamburg war einer der wichtigsten Umschlagplätze des transatlantischen Handels und zugleich einer der bedeutendsten Auswanderungshäfen. Hier im Jahre 1863.

The Hamburg harbor was one of the busiest ports in transatlantic trade and emigration. Here a view of 1863.

Die Wartehalle des Norddeutschen Lloyd, einer der wichtigsten Schiffahrtslinien, die Emigranten aus allen Teilen Europas nach Amerika brachte.

The waiting room of the Norddeutscher Lloyd, one of the most important shipping lines, transporting emigrants from all over Europe.

einem Erwachsenen beim billigsten Tarif nur 47 Zentimeter zustanden – Kindern die Hälfte! Während der ganzen Überfahrt, die mit Segelschiffen etwa 6 Wochen dauerte, diente dieses Gefängnis als Schlaf-, Eß- und Aufenthaltsraum, und man konnte von Glück sagen, wenn verdorbene Lebensmittel währenddessen keine Epidemie auslösten. Nicht besser erging es den Auswanderern in den Häfen, wo sie, kaum daß ihre Zahl bedeutend geworden war, dem Erwerbstrieb der ansässigen Geschäftsleute in die Hände fielen. Nepper und Schlepper – in Bremen „Litzer", in New York „runners" geheißen – zogen ihnen für überteuerte Herberge, unnötige Ausrüstungsgegenstände oder gar ungültige Fahrkarten das mühsam Ersparte aus der Tasche, ohne daß die einfachen Leute, von denen viele noch nie eine Großstadt gesehen hatten, wußten, wie ihnen geschah. Erst als die Behörden die Abwicklung des Auswandererverkehrs in die Hand nahmen – 1847 in New York, 1851 in Bremen – gelang es, solche Auswüchse einzudämmen. In New York wurde Castle Garden, ein ehemaliges Fort, das auch schon als Konzertsaal gedient hatte, zur Durchgangsstation für Generationen von Einwanderern,

passengers were lucky if spoiled food did not result in an epidemic. The emigrants did not fare any better in the ports on both sides of the Atlantic; as soon as there was a sufficient number of them, they fell prey to the greed of the local racketeers. Con-men and swindlers – called "Litzers" in Bremen, "runners" in New York, robbed them of their hard-earned savings by overcharging them for lodgings, selling them unneeded equipment or even phoney tickets, before the poor "greenhorns", many of whom had never seen a city in their lives, had a chance to realize what was going on. Not until the respective governments took over the processing of the immigrants – in New York in 1847, in Bremen in 1851 – could excesses of this sort be controlled. In New York, Castle Garden, a former Fort which had in the meantime been used as a concert hall, was converted to a way station for generations of immigrants, who were thus given the opportunity not only to get cleaned up and provide themselves with food, but also to obtain advice and job counseling. In 1892, this task was taken over by a new building on Ellis Island, where on peak days up to 8,000 immigrants were "processed".

Ankunft des Postdampfers „Washington" auf der Reede zu Bremerhaven am 19. 6. 1847. Der Raddampfer gehörte zu der unter deutscher Beteiligung gegründeten „Ocean Steam Navigation Company". Mit ihm wurde die erste regelmäßig befahrene Dampfschiffahrtslinie zwischen Nordamerika und dem europäischen Festland eröffnet.

The first arrival of the steamship Washington in Bremerhaven harbor on June 19, 1847. The Washington is almost fully rigged with sails. The paddle wheeler was the first vessel to set sail on a regular basis between the two shores of the Atlantic. She belonged to a German-American commercial cooperation, the "Ocean Steam Navigation Company".

Die Freiheitsstatue 1886, kurz vor der Fertigstellung. Mit „deutscher Gründlichkeit" betrachtet, steht sie auf europäischem Boden; Bedloes Island – 1956 in Liberty Island umbenannt – bestand großenteils aus Ballast, den Schiffe vor der Einfahrt in den New Yorker Hafen entladen hatten.

"Miss Liberty". From a literal point of view she could be said to be standing on European soil; Bedloes Island – renamed Liberty Island in 1956 – consisted largely of ballast ships had dropped before entering New York harbor.

Fahrplan der Atlantiküberquerungen der Schiffe des Norddeutschen Lloyd aus dem Jahre 1879.

Schedule of ocean crossings issued by Norddeutscher Lloyd, 1879.

die sich dort nicht nur waschen und verpflegen, sondern vor allem auch beraten und Arbeit vermitteln lassen konnten. 1892 übernahm diese Aufgaben ein Neubau auf Ellis Island, wo an Spitzentagen bis zu 8000 Immigranten ‚abgefertigt' wurden. Die Einführung der Dampfschiffe im letzten Jahrhundertdrittel verbesserte die Beförderungsbedingungen in der billigsten Klasse übrigens nur soweit, als sich die Reisedauer auf zwei Wochen verringerte. Die Raumverhältnisse an Bord waren gegen Ende des 19. Jahrhunderts noch kaum besser, als an seinem Anfang.

Mit dem rasanten ökonomischen Aufschwung der USA nach dem Ende des Bürgerkrieges hatte mittlerweile auch die dritte und größte Welle der deutschen Einwanderung eingesetzt. Der alte Mythos von der Neuen Welt schien nun handfeste wirtschaftliche Realität geworden zu sein: Ein deutscher Kaufmann hat angeblich 1902 das Wort vom „Land der unbegrenzten Möglichkeiten" geprägt; die Vermutung liegt nahe, daß er dabei an etwas anderes dachte als die Stürmer und Dränger, die 100 Jahre zuvor die amerikanische Demokratie besungen hatten. „Meine Fackel leuchtet euch durchs goldne Tor" – schnellen Reichtum, ein säkularisiertes Eldorado, versprach die Freiheitsstatue mit diesen Worten, die Emma Lazarus ihr 1883 in den Mund legte. Im europäischen Bewußtsein begannen die USA, vom Land der großen Ideen zum Land der großen Zahlen zu werden – und entsprechend groß wurden auch die Einwanderungsraten. Hatten zwischen 1830 und 1860 die Iren das größte Immigrantenkontingent gestellt, so waren es in den dreißig Jahren zwischen 1866 und 1896 die Deutschen. Der absolute Höhepunkt wurde 1882 erreicht, als von den 700000 Menschen, die in diesem Jahr in die USA übersiedelten, mehr als zwei Drittel, nämlich 500000, aus dem deutschsprachigen Raum kamen. Sie ließen sich größtenteils im Städteviereck New York–Minneapolis–St. Louis–Baltimore nieder, wo „Little Germanies" entstanden: Deutsche Stadtviertel mit eigenen Schulen, Kirchen, Krankenhäusern, Zeitungen und natürlich einem regen Vereinsleben. Das Zusammengehörigkeitsgefühl in der Fremde war nicht zuletzt deshalb so groß, weil viele Einwanderer die Sprache der neuen Heimat noch nicht beherrschten. So dauerte ihre Integration im „Schmelztiegel der Nationen" länger, erfolgte aber meistens schon in der zweiten Generation. Obwohl die Deutschen in der Gesamteinwanderung zwischen 1820 und 1950 die größte Gruppe ausmachen – vor Italienern, Iren und Engländern – und heute schätzungsweise ein Sechstel der Bevölkerung der USA deutschstämmig ist, sind sich doch nur noch 10% dieser Abkunft bewußt. Sauerkraut und verwandte Germanica wurden nicht zu Fossilien kultureller Eigenbrötlerei, sondern zu einem Teil des amerikanischen Alltags.

Ernstgemeinte Versuche, in Amerika ein ‚junges Deutschland' zu errichten, waren schon im frühen 19. Jahrhundert gescheitert: Die demokratische „Gießen-Gesellschaft" von 1835 oder der „Mainzer Adelsverein", der 1844 Neu-Braunfels in Texas als separatistische deutsche Siedlung gründete, waren kein Vorbild für die späteren Massenauswanderer, die ein neues Leben beginnen und sich rasch amerikanisieren wollten. An diese große Mehrheit erinnern heute nur noch die deutschen Namen, die den von ihnen gegründeten Orten geblieben sind und dank derer dem Reiseschriftsteller K. Goetz das Kunststück gelang, in zwei

When steam ships came into use during the last third of the century, conditions in the steerage class were improved only insofar as the passage now took only two weeks. Accommodations aboard were not much better toward the end of the century than they had been at its beginning.

With the very rapid economic development of the U. S. following the War between the States came the third and largest wave of German immigrants. The ancient myth of the New World now apparently had become a tangible economic reality. Tradition has it that a German businessman coined the phrase of "Land of boundless possibilities" (Land der unbegrenzten Möglichkeiten) in 1902; it may be assumed that what he had in mind was very different from the ideas of the "Sturm und Drang" poets who had sung the praises of American Democracy a hundred years earlier. "I lift my lamp beside the golden door . . .", such was the promise of the Statue of Liberty, in the words ascribed to her in 1883 by Emma Lazarus. And to the immigrants of that time, that meant quick wealth, a secularized Eldorado. In the eyes of Europe, America had changed from the Land of Great Ideas to the Land of Big Money – and the immigration rate increased in proportion. While between 1830 and 1860, most of the immigrants had come from Ireland, the Germans were in the majority during the 30 years between 1866 and 1896. The peak figure was achieved in 1882, when 500,000, or more than two thirds of the 700,000 people who came to the U. S. during that year, came from German-speaking countries. Most of them settled within the quadrangle New York – Minneapolis – St. Louis – Baltimore, where "Little Germanies" sprang up complete with their own schools, churches, hospitals, newspapers and of course a large and thriving number of clubs or "Vereine". This clannishness was largely due to the fact that many of the immigrants still could not speak the language of their new homeland. Thus their integration within the "melting pot" took somewhat longer, but was usually completed within two generations. Although the Germans were the largest single group in the total immigration between 1820 and 1950 – leading the Italians, the Irish and the English – and today an estimated one-sixth of the population of the U. S. is of German descent, only 10 % are still aware of that fact. "Sauerkraut" and similar German "institutions" did not degenerate to ethnic fossils, but became a part of American everyday life.

Some serious attempts to found a "young Germany" in America had already failed in the early 19th century. The democratic "Giessen-Gesellschaft" of 1835 or the "Mainzer Adelsverein" which in 1844 founded Neu-Braunfels in Texas as a purely German settlement failed to impress the immigrants of the later "mass emigrations", who wanted to start a new life and become "Americanized" as rapidly as possible. All that remains today of this great majority are the German names given by them to their settlements, which enabled K. Goetz, the author of many successful

Castle Garden, bis 1892 Durchgangsstation aller Einwanderer, die in New York landeten.

Castle Garden, until 1892 the processing station for all immigrants who landed in New York.

Der Hafen von Philadelphia, der „Stadt brüderlicher Liebe".

The harbor of Philadelphia, "City of Brotherly Love".

Immigranten am Geldwechselschalter von Ellis Island, Anfang des 20. Jahrhunderts.

Immigrants exchanging money at Ellis Island at the beginning of this century.

1902 wurde der Passagierverkehr über den Atlantik bereits fast ausschließlich mit Dampfschiffen durchgeführt.

By 1902 almost all transatlantic passenger traffic was handled by steam ships.

1949 wurde auch Ellis Island geschlossen: Einige der letzten dort abgefertigten Einwanderer beim Verlassen der Insel.

The Ellis Island station was closed in 1949. Here, some of the last immigrants to pass through the facility leave the island.

Stunden von Ohio nach Hamburg zu reisen: „Wenn man aus Hannover, vierzig Minuten südwestlich von Cincinnati, eine Stunde mit dem Auto fährt, kommt man nach Oldenburg. Dort beachte man einen Wegweiser nach Hamburg, das leicht in etwa 7 Minuten zu erreichen ist. Über Elsass kommt man dann – ohne die Grenze von Ohio zu überschreiten – durch Münster und Neu-Bayern in das Hannover-Settlement, wo 208 Familien siedeln, Enkel der Auswanderer aus Visselhövede im Kreise Rotenburg. Umgangssprache Plattdeutsch, Wege gut."

books on travel, to go from Hannover to Hamburg without leaving Ohio. "After leaving Hannover, forty minutes south of Cincinnati, you travel one hour by car. That takes you to Oldenburg. There you will find a sign directing you to Hamburg, which you will reach within 7 minutes. By way of Elsass, you then – without leaving Ohio – go through Munster and Neu-Bayern and arrive at the Hannover-settlement, where there are 208 families, the grandchildren of immigrants from Visselhövede. Language spoken: Low German, Roads good."

New York war der wichtigste Einwanderungshafen für deutsche Umsiedler. Dieses Bild Manhattans erschien 1883 – auf dem Höhepunkt der Einwanderungswelle – in der Zeitschrift „Illustrirte Welt". Links unten der runde Bau des Durchgangslagers Castle Garden, rechts der Hafen und die im selben Jahr eröffnete Brooklyn Bridge.

Most German immigrants entered through New York harbor. Here, a drawing of Manhattan from "Illustrirte Welt", 1883, at the apex of the immigration wave. The round building, lower left, is the processing station Castle Garden. At right is the newly opened Brooklyn Bridge.

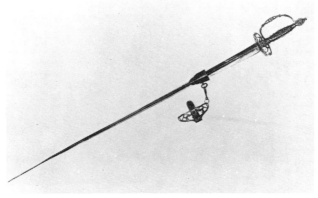

Oben: George Washington mit seiner Frau und ihren Kindern aus erster Ehe. König Friedrich II. von Preußen (unten) soll Washington den abgebildeten Degen mit der Widmung verehrt haben: „Vom ältesten General der Welt an den größten". Heute ist er Ausstellungsstück in der New York State Library in Albany.

George Washington, shown above with his wife and her children from her first marriage, is said to have received this ceremonial sword from King Frederick II of Prussia, shown below. Today the weapon is on display in the New York State Library in Albany.

Erste staatliche Beziehungen: Der Freundschafts- und Handelsvertrag von 1785

First Official Relations: The Treaty of Amity and Commerce of 1785

Die wechselvolle Geschichte der deutsch-amerikanischen Beziehungen begann gleich nach dem Ende des Unabhängigkeitskrieges. Es vergingen nur zwei Jahre seit der Pariser Friedensregelung, bis Preußen – im letzten Jahr der Regentschaft Friedrichs des Großen – als erster deutscher Staat einen Vertrag mit der jungen Republik abschloß. Zwar belebten die Vereinbarungen den beiderseitigen Handel, vor allem den Austausch von schlesischem Leinen gegen Tabak aus Virginia; ihre eigentliche Bedeutung aber lag in der fortschrittlich-humanitären Gesinnung, die den Charakter des Vertrags bestimmte und ihn zu dem Dokument machte, das die Entwicklung des internationalen Rechts so nachhaltig beeinflußte. Schon die Präambel zeigt das deutlich: „Von dem Wunsch beseelt, auf dauernde und gerechte Art und Weise die Regeln festzulegen, die im Verkehr und Handel zwischen ihren Ländern herzustellen ihr Bestreben ist, sind seine Majestät, der König von Preußen und die Vereinigten Staaten von Amerika zu dem Schluß gekommen, daß dieses Ziel nicht besser erreicht werden kann, als durch die Anerkennung des Prinzips vollkommenster Gleichheit und Gegenseitigkeit als Grundlage dieser Übereinkunft."

Auf amerikanischer Seite waren drei der hervorragendsten Politiker ihrer Zeit an den Verhandlungen beteiligt: Benjamin Franklin, der erste Gesandte des Kongresses am französischen Hof, sowie die späteren Präsidenten Thomas Jefferson und John Adams. Ihnen kam es vor allem darauf an, das Privateigentum im Seekrieg vor Konfiszierung zu schützen. Durch die Formel „Frei Schiff – Frei Gut" konnte eine Beschlagnahme auf hoher See ausgeschlossen werden. Ähnliche Bestimmungen galten an Land: Im Falle von kriegerischen Auseinandersetzungen zwischen den Vertragspartnern sollte den jeweils im anderen Land niedergelassenen Kaufleuten eine Frist von neun Monaten zur Abwicklung ihrer laufenden Geschäfte eingeräumt werden; Kinder, Frauen, Gelehrte und alle Personen, die dem gemeinsamen

The eventful history of German-American relations began soon after the end of the War of Independence. Only two years had elapsed since the Treaty of Paris before Prussia, in the last year of the reign of Frederick the Great, became the first German state to conclude a treaty with the young republic. The provisions of the treaty helped to encourage trade between the two partners, especially the exchange of Silesian linen for Virginia tobacco. But its deeper meaning lay in its progressive humanitarian concept, making it a document which was to become of lasting importance in the development of international law. This concept is apparent even in the preamble: ". . . desiring to fix, in a permanent and equitable manner, the rules to be observed in the intercourse and commerce they desire to establish between their respective countries, His Majesty and the United States have judged that the said end cannot be better obtained than by taking the most perfect equality and reciprocity for the basis of their agreement."

Three of the most prominent and distinguished politicians of the time represented America in the negotiations: Benjamin Franklin, the first congressional ambassador to France, as well as future presidents Thomas Jefferson and John Adams. Their main concern was the protection of private property from confiscation in the event of a naval war between one of the treaty partners and a third power. The non-involved treaty partner is guaranteed neutrality under Article XII ("free vessels – free cargo"). Other provisions dealt with conduct on land: in the event that war should break out between the treaty partners themselves, a moratorium of nine months was to be granted to foreign merchants residing in the enemy country to conclude any current business transactions. Women, children, scholars, and all persons contributing to the public good would be allowed to pursue their functions without interference, as stated in Article XI: "The most perfect freedom of conscience and of worship is granted to the

Benjamin Franklin, Thomas Jefferson und John Adams (von links nach rechts) nahmen an den Verhandlungen über die Handelsvereinbarungen zwischen Preußen und den Vereinigten Staaten teil und unterzeichneten 1785 gemeinsam das Vertragswerk.

Benjamin Franklin, Thomas Jefferson and John Adams (from left to right) negotiated and signed the Treaty of Amity and Commerce between Prussia and the United States.

Wohl dienen, sollten ungehindert ihrer Beschäftigung weiter nachgehen können. „Die weitestgehende Freiheit des Gewissens und der Religionsausübung" wurde allen Untertanen und Bürgern der einen Partei im Zuständigkeitsbereich der anderen durch § XI zugesichert. Durch eine andere Klausel wurde das Prinzip der Meistbegünstigung eingeführt, das auch heute noch in keinem internationalen Wirtschaftsvertrag fehlt. Es besagt, daß der eine Partner dem anderen alle handelspolitischen Vergünstigungen gewährt, die er dritten Staaten einräumt.

Die Bestimmungen über die Behandlung von Kriegsgefangenen stammten aus der Feder Jeffersons. Sie verboten es ausdrücklich, in Gefangenschaft geratene Soldaten in ferne Länder zu verschleppen, unter gesundheitsgefährdenden Bedingungen festzuhalten, in dunkle Verliese zu sperren und anzuketten. Vielmehr sei für ausreichende Ernährung und gesunde Lager zu sorgen. So konnte George Washington diesen „Treaty of Amity and Commerce" zu Recht als den freisinnigsten Vertrag bezeichnen, der – bis zu seiner Zeit – je von unabhängigen Mächten abgeschlossen worden war.

1799 noch einmal für zehn Jahre verlängert, blieb dieses Vertragswerk doch bis zum Ende des 19. Jahrhunderts Vorbild aller handelspolitischen Vereinbarungen, die zahlreiche deutsche Kleinstaaten im Gefolge Preußens mit den Vereinigten Staaten abschlossen. Und was die Regierungen im § I nur hatten dekretieren können, wurde im Lauf der Jahre Wirklichkeit: „Es soll fester, unverletzlicher und allgemeiner Friede und wahre Freundschaft zwischen seiner Majestät, seinen Erben und Nachfolgern, sowie seinen Untertanen einerseits und den Vereinigten Staaten und ihren Bürgern andererseits ohne irgendwelche Ausnahme hinsichtlich der Gebiete und Personen bestehen."

citizens or subjects of either party within the jurisdiction of the other", the only exception being religious insults. Another very important clause was that of the "most-favored-nation", which states that each partner shall guarantee the other any and all economic concessions granted to a third state. This clause is still contained in all international commercial treaties.

The provisions pertaining to the treatment of prisoners of war stem from the pen of Thomas Jefferson. It is expressly forbidden to transport prisoners of war to foreign lands; to incarcerate them under conditions dangerous to their health; to confine them in dungeons, or to put them in chains – what is important is that they have adequate food, and lodging worthy of human habitation. Thus George Washington could rightfully point to the "Treaty of Amity and Commerce" as the most liberal treaty so far concluded between two independent powers.

The treaty itself was renewed for another ten years in 1799. Its basic framework was to remain the model for all economic agreements between the various German states (following in Prussia's footsteps) and the United States until the end of the 19th century. And the words of Article I, instead of becoming obsolete and yellow with age, acquired a deeper meaning with the passage of time: "There shall be a firm, inviolable, and universal peace and sincere friendship between His Majesty the King of Prussia, his heirs, successors, and subjects, on the one part, and the United States of America and their citizens on the other, without exception of persons or places."

Die ,,Bill of Rights'' und die Folgen

The ,,Bill of Rights'' and its Consequences in Europe

Die Vereinigten Staaten von Nordamerika konstituierten sich als erste moderne Demokratie: Hier hatte die Gedankenwelt der europäischen Aufklärung erstmals konkrete politische Folgen. Das amerikanische Experiment bewies in der Praxis, was die Philosophen postuliert hatten: die Fähigkeit des Volkes, sich selbst zu regieren. Der ,,Ausgang des Menschen aus seiner selbstverschuldeten Unmündigkeit'' – so Kants Definition der Aufklärung – versprach endlich, politische Realität zu werden.

Einen notwendigen Schritt zur politischen Verjüngung der Menschheit sah der Historiker George Bancroft (1800–1891) in der amerikanischen Revolution. Verjüngung – das bedeutete, sich der überalterten absolutistischen Regierungsformen zu entledigen und in freier Entscheidung in einen Gesellschaftsvertrag einzuwilligen, in dem die Befugnisse der Regierung eindeutig definiert und von der Zustimmung der Regierten abhängig waren. Schon in der Unabhängigkeitserklärung hatte Thomas Jefferson 1776 erstmals das Recht auf Widerstand gegen eine Regierung formuliert, die die Naturrechte auf Leben, Freiheit und das Streben nach Glück mißachtet. Der 1787 verabschiedeten Verfassung wurden 1791 zehn Zusatzartikel angefügt, die diese globale Umschreibung der Grundrechte genau spezifizieren: Die sogenannte ,,Bill of Rights'', das Muster aller Menschenrechtserklärungen, die bis heute in die Verfassungen der meisten Staaten eingegangen sind.

Die ,,Bill of Rights'' sollte, in Jeffersons Worten, festlegen, ,,was für Rechte dem Volk gegen jegliche Regierung der Erde zustehen''. Im einzelnen schützen die Artikel die freie Religionsausübung, die Rede- und Pressefreiheit, das Recht auf einen fairen und öffentlichen Prozeß vor einem ordentlichen Gericht, das Petitionsrecht gegenüber der Regierung, und das Recht, Waffen zu tragen; sie verbieten die Einquartierung von Truppen ohne Zustimmung des Hauseigentümers, grausame und ungewöhnliche Strafen sowie willkürliche Haussuchung, Verhaftung und Beschlagnahme. Eine zusätzliche Absicherung enthalten die Artikel 9 und 10, in denen ausdrücklich erklärt wird, daß die hier aufgezählten Rechte andere, nicht erwähnte Rechte des Volkes nicht einschränken und daß Machtbefugnisse, die die Verfassung weder den Vereinigten Staaten überträgt, noch den Einzelstaaten abspricht, dem Volk und den einzelnen Staaten der USA vorbehalten bleiben.

Die demokratischen Grundsätze der ,,Bill of Rights'' wurden sofort auch in Europa bekannt – teilweise durch ihren Initiator selbst. Thomas Jefferson, als amerikanischer Gesandter von 1785 bis 1789 in Paris, soll zusammen mit Lafayette auch am Zustandekommen des französischen Pendants, der ,,Erklärung der Menschen- und Bürgerrechte'' vom 26. August 1789 beteiligt gewesen sein. Verfaßt wurde dieses wichtigste Dokument der französischen Revolution von J. J. Mounier, von dem bekannt ist, daß er die amerikanische Regierung für die beste der Welt hielt. Doch nicht nur in Frankreich wurde das amerikanische Beispiel diskutiert: Im angrenzenden Belgien beispielsweise entwickelte sich eine lebhafte Zeitschriftenliteratur über die amerikanische Verfassung; in der Schweiz hob ein Verfassungsgeschichtler die Bedeutung der Tatsache hervor, daß der Menschenrechtskatalog endlich

The American experiment, influenced by the enlightenment thinkers of Europe, proved that man was indeed capable of self-government. The American historian George Bancroft (1800 to 1891) looked back at the American Revolution as a necessary step towards the political regeneration of mankind. Europeans fled to the new continent in their attempt to overcome the wickedness of European history and joined in the new social contract society based on the strict limitation of the powers of government. No more would mankind be subject to the cruel and irrational whims of a Monarch. The Americans were setting up a government which would guarantee the rights of the people. The power of the government was limited by law and the safeguard of civil liberties was insured through constitutional guarantees, as spelled out by the Bill of Rights incorporated into the Constitution and regarded as its most important part.

In ratifying the Constitution there was a plea from several states for a bill of rights. A bill of rights, as Thomas Jefferson remarked, was "what the people are entitled to against every government on earth, general or particular, and what no just government should refuse, or rest on inference." James Madison, a good friend of Jefferson, originally against a bill of rights, took it upon himself to draft a bill when it became clear that the people of the United States were determined to have one. From his proposals presented to Congress in June 1789, there emerged the first ten amendments to the Constitution. These amendments became known as the Bill of Rights and protected freedom of religion, of speech, of the press, and the right to assemble, to petition the government, to bear arms, to be tried by a jury, and to enjoy the protection of the law from excessive bail, cruel or unusual punishment, and the quartering of troops in private houses. The ninth amendment makes it clear that the government can never claim that the people have no rights except those specifically listed: "The enumeration in the Constitution of certain rights shall not be construed to deny or disparage others retained by the people". The tenth amendment says that "the powers not delegated to the United States by the Constitution, nor prohibited by it to the States, are reserved to the States respectively, or to the people."

The spirit of democratic principles contained in the Bill of Rights spread across the Atlantic and was deposited in the heart of Europe – France. The French were well aware of the American Bill of Rights. Jefferson was in Paris and active with Lafayette in the preparation of the French document. The French "Declaration of the Rights of Man and Citizen" (August 26, 1789) was written not by Lafayette but by J. J. Mounier who also was fully familiar with the United States and thought it had the best government in history. A detailed discussion of American government took place all over France. The American state constitutions were published in France on five different occasions between 1776 and 1778. In the rest of Europe, the U. S. Constitution was published in Dutch and in Belgium an active periodical literature displayed a lively interest in the Constitution and Bill of Rights. In Switzerland an authority on constitutional history emphasized the importance of the

Die ersten zehn Zusatzartikel zur amerikanischen Verfassung, allgemein bekannt als die ,,Bill of Rights'' (Erklärung der Menschenrechte), beeinflußten auch das deutsche Grundgesetz von 1949.

The first ten amendments to the American Constitution, popularly known as the "Bill of Rights", influenced the Constitution of the Federal Republic of Germany, drawn up after the Second World War.

aus der Philosophie in die Politik transplantiert worden war; in England publizierte Richard Price ein Buch, in dem das amerikanische Experiment als Vorbild für alle Staaten der Erde empfohlen wurde. Später rühmte der englische Premier Gladstone die U. S.-Verfassung mit der „Bill of Rights" als „das Großartigste, was menschlicher Verstand und Wille je hervorgebracht haben". In Deutschland konnte man nur neidisch über den Atlantik blicken: Bezeichnend für den unterschiedlichen politischen Entwicklungsstand der Länder war der Freundschafts- und Handelsvertrag von 1785, der ausdrücklich zwischen den amerikanischen Bürgern auf der einen, und den preußischen Untertanen auf der anderen Seite abgeschlossen wurde. Auch in den Verfassungen der deutschen Kleinstaaten des 19. Jahrhunderts, und sogar in der Verfassung des Deutschen Reiches von 1871, waren noch nicht alle menschlichen Grundrechte verbrieft. Die Revolution von 1848 war ja gescheitert – und mit ihr der erste Versuch, eine „Bill of Rights" auch für Deutschland verbindlich zu machen. Erst 1919 verabschiedete die Weimarer Nationalversammlung eine deutsche Verfassung, die den Katalog der Menschenrechte nach dem amerikanischen und französischen Vorbild enthielt. Heute lebt er in den Artikeln 1–19 des Grundgesetzes der Bundesrepublik Deutschland ebenso weiter, wie in der „Erklärung der Menschenrechte" der Vereinten Nationen (1948) oder den „Europäischen Konventionen der Menschenrechte und Grundfreiheiten", die der Europarat 1950 erarbeitete.

inclusion of a bill of rights in the American Constitution. In Britain Parliamentary reformers were sympathetic to the American political experiment. Richard Price published a short book in England on how the American experience could be a benefit to the world. Later Gladstone would say that the Constitution with the Bill of Rights was "the most wonderful work ever struck off at a given time by the brain and purpose of man."

In Leipzig the U. S. Constitution was translated from the French. Events in America stirred up political commentary throughout Germany, albeit partially negative. Nevertheless there were many, such as J. C. Schmohl, who wrote *Nordamerika und Demokratie*, who summoned their fellow Germans "to rise to a realization of the dignity of a free man." Schmohl emigrated to America, but died at sea. The German revolutionaries of 1848 worked on a bill of rights but not until the Weimar Republic did Germany see another bill of rights which was written into the Weimar Constitution. The Democrats, the smallest of the parties in the Assembly in 1919, without force and without backing wrote the Constitution. They possessed to the full the "spirit of 1848".

The impact of the Bill of Rights, the first ten amendments of the U. S. Constitution, was to be felt around the world. The bells had tolled for Monarchy. The spirit of democratic revolution which spread throughout Europe, influenced by events in France which were in turn influenced by events in America, was instrumental in bringing down the Old Regime of Europe.

Zeitgenössische Darstellung des Sturms auf die Bastille am 14. Juli 1789: Das amerikanische Beispiel begann in Europa zu wirken.

The success of the American Revolution, and the ideas it espoused, set off a wave of armed rebellions throughout the European continent. In France, the people stormed the Bastille prison in Paris, thus giving the signal for the French Revolution of 1789.

Die Achtundvierziger in den USA

The "48ers": German Revolutionaries in the USA

Wenige Revolutionen endeten je damit, daß einem König die Kaiserkrone angetragen wurde – und selbst das noch vergeblich. Deutschland brachte dieses Kunststück 1848 fertig, als der Versuch mißlang, aus dem Mosaik monarchistisch regierter Kleinstaaten zwischen Preußen und Österreich einen demokratischen Nationalstaat zu machen.

Der auslösende Funke kam von der französischen Februarrevolution, deren unmittelbarer Anlaß das Verbot einer Demonstration an Washingtons Geburtstag gewesen war. Im März folgten Erhebungen in den meisten deutschen Staaten. In Wien wurde Metternich gestürzt, in München dankte König Ludwig I. ab, liberale „Märzministerien" entstanden, der Ruf nach einer demokratisch gewählten Vertretung des ganzen deutschen Volkes wurde unüberhörbar.

Am 18. Mai trat dann die Frankfurter Nationalversammlung in der Paulskirche zusammen. Mit dem Enthusiasmus eines nach jahrzehntelanger Unterdrückung freigesetzten Reformeifers ging das Bürgerparlament, das überwiegend aus Akademikern, wenigen Bauern, keinen Arbeitern bestand, an den Entwurf einer Verfassung, die als erste deutsche auch den vollständigen Katalog der Menschenrechte enthielt. Sie sollte nicht in Kraft treten: Denn während Frankfurt debattierte, formierte sich in Wien und Berlin die Reaktion. Das Parlament verfügte über keinerlei Exekutivgewalt, und als im März 1849 der Verfassungsentwurf fertig war, brauchte Preußens Friedrich Wilhelm IV. die ihm vorgeschlagene Kaiserwürde nur abzulehnen, um die Reichsidee zusammenbrechen zu lassen. Die „Paulskirche" löste sich auf, ein radikaldemokratisches Rumpfparlament wurde mit Waffengewalt auseinandergetrieben, die bürgerliche Revolution war gescheitert.

Few revolutions have ever ended with a king being offered an emperor's crown – which he then proceeds to refuse. But this actually happened in Germany in 1848, and the attempt to create one democratic national state out of the mosaic of small territorial principalities between Prussia and Austria ended in failure.

In 1848, the democratic spark was kindled by the French February Revolution, which itself had been triggered off by a ban forbidding a demonstration on Washington's Birthday. Uprisings in most of the German states followed in March. Metternich was toppled in Vienna; Ludwig I abdicated in Munich; liberal "March Ministries" sprang up; the cry for democratic representation for all Germans could no longer be silenced.

The National Assembly convened on May 18 at St. Paul's Church in Frankfurt. Inspired with the enthusiasm of reformatory zeal set free after decades of suppression, the Frankfurt Parliament, consisting primarily of intellectuals ,a few peasants, and no workers, began to draw up the first German constitution to contain a complete bill of human rights. It was not destined to go into effect, for while those in Frankfurt were busy debating, rebellious elements were gathering in Vienna and Berlin. When the draft of the constitution was ready in March 1849, the emperor's crown was offered to Frederick William IV of Prussia, who rejected it. The Parliament, having absolutely no executive powers, could do nothing, and the whole idea of one national state went up in smoke. The "Parliament of Professors" was dissolved; a radical democratic rump parliament was dispersed by force; revolt against authoritarian rule had failed.

Das Hambacher Fest war die erste Massenversammlung der demokratischen Einheitsbewegung, die 1848 die deutschen Revolutionen auslöste. Zug zum Hambacher Schloß am 27. Mai 1832.

The "Hambach Festival" in May 1832 was the first mass-meeting of the nationalists, who later promoted the German Revolution of 1848.

Ihre Exponenten und Sympathisanten flohen, einige Tausend an der Zahl, die meisten in die USA. Die Vereinigten Staaten zählten zu den wenigen Ländern, die der Versammlung in der Paulskirche eine Grußadresse geschickt hatten und die deutsche „Revolution" interessiert verfolgten. Die Ideale der amerikanischen Revolution waren den Achtundvierzigern Vorbild gewesen – jetzt wurden die USA ihr Exil. Mit den großen Gruppen der Familieneinwanderer hatten sie keine Ähnlichkeit: Der typische „Forty-Eighter" war Anfang zwanzig, ein Freidenker und Burschenschaftler, der sein Leben für die Freiheit riskiert hatte und nun, ohne Familienanhang und ohne Gepäck, in Amerika ankam. Oft war er nur knapp der Polizei entkommen oder aus dem Gefängnis ausgebrochen. Sein Äußeres entsprach, mit Schlapphut und Bart, dem romantischen Helden der Revolution und einem der ersten Ankömmlinge: Dem Münchener Juraprofessor Friedrich Hecker, der bei seiner Ankunft in New York von über 20000 Menschen mit einem Meer von schwarz-rot-goldenen Fahnen empfangen wurde.

In ihren politischen Zielsetzungen waren die emigrierten Achtundvierziger ebenso gespalten, wie es das Frankfurter Parlament – dem einige angehört hatten – gewesen war. Zu ihnen gehörten Nationalisten, Humanisten, Radikale, Träumer und Utopisten. Alle waren sie vom Glauben an Freiheit, sozialen Fortschritt und Demokratie durchdrungen. Zunächst hofften sie auf einen Umsturz in Deutschland, der es ihnen erlauben würde, zurückzukehren. Als die politische Wetterlage in Europa diese Erwartung zunichte machte, übertrugen sie ihren Reformwillen und Enthusiasmus auf Amerika. Als Journalisten engagierten sie sich in der amerikanischen Innenpolitik – so Oswald Ottendorfer als Herausgeber und Miteigentümer der vielgelesenen, deutschsprachigen *New Yorker Staatszeitung*. Sie setzten sich für die Abschaffung der Negersklaverei ein, unterstützten die junge Republikanische Partei und kämpften im Sezessionskrieg auf der Seite der Nordstaaten. Friedrich Hecker stellte aus eigener Initiative ein rein deutsches Regiment auf; andere, die für Lincoln kämpften, waren Heckers ehemaliger Bundesgenosse Franz Sigel, 1848 Führer der „Badischen Revolutionsarmee", und Carl Schurz.

Carl Schurz (1829–1906), wohl einer der bekanntesten Deutsch-Amerikaner überhaupt, war die herausragende Persönlichkeit unter den „Forty Eighters". Mit 19 Jahren hatte er sich, als Student, der demokratischen Bewegung angeschlossen; mit 21 befreite er seinen ehemaligen Lehrer, Gottfried Kinkel, auf abenteuerliche Weise aus der Festungshaft in Spandau, floh anschließend über England in die USA und ließ sich zunächst als Farmer nieder. 1858 gelang es ihm, als Anwalt Fuß zu fassen. Er trat der Republikanischen Partei bei, unterstützte Abraham Lincoln im Wahlkampf und wurde 1861 dessen erster Gesandter in Madrid. Auf eigenen Wunsch ließ er sich von diesem

Revolutionaries and sympathizers fled by the thousands, most of them to the United States. America was one of the few countries which had sent a message of encouragement to the Assembly in St. Paul's Church, and also one of the few which had followed the happenings of the German "Revolution" with interest. The ideals of 1776 had been, and still were, the ideals of the Forty-Eighters, and the country where these ideals prevailed was now their home in exile. They had nothing in common with the large groups of immigrant families: the typical Forty-Eighter was in his early twenties; he was a freethinker and a member of the "Burschenschaft" (a student organization with nationalistic aims); he had risked his life for freedom, and had now arrived in America without family or belongings. He had often barely managed to avoid arrest, and sometimes he had escaped from prison. His physical appearance with slouch hat and beard fitted the image of a romantic hero of the Revolution, and one of the first Forty-Eighters to arrive answered this description perfectly: the Munich law professor Frederick Hecker, whose arrival in New York was cheered by more than 20,000 people, all waving black-red-gold flags.

The immigrant Forty-Eighters were just as divided in their political aims as the Frankfurt Assembly had been (a number of them had been members). Their ranks included Humanists, Nationalists, radicals, dreamers, and Utopians. They were intoxicated by the thought of freedom, social progress, and democracy. At first they hoped for an upheaval in Germany, which would enable them to return. But when the political climate in Europe showed no signs of changing, they transferred their enthusiasm and zeal for reform to the United States. As journalists, they became involved in American domestic policy. One such man was Oswald Ottendorfer, the publisher and part-owner of the widely read German-language newspaper, the *New Yorker Staatszeitung*. These men spoke out for the abolition of slavery, supported the young Republican Party, and fought in the Civil War on the side of the North. On his own initiative, Frederick Hecker mustered an all-German regiment; among the others who fought for Lincoln were Hecker's former comrade-at-arms Franz Sigel, leader of the Baden Revolutionary Army in 1848, and Carl Schurz.

Carl Schurz (1829–1906), one of the most famous German-Americans, was the towering figure among the Forty-Eighters. At the age of nineteen, as a student, he joined the democratic movement; at twenty-one, he courageously freed his former professor, Gottfried Kinkel, from imprisonment in the fortress of Spandau; he then fled by way of England to the United States, where he temporarily settled down as a farmer. In 1858, he was able to establish himself as a

Der "Barrikadenaufstand" in Berlin am 18. März 1848. The uprising at Berlin on March 18, 1848.

48

Carl Schurz (rechts) als General im Bürgerkrieg.

Carl Schurz (extreme right) served in the Civil War as a Union General. The dedication on the back of the picture is to Schurz's sister-in-law, Bertha Ronge.

Friedrich Hecker, der Anführer der badischen Revolutionäre. Nach ihrer militärischen Niederlage floh er über die Schweiz nach New York.

Friedrich Hecker was one of the most celebrated "forty-eighters". The legend to this picture reads: "For Unity, For Freedom, Against Slavery, Against Sanctimonious Hypocrites".

Weihnachtsfest im Bürgerkrieg: Dieses gefühlvolle Motiv von Thomas Nast wurde zu einer der populärsten Grafiken des 19. Jahrhunderts.

Christmas in a nation divided: Civil War sentimentality illustrated by the German-born Thomas Nast.

Der junge Graf Zeppelin (zweiter von rechts) im amerikanischen Bürgerkrieg. Hier machte der spätere Pionier des Luftschiffbaus seinen ersten Ballonaufstieg.

The young Graf Zeppelin (second from right) acted as an observer during the American Civil War It was in America that the subsequent aircraft pioneer made his first ascent in a balloon.

49

Posten abberufen, um als Divisionskommandeur der Union am Bürgerkrieg teilzunehmen. Als Innenminister in der Regierung von Präsident Rutherford Hayes (1877–1881) setzte er die Zivildienstreform durch und gab erste Anstöße zu einer Integrierung der Indianer in die amerikanische Gesellschaft – was ihn zu diesem Zeitpunkt, nur wenige Jahre nach Little Bighorn, zahlreichen Mißverständnissen und Anfeindungen aussetzte.

Die glänzende Karriere von Carl Schurz, von dem es heißt, er sei mit seiner kosmopolitischen Einstellung schon vor der Ankunft in Amerika ein Amerikaner gewesen, ist nur für einen kleinen Teil der geflohenen Achtundvierziger typisch. Sicher war die Eingliederung der Emigranten in die amerikanische Gesellschaft eine Existenzfrage, ihre intensive Teilnahme am öffentlichen Leben Selbstschutz. Aber nicht jedem gelang es, die Sprachschwierigkeiten zu überwinden oder einen seiner Ausbildung entsprechenden Arbeitsplatz zu finden. So gab es bald die wegen ihrer hier überflüssigen klassischen Bildung sogenannten „Lateinfarmer", deren landwirtschaftliche Unternehmungen meist unter keinem guten Stern standen. Andere Schwarmgeister fanden das idealisierte Amerika ihrer Träume in der rauhen Realität des Alltags nicht wieder. Dennoch gab es unter den Einwanderern kaum eine andere Gruppe, die so geschlossen und loyalitätsbereit wie die Achtundvierziger ihre Ideale und Ziele in die neue Existenz miteingebracht und verwirklicht hat.

lawyer. He then joined the Republican Party, supported the presidential campaign of Abraham Lincoln, and in 1861 became Lincoln's first ambassador to Madrid. At his own request, he was relieved of this post, so that he might serve as a division commander for the Union in the Civil War. As Secretary of the Interior in the administration of President Rutherford B. Hayes, he pushed through the civil service reform, and also made the first moves towards integrating the Indians into American society, which at the time, only a few years after Little Bighorn, made him many enemies and involved him in many misunderstandings.

The brilliant career of Carl Schurz, of whom it has been said that his cosmopolitan outlook made him an American before he ever arrived in the country, was not typical for the majority of the Forty-Eighters. For most of them, integration into the new society was a necessity for survival, and active participation in public affairs a form of self-defense. Some were not able to overcome the language barrier, or to find the kind of work for which they had been trained or educated. There were the "Latin Farmers", so called because of their classical academic backgrounds, which were of no use in coping with the demands of life on a farm, as most of their agricultural attempts showed. Others never found the idealized America of their dreams in the hard drab reality of everyday life. But in spite of everything, the Forty-Eighters were one of the few groups of immigrants to work so consistently and loyally towards the realization of their ideals and goals in a country other than their homeland.

Noch ein weiteres Mal nach 1848 wurden die USA der Zufluchtsort politischer Flüchtlinge aus Deutschland: Während der „tausend Jahre" zwischen 1933 und 1945. Politisch Andersdenkende, Intellektuelle jeder Schattierung und vor allem Juden waren im nationalsozialistischen „Dritten Reich" einer Verfolgung ausgesetzt, die von nichts Vergleichbarem in der Geschichte übertroffen wird. Über eine Million Menschen flohen noch vor Kriegsbeginn; ungefähr 200000, davon etwa die Hälfte Juden, gingen in die USA.

Oft genug zögerte gerade das jüdische Bürgertum, Deutschland zu verlassen – die Gefährdetsten fühlten sich ihrer kulturellen Heimat am engsten verbunden. Schriftsteller und Wissenschaftler, die schon 1933 mit Publikationsverboten belegt und deren Bücher öffentlich verbrannt wurden, erkannten rascher, daß es hoffnungslos war, im Lande zu bleiben: Viele flohen unmittelbar nach Hitlers Machtübernahme am 30. Januar 1933. Bereits im Sommer dieses Jahres wurde den Exilanten durch Gesetz die deutsche Staatsbürgerschaft aberkannt.

„Der Paß ist der edelste Teil von einem Menschen. Er kommt auch nicht auf so einfache Weise zustand wie ein Mensch." So schrieb einer, der es wissen mußte, der Flüchtling Bertolt Brecht. Die Situation der paß- und staatenlosen Emigranten war verzweifelt: Ohne Arbeitserlaubnis, ohne Einnahmen, von befristeten Aufenthaltsgenehmigungen oder entwürdigenden Auflagen getrieben, flohen sie von Grenze zu Grenze, „öfter als die Schuhe die Länder wechselnd". Kaum ein Staat in Europa, der sie nicht aus Angst vor Hitler weitergeschickt hätte, kaum ein Staat schließlich, der nach Kriegsbeginn noch vor Hitlers Zugriff sicher war.

So richteten sich ihre Hoffnungen auf die USA, wurden, wie ein Zeitgenosse berichtete, oft „maßlos und messianisch". Doch die USA waren längst kein Einwanderungsland mehr. Die wirtschaftliche Depression – 15 Millionen Arbeitslose 1932 – zwang zu einer drastischen Beschränkung der Einwanderungsquoten. Zwar ordnete Präsident Roosevelt schon 1934 an, die Bestimmungen gegenüber politischen Flüchtlingen möglichst großzügig auszulegen – aber der Akzent lag auf „möglichst". Ohne weiteres gelang es nur prominenten Exilierten, etwa Einstein oder Thomas Mann, in die USA einzureisen. Hier liegt ein weiterer Grund dafür, daß das Bild der deutschen US-Emigration der 30er-Jahre überwiegend von Künstlern und Wissenschaftlern bestimmt wurde. Sie konnten die notwendigen Bürgschaften leichter erhalten oder, unter Umgehung des Diktats der Quote, direkt an Universitäten berufen werden. So sammelte sich die geistige Elite Deutschlands in den USA: „Praktisch alle, die in der Weltmeinung für das stehen, was vor 1933 als deutsche Kultur geläufig war, sind heute Flüchtlinge", schrieb die Kolumnistin Dorothy Thompson bereits 1938. Die Präsenz der deutschen Hitler-Gegner in den USA legte einen Grundstein zur späteren Entwicklung der deutsch-amerikanischen Freundschaft. Im Exil begann, mitten im Krieg, der Frieden.

German political exiles found refuge in the United States not only in the years after 1848, but once again in the "thousand years" between 1933 and 1945. Political dissidents, intellectuals of every hue, and particularly Jews were the objects of a persecution by the national socialist "Third Reich" unparalleled in the annals of history. There were over a million refugees even before the outbreak of war; approximately 200,000 (about half of whom were Jews) fled to the U. S. But often enough, Jews were the very ones who hesitated to leave Germany; imperilled though they were, they felt too culturally bound to their German homeland. Writers and scientists, whose publications were already banned in 1933 and whose books were burned, were quicker to realize the hopelessness of remaining in the country. Many fled immediately upon Hitler's coming to power on January 30, 1933. In the summer of that same year, a law was already passed rescinding the German citizenship of those going into exile.

"The noblest part of a person is his passport. Getting one is not as simple a procedure as begetting future passport-holders," wrote a man who had every reason to know what he was talking about: the refugee Bertolt Brecht. The emigrés without passport or citizenship were in a desperate situation. Often without work-permits, without a source of income, their visas were either limited or subject to degrading restrictions. They were driven from border to border, "changing countries more often than shoes". There was hardly a European nation which, out of fear of Hitler, didn't expel the refugees; hardly a nation which, after the outbreak of hostilities, was safe from possible take-over by Hitler.

Thus the exiles put all their hopes on America, often, in the words of a contemporary, "beyond all measure and messianically". But the U. S. had long since ceased to be a land of open immigration. The Depression (15 million unemployed in 1932) had made a drastic reduction in the immigration quota necessary. Although in 1934 President Roosevelt requested the restrictions to be applied as liberal as possible in the case of political refugees, the accent was on the words "as possible". Celebrities such as Einstein and Thomas Mann had no problem entering the U. S. That is one reason why the list of refugees in the 30's seems to be a list of artists and scientists. It was easier for them to find sponsors or to avoid the quota restrictions by directly receiving university positions. Thus the United States became a gathering-place for the intellectual elite of Germany. In 1938, the columnist Dorothy Thompson already could write, "Practically everyone whom the world considers to be representative of German culture before 1933, is now a refugee."

It is interesting to note that the very presence of the anti-Hitler forces in the U. S. helped lay the foundation for the postwar development of German-American friendship. In exile, in the middle of war, peace had already begun.

In die USA emigrierten:

Prominent Emigrés to the United States:

1933

Josef Albers (Maler/painter), Richard Bernheimer (Kunsthistoriker/art historian), Arnold Brecht (Politologe/political scientist), Gerhard Colm (Nationalökonom/political economist), Helene Deutsch (Psychoanalitikerin/psychoanalyst), Albert Einstein (Physiker/physicist), Hanns Eisler (Komponist/composer), Erik H. Erikson (Psychologe/psychologist), James Franck (Physiker/physicist), George Grosz (Maler/painter), Werner Hegemann (Architekt/architect), Hermann Kantorowicz (Politologe/political scientist), Otto Klemperer (Dirigent/conductor), Carl Landauer (Nationalökonom/political economist), Paul F. Lazarsfeld (Soziologe/sociologist), Emil Lederer (Nationalökonom/political economist), Kurt Lewin (Psychologe/psychologist), Otto Nathan (Nationalökonom/political economist), Johann von Neumann (Mathematiker/mathematician), Eugen Rosenstock-Huessy (Philosoph/philosopher), Albert Salomon (Soziologe/sociologist), Hans Simons (Jurist/jurist), Hans Speier (Soziologe/sociologist), Otto Stern (Physiker/physicist), Gustav Stolper (Nationalökonom/political economist), Paul Tillich (Theologe/theologian), Alfred Vagts (Historiker/historian), Heinz Werner (Psychologe/psychologist), Hermann Weyl (Mathematiker/mathematician), Billy Wilder (Filmregisseur/film director)

1934

Margarete Bieber (Archäologin/archaeologist), Felix Bloch (Physiker/physicist), Erich Fromm (Psychologe/psychologist), Albrecht Goetze (Assyrologe/assyriologist), Hajo Holborn (Historiker/historian), Max Horkheimer (Soziologe/sociologist), Guido Kisch (Rechtshistoriker/historian of jurisprudence), Erich Korngold (Komponist/composer), Leo Lowenthal (Soziologe/sociologist), Herbert Marcuse (Philosoph/philosopher), Fritz Morstein Marx (Politologe/political scientist), Sigmund Neumann (Politologe/political scientist), Erwin Panofsky (Kunsthistoriker/art historian), Curt Riess (Schriftsteller/author), Kurt Riezler (Geschichtsphilosoph/historian), Kurt Rosenfeld (sozialist. Politiker/socialist politician), Gerhard Seger (SPD-Politiker/SPD-politician), Ernst Toch (Komponist/composer), Robert Ulich (Pädagoge/educator), Max Wertheimer (Psychologe/psychologist), Karl August Wittfogel (Politologe/political scientist)

1935

Hans A. Bethe (Physiker/physicist), Rudolf Carnap (Philosoph/philosopher), Alfred Eisenstaedt (Photograph/photographer), Hermann Frankel (Philologe/philologist), Walter Friedlaender (Kunsthistoriker/art historian), Frieda Fromm-Reichmann (Psychoanalytikerin/psychoanalyst), Stefan Heym (Schriftsteller/author), Rudolf Katz (SPD-Politiker/SPD-politician), Richard Krautheimer (Kunsthistoriker/art historian), Heinrich Kronstein (Jurist/professor of law), Fritz Lang (Filmregisseur/film director), Lotte Lenya (Schauspielerin/actress), Wolfgang Pauli (Physiker/physicist), Otto Rank (Psychologe/psychologist), Hans Rosenberg (Historiker/historian), Tony Sender (SPD-Politikerin/SPD-politician), Edward Teller (Atomphysiker/atomic physicist), Kurt Weill (Komponist/composer)

1936

Willi Apel (Musikwissenschaftler/musicologist), Arnold Bergstraesser (Historiker/historian), Konrad Bloch (Biochemiker/biochemist), Max Brauer (SPD-Politiker/SPD-politician), Heinz Fraenkel-Conrat (Biochemiker/biochemist), Felix Gilbert (Historiker/historian), Richard Goldschmidt (Zoologe/zoologist), Werner Jaeger (Philologe/philologist), Hubertus Prinz zu Löwenstein (Zentrumspolitiker/politician), Erika und Klaus Mann (Schriftsteller/authors), Arnold Schönberg (Komponist/composer), Leo Spitzer (Philologe/philologist), Ernst Toller (Schriftsteller/author), Karl Vietor (Literaturwissenschaftler/literary scholar)

1937

Heinrich Brüning (ehem. Reichskanzler/former chancellor), Max Delbrück (Biophysiker/biophysicist), Peter F. Drucker (Nationalökonom/political economist), Bruno Frank (Schriftsteller/author), Walter Gropius (Architekt/architect), Waldemar Gurian (Politologe/political scientist), Wolfgang Hallgarten (Historiker/historian), Carl G. Hempel (Philosoph/philosopher), Ernst Krenek (Komponist/composer), Erich Leinsdorf (Dirigent/conductor), Hans J. Morgenthau (Politologe/political scientist), Kurt Pinthus (Literaturwissenschaftler/literary scholar), Curt Sachs (Musikwissenschaftler/musicologist), Wilhelm Sollmann (SPD-Politiker/SPD-politician), Walter Sulzbach (Nationalökonom/political economist), Leo Szilard (Atomphysiker/atomic physicist)

1938

Theodor W. Adorno (Soziologe/sociologist), Hans Baron (Historiker/historian), Reinhard Bendix (Soziologe/sociologist), Ernst Bloch (Philosoph/philosopher), Hermann Broch (Schriftsteller/author), Ernst Caspari (Genetiker/geneticist), Karl Deutsch (Politologe/political scientist), Herbert Dieckmann (Literaturhistoriker/literary historian), Ernst Fraenkel (Politologe/political scientist), Manfred George (Journalist/editor), Alexander Gerschenkorn (Wirtschaftshistoriker/economic historian), Oskar Maria Graf (Schriftsteller/author), Erich von Kahler (Philosoph/philosopher), Robert Kempner (Jurist/jurist), Fritz Kortner (Schauspieler/actor), Thomas Mann (Schriftsteller/author), Ludwig Mies van der Rohe (Architekt/architect), Franz Oppenheimer (Nationalökonom/political economist), Frederick Praeger (Verleger/book publisher), Theodor Reik (Psychiater/psychiatrist), Max Reinhardt (Regisseur/theatrical producer), Arthur Rosenberg (Historiker/historian), William Steinberg (Dirigent/conductor), Leo Strauss (Philosoph/philosopher), Eric Vögelin (Philosoph/philosopher), Hans Wallenberg (Redakteur/editor), Max M. Warburg (Bankier/banker), Joseph Wechsberg (Schriftsteller/author), Franz Carl Weiskopf (Schriftsteller/author), Stefan Zweig (Schriftsteller/author)

1939

Bruno Bettelheim (Psychologe/psychologist), Herbert Bloch (Historiker/historian), Moritz Julius Bonn (Politologe/political scientist), Adolf Busch (Geiger/violinist), Joseph Buttinger (sozialist. Politiker/socialist politician), Alfred Einstein (Musikwissenschaftler/musicologist), Julius Epstein (Journalist/journalist), Ossip K. Flechtheim (Politologe/political scientist), Karl B. Frank (sozialist. Politiker/socialist politician), Curt Goetz (Dramatiker/playwright), Kurt R. Grossmann (Organisator der Flüchtlingshilfe/organizer of refugee aid programs), Albert C. Grzesinski (SPD-Politiker/SPD-politician), Paul Hertz (SPD-Politiker/SPD-politician), Wieland Herzfelde (Schriftsteller/author), Ernst Kantorowicz (Historiker/historian), Adolf Katzenellenbogen (Kunsthistoriker/art historian), Karl Löwith (Philosoph/philosopher), Ludwig Marcuse (Schriftsteller/author), Erwin Piscator (Regisseur/director), Wilhelm Reich (Psychologe/psychologist), Artur Schnabel (Pianist/pianist), Robert Siodmak (Filmregisseur/film director), Samuel P. Spiegel (Filmregisseur/film director), Fritz Sternberg (Nationalökonom/political economist), Veit Valentin (Historiker/historian), Berthold Viertel (Schriftsteller/author), Carl Zuckmayer (Dramatiker/playwright)

1940

Rudolf Arnheim (Kunstpsychologe/psychologist of art), Siegfried Bernfeld (Psychologe/psychologist), Charlotte und Karl Bühler (Psychologen/psychologists), Richard Graf Coudenhove-Calergi (Paneuropa-Politiker/politician), Alfred Döblin (Schriftsteller/author), Lion Feuchtwanger (Schriftsteller/author), Ruth Fischer (ehem. kommunist. Politikerin/former communist politician), Friedrich Wilhelm Foerster (Pädagoge/educator), Konrad Heiden (Historiker/historian), Paul Hindemith (Komponist/composer), Hans Jacob (Journalist/editor), Ernst Jaeckh (Publizist/publicist), Fritz Kahn (Populärautor/author), Hans Kelsen (Jurist/professor of law), Hermann Kesten (Schriftsteller/author), Egon Erwin Kisch (Journalist/journalist), Adolf Löwe (Nationalökonom/political economist), Otto Loewi (Pharmakologe/pharmacologist), Emil Ludwig (Schriftsteller/author), Heinrich Mann (Schriftsteller/author), Alma Mahler-Werfel (Schriftstellerin/author), Otto Meyerhof (Biochemiker/biochemist), Ludwig von Mieses (Nationalökonom/political economist), Ferenc Molnár (Dramatiker/playwright), Norbert Mühlen (Journalist/journalist), Alfred Neumann (Schriftsteller/author), Max Nußbaum (Rabbiner/rabbi), Karl Otto Paetel (Publizist/publicist), Stefan T. Possony (Politologe/political scientist), Erich Maria Remarque (Schriftsteller/author), Alexander Roda-Roda (Schriftsteller/author), Hans Rothfels (Historiker/historian), Leopold Schwarzschild (Journalist/editor), Friedrich Stampfer (SPD-Politiker/SPD-politician), Fritz von Unruh (Schriftsteller/author), Bruno Walter (Dirigent/conductor), Herbert Weichmann (SPD-Politiker/SPD-politician), Franz Werfel (Schriftsteller/author)

1941

Erwin Ackerknecht (Medizinhistoriker/historian of medicine), Hannah Arendt (Philosophin/philosopher), Bertolt Brecht (Schriftsteller/author), Ernst Cassirer (Philosoph/philosopher)), Julius Deutsch (Politiker/politician), Max Ernst (Maler/painter), Heinz Hartmann (Psychoanalytiker/psychoanalyst), Joachim Joesten (Journalist/journalist), Siegfried Kracauer (Filmwissenschaftler/film historian), Alfred Kantorowicz (Journalist/journalist), Leo Lania (Publizist/publicist), Fritz Lipmann (Biochemiker/biochemist), Hans J. Meyer (Bankier/banker), Hermann Rauschning (konservat. Politiker/politician), Franz Schoenberner (Redakteur/editor), Konrad Wachsmann (Architekt/architect), Kurt Wolff (Verleger/publisher)

Das Ende des Ersten Weltkriegs: Am 10. November geht Kaiser Wilhelm ins holländische Exil. Am 11. November wird der Waffenstillstand in einem Eisenbahnwagen in der Nähe von Compiègne in Frankreich unterzeichnet. Das Bild zeigt Marschall Foch vor dem Wagen.

The End of World War I. On November 10 Kaiser Wilhelm crossed the border into the Netherlands. On November 11, the armistice was signed in a railway car near Compiègne in France. The picture shows Marshall Foch in front of the car.

Als Repräsentant Deutschlands unterzeichnet Generaloberst Alfred Jodl die bedingungslose Kapitulation in General Eisenhowers Hauptquartier zu Reims.

General Jodl representing Germany signs the Unconditional Surrender in General Eisenhower's headquarters in Reims.

Zwischen den Kriegen schuf die bekannte Künstlerin Käthe Kollwitz diese berühmtgewordene Kohlezeichnung mit dem Titel „Nie wieder Krieg!"

Between the two wars, the German illustrator Käthe Kollwitz drew this famous charcoal sketch entitled "War – Never Again!"

Friedensregelungen für Europa 1918 und 1945

Zweimal im zwanzigsten Jahrhundert waren die USA und Deutschland Kriegsgegner; zweimal waren die staatlichen und menschlichen Beziehungen zwischen beiden Ländern Belastungen ausgesetzt, deren Überwindung damals kaum für jemand für möglich gehalten hätte. Und doch ging aus dem schmerzlichen historischen Prozeß, der das Gesicht Europas zwischen 1917 und 1945 von Grund auf veränderte, letztlich die engste Freundschaft hervor, die jemals zwischen den Vereinigten Staaten und Deutschland bestand.

Während des Ersten Weltkriegs sahen sich die USA unter Präsident Wilson erstmals in der Rolle des internationalen Vermittlers: Schon 1916 versuchte Wilson, einen Meinungsaustausch der kriegführenden Mächte über die Bedingungen eines Friedensschlusses anzuregen. Deutschlands Erklärung des unbeschränkten U-Boot-Krieges enttäuschte diese Bemühungen um einen allseitigen „Frieden ohne Sieg" und führte im April 1917 zum Kriegseintritt der USA. Ihr Kriegsziel war, in Wilsons Worten, zu einer „demokratischen Weltrevolution" beizutragen.

Während das Engagement der amerikanischen Großmacht das Kriegsende beschleunigte, bemühte sich Wilson mit seinen ‚14 Punkten' vom Januar 1918 bereits um die Perspektiven einer künftigen Friedensordnung: Die Wiederherstellung politisch unabhängiger Staaten in unverletzlichen Grenzen sollte den Krieg abschließen, das Verbot jeglicher Geheimdiplomatie und die Gründung eines Völkerbundes den Frieden für alle Zukunft sichern. Die amerikanischen Soldaten, die Ende 1918 aus Europa zurückkehrten, glaubten fest, im letzten großen Krieg der Weltgeschichte gekämpft zu haben. Doch der politische Weitblick der 14 Punkte setzte sich bei den Friedensverhandlungen von Versailles nicht durch. Die USA lehnten den dort ausgehandelten Vertrag ab, schlossen 1921 einen Sonderfrieden mit Deutschland und zogen sich enttäuscht in eine isolationistische Politik zurück. Sie waren endgültig als Weltmacht etabliert, hatten ihre demokratische Revolution aber nicht durchsetzen können. Europa hatte sich den Weg in den zweiten Weltkrieg vorgezeichnet.

Amerikas politische Neutralität gegenüber dem nationalsozialistischen Deutschland war nicht, wie im Ersten Weltkrieg, eine Neutralität aus Überzeugung, sondern ein Warten auf das Unvermeidliche. Nach der deutschen Kriegserklärung im Dezember 1941 ging es nicht nur um eine Auseinandersetzung zwischen Staaten, sondern um einen Kampf der Demokratie gegen die Diktatur. Das „Dritte Reich" Adolf Hitlers, das die Welt in die größte Katastrophe der Neuzeit verstrickte, ist später als ‚Verhängnis', als ‚Unfall der Geschichte' bezeichnet worden. Diese hilflosen Metaphern vernebeln Zusammenhänge und erklären nichts – doch daß man sich ihrer bedienen möchte, ist zumindest verständlich. Als Präsident Truman nach dem Krieg erklärte, die USA hätten nicht gegen Deutschland gekämpft, sondern gegen Hitler, ebnete dies den Weg zu einem neuen, gemeinsamen Anfang. Heute, da die dunkelste Phase der deutsch-amerikanischen Beziehungen der Vergangenheit angehört, gewinnt ein Wort des Nobelpreisträgers Heinrich Böll an Bedeutung: „Ein Volk ohne Erinnerung richtet sich selbst".

Peace Settlements in Europe, 1918 and 1945

Twice during the twentieth century, the U. S. and Germany fought on opposite sides during a war. Twice, the diplomatic and human relationships between the two countries were strained to a point where it seemed impossible that they would ever again be normal. And yet this painful historical process, which completely changed the face of Europe between 1917 and 1945, in the end resulted in the closest friendship that had ever existed between Germany and the United States.

During World War I, the U. S., led by President Wilson, first saw itself in the role of international mediator. As early as 1916, Wilson tried to induce the warring powers to discuss the conditions of a negotiated peace. Germany's declaration of unlimited submarine warfare brought about the failure of this attempt at a universal "peace without victory", and in April 1917 resulted in the U. S. joining the war on the side of the Allies. Its intention was, in the words of Wilson, to contribute to a "democratic world revolution".

While the contribution made by the force of arms on the part of the U. S. helped to bring about the end of the war, Wilson, with his "14 Points" of January 1918, was already considering the aspects of the peace to come; the end of the war was to be marked by the re-establishment of politically independent states within inviolable borders, while the prohibition of any secret diplomacy, together with the foundation of a League of Nations, was to secure a peace that would last for all time to come. The American soldiers who returned from overseas late in 1918 were convinced that they had been fighting the last major war in history. However, the political far-sightedness which had led to the program of the "14 Points" failed to carry the day during the peace conference at Versailles. The U. S. refused to accept the treaty negotiated there, made a separate peace with Germany in 1921, and, thoroughly disillusioned, withdrew behind a wall of isolationism. Though the U. S. was now established as a major power, it had been unable to carry out its plan of a democratic revolution. Europe had embarked on the course that was to lead to the Second World War.

The neutrality of America toward Nazi-Germany was not, as in World War I, a neutrality based on conviction – it was simply a waiting for the inevitable. After the German declaration of war in December 1941, the issue was not merely the settling of differences between two states, but a struggle between Democracy and Dictatorship. The "Third Reich" of Adolf Hitler, which brought about the greatest worldwide catastrophe of modern times, has since been described as "an inexorable doom", or as "an accident of history". These hapless metaphors merely obscure the logical succession of historical facts and explain nothing, although the temptation to use them is at least understandable. When President Truman declared, after the war, that the U. S. had been fighting not against Germany but against Hitler, his words smoothed the way for a new beginning of cooperation between the two nations. Today, when the darkest phase of German-American relationships is a thing of the past, Nobel Prize winner Heinrich Böll's statement gains new significance: "A people without a memory condemns itself!"

Der historische Handschlag an der Elbe, wo sich 1945 die Soldaten der amerikanischen und der Roten Armee trafen.

The famous handshake when the American soldiers met soldiers of the Red Army at the Elbe River in 1945.

Humanitäre Hilfe nach den Kriegen   Postwar Humanitarian Aid

Viele der so zahlreichen freundschaftlichen Beziehungen, die heute über den Atlantik hinweg bestehen, verdanken die Amerikaner ihrer fast sprichwörtlichen Bereitschaft, dort Hilfe zu leisten, wo andere Völker in Not geraten sind. Gerade die Europäer hatten in ihrer jüngsten Vergangenheit mehrmals die Gelegenheit, diese Eigenschaft kennen und schätzen zu lernen. Und die Deutschen durften erfahren, daß Beistand auch ehemaligen Gegnern nicht verweigert wird. Das hatte der spätere Präsident Herbert Hoover schon 1919 in seiner Schrift *Warum wir Deutschland ernähren* mit dem Hinweis bekräftigt: „Wir versetzen niemandem einen Stoß in den Bauch, nachdem wir ihn besiegt haben".

Wie schnell und großzügig sich diese Hilfsbereitschaft äußert, zeigte beispielhaft das „Amerikanische Hilfswerk". Schon kurz nach Beginn des ersten Weltkriegs von Hoover 1914 ins Leben gerufen, leitete es bis 1921 Nahrungsmittel, Medikamente und Kleidung im Wert von mehreren hundert Millionen Dollar nach Europa. Anschließend wurde diese Aktion durch private Organisationen, vor allem der Quäker, fortgeführt. Sie bemühten sich in Deutschland durch die täglich in den Schulen ausgeteilte Quäkerspeisung so erfolgreich um die Ernährung der Kinder, daß „quäkern" in dieser Zeit geradezu ein Synonym für „essen" wurde.

Der Maxime Hoovers folgten die Amerikaner auch nach dem Zweiten Weltkrieg. Wiederum organisierten sie Hilfsaktionen gewaltigen Ausmaßes. Was als spontane Reaktion auf die Notlage von Bekannten und Verwandten begonnen hatte, wurde wenig später durch die amerikanischen Wohlfahrtsverbände zu einer festen Einrichtung gemacht. Sie gründeten die „Kooperative der amerikanischen Hilfssendungen für Europa", kurz CARE genannt. Durch sie konnte jeder hilfswillige Amerikaner gegen Einzahlung von zehn Dollar eine Lebensmittel- oder Kleider-Sendung an gewünschte Adressaten in Europa verschicken lassen. Wir können uns heute kaum noch vorstellen, was diese CARE-Pakete in der damaligen Zeit für Millionen von Deutschen bedeuteten, die oft nicht einmal das Nötigste zum Leben hatten. Wenn ein Paket eintraf, versammelte sich die ganze Familie wie zu Weihnachten, um den Inhalt Stück für Stück auszupacken. Neben den

Many of the numerous friendly ties between the U. S. and Europe are due to the almost proverbial readiness of the Americans to provide help to any country that needs it. Especially the Europeans had the opportunity to experience and appreciate this quality of "good-neighborliness" in the recent past. And the Germans discovered that even a former enemy is not denied aid. As early as 1919, the future president Herbert Hoover dryly stated in his pamphlet *Why We Feed Germany* that the U. S. doesn't kick a man when he's down. How swiftly and liberally this readiness to help could be translated into action may be seen by the example of the American Relief Administration. Founded by Hoover shortly after the beginning of the First World War, in 1914, it had sent food, medicines and clothing worth several hundred million dollars to Europe by 1921. The work was then carried on by private organizations, primarily by the Quakers. They were so successful in their project of feeding children by means of the "Quaker meals" distributed in the schools that "quakering" became practically a synonym for "eating" at the time.

After World War II, America still followed the precepts of Herbert Hoover. It again organized aid on a gigantic scale. What had begun as a spontaneous response to the need of friends and relations soon became a regular institution administered by the American welfare organizations. They founded the "Cooperative for American Relief Everywhere", CARE for short. Through CARE, any American wishing to help could send a package of food or clothing to any person or persons in Europe simply by paying $ 10. Nowadays, we can hardly imagine what those CARE packages meant to millions of Germans, who at that time often did not even have the barest necessities. When one of the packages arrived, the entire family would gather around, as at Christmastime, to unpack everything piece by piece. Besides staples, there were luxuries undreamed-of for years: butter, coffee and cigarettes for the grown-ups, cocoa and candy bars for the children. There were even some things never seen before, such as powdered milk and chewing gum.

Der spätere Präsident Herbert Hoover organisierte schon 1914 das „Amerikanische Hilfswerk", das Europa bis 1921 mit dringend benötigten Nahrungsmitteln versorgte.

President Herbert Hoover, here shown during a campaign speech in 1928, organized The American Relief Administration which provided desperately needed food for Europe from 1914 to 1921.

Die Ausgabe von Quäkerspeisen in einer Münchner Schule.

"Quakering" at an elementary school in Munich.

Berlins Regierender Bürgermeister von 1948 bis 1953, Dr. Ernst Reuter, übergibt das millionste CARE-Paket.   *Berlin's Governing Mayor from 1948 to 1953, Dr. Ernst Reuter, takes delivery on the millionth CARE package.*

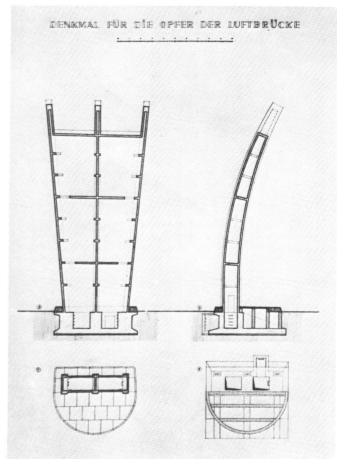

Das Mahnmal vor dem Flughafen Berlin-Tempelhof, entworfen von dem Architekten Eduard Ludwig, wurde 1952 zum Gedenken an die 97 Amerikaner, Engländer und Deutschen errichtet, die ihr Leben während der „Luftbrücke" verloren hatten. Der aufstrebende Betonbogen, im Volksmund „Hungerharke" genannt, symbolisiert die drei Luftkorridore von und nach Berlin. Das Bild darunter entstand bei einer der alljährlich stattfindenden Gedenkfeiern.

This monument designed by Eduard Ludwig in 1951 was built in memory of the 97 Americans, British and Germans who lost their lives in the Berlin Air Lift. The three points on the top of the incomplete bridge symbolize the three air corridors from West Germany to the beleaguered city. The photograph beneath shows one of the annual memorial ceremonies held here.

Walter Gropius (Mitte) besucht eine Bauhaus-Ausstellung an der Harvard Universität, die vom Goethe Institut Boston zusammengetragen worden war.

Walter Gropius (middle) attending the Bauhaus Exhibition put on by the Goethe Institute of Boston at Harvard University.

Der Referent für Fragen der Städteplanung beim Hamburger Senat, Werner Hebebrand, besucht Frank Lloyd Wright im November 1956 in Taliesin West, Wrights Wohnsitz bei Phoenix, Arizona.

Werner Hebebrand, Head of City Planning for the City of Hamburg, visiting Frank Lloyd Wright at Taliesin West, Wright's home near Phoenix, Arizona, in November of 1956.

Die Ausstellungshalle der „Internationalen Gartenschau" von 1963 in Hamburg. Die Zeltdachkonstruktion gehört zu den vielen deutschen Nachkriegserfindungen, durch die sich auch amerikanische Architekten anregen tionsprinzipien, die von Professor Frei Otto entwickelt wurden.

Exhibition Hall at the International Garden Fair in Hamburg, 1963. The tent roof design was one of many post-war German ideas now inspiring American architects as well. The design is based on principles developed by Professor Frei Otto.

1937 kam Walter Gropius über England in die Vereinigten Staaten und wurde Leiter der Architekturabteilung an der „Harvard Graduate School of Design". Er hatte dort Schüler aus aller Welt. Zusammen mit einer Architektengemeinschaft realisierte er zahlreiche Bauten, darunter das PanAm-Verwaltungsgebäude in New York.

1938 wurde Ludwig Mies van der Rohe zum Leiter der Architekturabteilung des späteren „Illinois Institute of Technology" (IIT) in Chicago berufen. Mit ihm kam der Städteplaner Ludwig Hilberseimer (1885–1967). Mies van der Rohes Einfluß war so überragend, daß von der „zweiten Chicago School of Architecture" gesprochen wird, die sich der großen Pionierleistung des 19. Jahrhunderts ebenbürtig an die Seite stellt: Seine Bauten und die seiner Schüler setzen heute in der Innenstadt von Chicago und in New York wichtige städtebauliche Akzente.

In Chicago wurde 1937 auch die Nachfolgeinstitution des Bauhauses gegründet: Laszlo Moholy-Nagy (1895–1946) leitete sie bis zu seinem Tode. An ihr arbeiteten so bedeutende Architekten wie Serge Chermayeff (geboren 1900), Konrad Wachsmann (geboren 1911) und Richard Buckminster Fuller (geboren 1895).

In der Nachkriegszeit haben sich die typischen Stilelemente des Neuen Bauens auf breitestem Raum durchgesetzt – häufig leider unter Vernachlässigung der sozialethischen Grundsätze ihrer Erfinder: Funktionalismus wurde als das Prinzip der schieren ökonomischen Rationalität mißverstanden. Die simplifizierte, phantasiearme Form, in der heute mit den Versatzstücken des Bauhausstiles Massenarchitektur betrieben wird, fordert zu Recht Kritik heraus. Weniger berechtigt ist es allerdings, die Pioniere aus Chicago und Weimar für das Elend unserer Städte verantwortlich zu machen: Die Rückbesinnung auf deren umfassenderen Rationalitätsbegriff, der mehr als bloße Rentabilität im Sinne hatte, könnte hier vieles richtigstellen.

In 1937, Walter Gropius came to the United States via England to head the Harvard Graduate School of Design's architecture department, where he taught students from all over the world. There, working in an architectural partnership firm, he designed numerous buildings, including the Pan Am Building in New York.

In 1938, Ludwig Mies van der Rohe answered a call to head the architecture department of what was later known as the Illinois Institute of Technology (IIT) in Chicago. With him came the city planner Ludwig Hilberseimer (1885–1967). Mies van der Rohe's influence was so great that people began to speak of the "second" Chicago School of Architecture, whose importance and accomplishments were as high as those of the 19th century pioneers. His own buildings and those of his students have left their unmistakable stamp on the present day skylines of Chicago and New York.

In 1937, an institution to succeed the Bauhaus was established in Chicago. Laszlo Moholy-Nagy (1895–1946) directed the institute until his death. Important architects such as Serge Chermayeff (b. 1900), Konrad Wachsmann (b. 1911), and Richard Buckminster Fuller (b. 1895), have worked there.

In the postwar period, the typical stylistic elements of the modern style found wide acceptance, but unfortunately were often applied without the social and ethical insights of their creators. Functionalism became misinterpreted to mean economic rationalization. The oversimplification and lack of imagination which mark so much of today's mass architecture have justifiably been criticized. However, it is less just to lay responsibility for the architectural and sociological failings of today's cities on the pioneers of Chicago and Weimar. A reexamination of their much broader concept of rationalization, which meant much more than simple profitability, would correct many false impressions.

Jenseits nationaler Grenzen: Die Kunst unserer Zeit

Nordamerikanische Kunst wurde in Europa erst nach dem Zweiten Weltkrieg bemerkt – bemerkt in dem Sinn, daß europäische Künstler auf das zu reflektieren begannen, was jenseits des Atlantik entstand. Für die Künstler in Amerika war dies der entscheidende Durchbruch nach einer Periode von knapp zweihundert Jahren, in der sie sich fast ausnahmslos an europäischen Stilentwicklungen orientiert hatten.

Es wäre jedoch falsch zu behaupten, die Tradition der Moderne habe in den Vereinigten Staaten erst vor dreißig Jahren ihren Anfang genommen. Sie läßt sich mindestens auf das Jahr 1913 zurückverfolgen, dem Datum der inzwischen bereits zur Legende gewordenen „Armory Show". Die elfhundert Bilder dieser Mammut-Show – eine repräsentative Auswahl der aktuellen Strömungen Europas vom Fauvismus bis Kubismus – lösten in New York, Chicago und Boston Skandale und Stürme der Begeisterung aus. Als auch noch viele der extravagantesten Werke wider alle Voraussagen Käufer fanden, galt das amerikanische Publikum unter den Avantgardisten der Alten Welt für unkonventioneller und aufnahmebereiter als das traditionsüberlastete Europa. Amerika begann, Anziehungskraft auf europäische Künstler auszuüben. Francis Picabia (1879–1953) und Marcel Duchamp (1887–1968) statteten den USA längere Besuche ab, Albert Gleizes (1881–1953) und Alexander Archipenko (1887–1964) ließen sich dort sogar nieder.

Die große Welle des Zuzugs aber kam mit der Emigration deutscher Maler in der Zeit nach 1933. Zu den ersten Auswanderern gehörten Josef Albers (geboren 1888) und George Grosz (1871–1959), ihnen folgten am Beginn der vierziger Jahre unter anderen Lyonel Feininger (1893–1956), Richard Lindner (geboren 1901) und Hans Richter (geboren 1888). Erst nach Kriegsende traf Max Beckmann (1884–1950) ein, der zunächst nach Holland emigriert war.

Transcending National Borders: Contemporary Art

It was not until after the Second World War that Europe took notice of North American art – and at first it was only European artists who grew attentive to what was happening on the other side of the Atlantic. For the artists in America, this was the critical breakthrough after a period of two centuries during which they almost without exception had oriented their styles to European trends.

It would be incorrect, however, to contend that the modern tradition in the United States had its beginnings only thirty years ago. We can trace it back at least as far as 1913, the year of the already legendary "Armory Show". The eleven hundred paintings of this mammoth show (a representative selection of current European styles from fauvism to cubism) brought about scandals but also a torrent of excitement from New York to Boston and Chicago. When, contrary to all expectations, many of the works displayed even found buyers, the members of the European avant-garde realized that the American public was more open-minded and unconventional than that of Europe. America began to attract European artists. Francis Picabia (1879–1953) and Marcel Duchamp (1887–1968) took extended trips to the USA; Albert Gleizes (1881–1953) and Alexander Archipenko (1887–1964) even settled there.

A whole wave of new arrivals came with the emigration of German artists after 1933. Among the first to arrive were Josef Albers (b. 1888) and George Grosz (1871–1959), followed in the early 40's by Lyonel Feininger (1893–1956), Richard Lindner (b. 1901), and Hans Richter (b. 1888). Max Beckmann (1884–1950), who first emigrated to Holland, did not arrive in America until after the war.

Although the creative atmosphere in America was heavily and invigoratingly influenced by the influx of European ideas, the younger generation soon grew dissatisfied with the state of affairs.

„Kathedrale" von Hans Hofmann, 1959.

"Cathedral" by Hans Hofmann – 1959.

Lyonel Feininger im Atelier: Segelschiffe und Städte waren zentrale Themen seiner kubistischen Kompositionen.

Lyonel Feininger in his studio. Sailing vessels and cities served as main themes in his cubistic compositions.

„Geschütztes Blau", von Josef Albers, 1957. Ein Beispiel der 1949 begonnenen Serie „Ehrung des Quadrats".

"Protected Blue" by Josef Albers, 1957. An example from the "homage to the square" series.

Werke von Andy Warhol, Claes Oldenburg und James Rosenquist auf der Kasseler documenta IV, 1968.

Exhibition hall at the documenta IV, 1968, in Kassel, featuring works of Andy Warhol, Claes Oldenburg and James Rosenquist.

Obwohl das Eindringen europäischer Ideen das kreative Klima in den USA nachhaltig belebt hatte, wurden die Maler der jüngeren Generation mit dem Stand der Dinge bald unzufrieden. Sie hatten das Gefühl, als sei zum wiederholten Male nur eine fremde Tradition mit ihrem totalen Anspruch übernommen worden. Dagegen richtete sich ihre Opposition. Einen Ausweg aus dieser Situation suchten sie in einer Malerei der spontanen Gestik, dem „action painting", mit dem sie die amerikanische Kunst auf eigene Füße stellten. Dieser Schritt war um so befreiender und fruchtbarer, als er auch die europäische Kunstszene beeinflußte und die Maler der Alten Welt zu einer Überprüfung ihrer Bild-Vorstellungen anregte. Die Entwicklung des „abstrakten Expressionismus" – als der die Malerei des „action painting" später berühmt wurde – begann in den vierziger Jahren und erreichte ihren Höhepunkt im darauffolgenden Jahrzehnt. Einem größeren Publikum in Europa wurde sie indessen erst auf der „documenta II" 1959 in Kassel vorgestellt. Dort konnte man sich einen Überblick verschaffen über die Leistungen der New Yorker Schule des „abstrakten Expressionismus", zu deren herausragendsten Meistern Jackson Pollock (1912–1956), Franz Kline (1910–1962) und der naturalisierte Holländer Willem de Kooning (geboren 1904) gehörten. Daneben machte die Ausstellung bekannt mit der ruhigen Flächenkunst eines Barnett Newman (geboren 1905) und Mark Rothko (1903–1970), sowie den vibrierenden Tafeln Mark Tobeys (geboren 1890).

Noch zweimal hat die amerikanische Kunst danach Einfluß auf die Szene in Europa ausgeübt: auf der „documenta IV" (1968) mit der Vorstellung amerikanischer Pop Art eines Andy Warhol (geboren 1928), Roy Lichtenstein (geboren 1923), Tom Wesselmann (geboren 1931), Robert Indiana (geboren 1928). Diese Arbeiten wurden jedoch übergewichtig von europäischen und amerikanischen Leistungen der „New Abstraction – Neuen Abstraktion" begleitet. Schließlich auf der „documenta V" (1972) mit ihrer Phalanx von Fotorealisten wie etwa Chuck Close (geboren 1940), Donald Eddy (geboren 1944), Ralph Goings (geboren 1928) und im dreidimensionalen Bereich: Duane Hanson (geboren 1925) oder John de Andrea (geboren 1941).

Während die informelle und neue Abstraktion (hard-edge, minimal) eine totale Wandlung der malerischen Auffassung brachte, führten die beiden späteren Tendenzen zu einer Wandlung der inhaltlichen Auffassung: die totgeglaubte gegenständliche Kunst war wieder erstanden. Diese zweite Revolution hat in Europa jedoch weit weniger adäquate Partner gefunden als die erste, wenn auch die Zahl der Mitläufer gewaltig ist. Heute ist noch nicht abzusehen, ob das Pendel der Wechselbeziehungen wieder zurückschwingt oder ob es vielleicht seinen Ausschwingpunkt noch gar nicht erreicht hat.

They felt they focused their entire attention on foreign traditions too often, and took their first steps in a new direction. Their first effort to get American painting to stand on its own feet was in "action painting", creating works by means of spontaneous gestures. This turned out to be all the more liberating and fruitful in that it began to influence the European art scene, and led the painters of the "Old World" to reassess their very basic concepts of painting. The development of "abstract expressionism" (which is what "action painting" later became famous as) began in the 40's and reached its high-point in the following decade. It was first presented to a large European audience during the "documenta II" exhibition in Kassel in 1959. There one could survey the achievements of the New York School of abstract expressionism, whose outstanding masters included Jackson Pollock (1912–1956), Franz Kline (1910–1962), and the naturalized Dutchman, Willem de Kooning (b. 1904). The exhibition also presented the placid surfaces of Barnett Newman (b. 1905) and Mark Rothko (1903 to 1970), as well as the vibrating panels of Mark Tobey (b. 1890).

American art twice again influenced the European scene: first, at the 1968 "documenta IV" with the presentation of American "Pop Art" by Andy Warhol (b. 1928), Roy Lichtenstein (b. 1923), Tom Wesselmann (b. 1931), and Robert Indiana (b. 1928), although their efforts were somewhat overshadowed by the European and American examples of "New Abstraction"; and secondly, at the "documenta V", (1972), by a contingent of "photorealists" like Chuck Close (b. 1940), Donald Eddy (b. 1944), or Ralph Goings (b. 1928), and in the three-dimensional field, by Duane Hanson (b. 1925), or John de Andrea (b. 1941).

While the "New Abstraction" (hard-edge, minimal) brought a total transformation in the concept of painting, the two other tendencies mentioned were only concerned with transforming the content, or subject-matter: representational painting was not dead. This second revolution failed to find many adequate advocates in Europe, although there are plenty who dabble in the technique. Today it is not yet possible to predict whether the pendulum of mutual influence is about to swing back, or whether it has perhaps not yet finished swinging out.

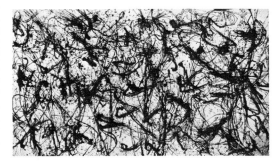

‚Action painting': Jackson Pollocks „Nummer 32". Kunstsammlung Nordrhein-Westfalen, Düsseldorf.

Jackson Pollock's "Number 32" which hangs in the Kunstsammlung Nordrhein-Westfalen in Düsseldorf.

Gruppenbild mit Galerist: 3 Plastiken von George Segal und Franz Dahlem, ein Darmstädter Galeriebesitzer.

Three sculptures by George Segal pose with Franz Dahlem, a Darmstadt gallery owner.

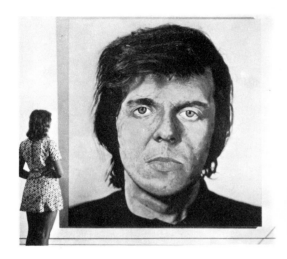

Beispiel des amerikanischen Fotorealismus auf der documenta V (1972): „Kent" von Chuck Close, 1970/71, Acryl auf Leinwand.

"Kent" by Chuck Close, an example of photo-realism, on display at the documenta V in 1972.

Der Deutsche Akademische Austauschdienst (DAAD) fördert Wissenschaften und Künste: Hier der amerikanische Bildhauer Edward Kienholz als „Artist in Residence" in Berlin.

The German Academic Exchange Service (DAAD) provides exchanges on all levels, including inviting such well known personalities as sculptor Edward Kienholz to serve as "artist in residence" in Berlin.

„Supermarket Lady" von Duane Hanson. Neue Galerie Aachen, Sammlung Ludwig.

Duane Hanson's "Supermarket Lady", now on display at the Neue Galerie Aachen, Sammlung Ludwig.

Deutsch-Amerikanische Malerei im 19. Jahrhundert

German-American Art in the 19th Century

Die enge Verflechtung mit dem europäischen Kunstbetrieb, aus der oft eine schöpferische Auseinandersetzung resultierte, war ein bestimmender Faktor für die amerikanische Kunstszene des 19. Jahrhunderts.

Europas Attraktivität lag vor allem in der Fülle des Studienmaterials, das die seit der Antike ununterbrochene kulturelle Tradition der Alten Welt für die amerikanischen Künstler bereithielt. Ebenso wichtig war die Möglichkeit, die aktuellen Stilrichtungen an der Quelle, in den Ateliers der großen Meister, kennenzulernen.

Eines dieser europäischen Reiseziele amerikanischer Künstler – und zwar der um die 20er Jahre des 19. Jahrhunderts geborenen Generation – war Düsseldorf am Rhein. Hier lehrten damals berühmte deutsche Romantiker: Wilhelm Schadow (1788–1862), der das Interesse auf das historische Genrebild lenkte; Karl Friedrich Lessing (1808–1880), das unbewußte Vorbild seiner Generation in ihren Bemühungen, literarische Werke für die Malerei nutzbar zu machen; schließlich Andreas Achenbach (1815–1910), der als erster mit der romantischen Empfindungsweise der Düsseldorfer Schule brach und Landschaften nicht als Träger symbolischer Bedeutung, sondern um ihrer selbst willen malte. Zu Achenbachs amerikanischen Schülern gehörten Worthington Whittredge (1820–1910) und Albert Bierstadt (1830–1902), der als Zweijähriger mit seinen Eltern aus Deutschland in die USA gekommen war. Beide waren vorwiegend Landschaftsmaler: man kann sie als romantische Realisten bezeichnen. Auch wenn sie in der amerikanischen Landschaftsmalerei auf Vorläufer zurückblicken konnten, war es doch ihre Generation, die diesem Genre in den USA zum Durchbruch verhalf. Vor allem Bierstadt ist hier hervorzuheben, der 1858 an einer Straßenvermessungsexpedition teilnahm und diese schließlich verließ, um einen Sommer lang unberührte Natur zu zeichnen. Mit Gemälden nach diesen Zeichnungen führte er der amerikanischen Öffentlichkeit die Schönheit des eigenen Landes vor Augen und erzielte einen durchschlagenden Erfolg: Bierstadts Kunst wurde so hoch geschätzt, daß er 1867 den Auftrag erhielt, zwei Bilder für das Capitol in Washington zu malen. Neben ihm wurde dieser Ehre ein anderer Amerikaner teilhaftig, der der Düsseldorfer Schule fast zwanzig Jahre als Schüler und Lehrer angehört hatte: der in Deutschland geborene Emanuel Gottlieb Leutze (1816–1868).

A decisive factor in American art of the 19th century was the creative impulse resulting from its interweaving with the contemporary European art scene.

What made Europe so attractive for American artists was firstly the unbroken tradition of the Old World, stemming from antiquity; and secondly, the chance to get acquainted with current styles right in the workshops of the great masters.

One of the European destinations of American artists born around the 1820's was Düsseldorf on the Rhine. It was here that two then famous German romanticists were teaching: Wilhelm Schadow (1788–1862), who directed attention to historical genre-painting, and Karl Friedrich Lessing (1808–1880), who prefigured an entire generation which strove to use works of literature as a source of inspiration for painting. Then there was Andreas Achenbach (1815–1910), the first to break with the romantic sentiment of the Düsseldorf school and paint landscapes for their own sake, and not as bearers of symbolic meanings. Among Achenbach's American pupils were Worthington Whittredge (1820–1910), and Albert Bierstadt (1830–1902), who was born in Germany, but whose family emigrated to the United States when he was two years old. Both were landscape painters, perhaps best characterized as "romantic realists". Although they were not without predecessors in American landscape painting, it was still their generation which achieved a breakthrough for the field in the States. Credit must be given in this realm especially to Bierstadt, who left a job as road-surveyor in 1858 to spend a summer sketching nature in an unspoiled state. The paintings which he then based on these sketches, showing the American public the beauty of its own country, were an enormous success. Bierstadt's work was so esteemed that in 1867 he was commissioned to paint two pictures for the Capitol in Washington. This honor was also given to another American who had been a member of the Düsseldorf School for over twenty years as student and teacher: the German-born Emanuel Gottlieb Leutze (1816–1868). A member of K. F. Lessing's circle, he helped popularize the sentimental narrative painting in America. "Westward the Course of Empire takes its Way" was the theme of the commision Leutze received in 1860 for the frescoes decorating the southwest staircase of the Capitol. This topic, as that of

Urfassung von Leutzes „George Washington überquert den Delaware"; das Bild hing in der Bremer Kunsthalle, bis es im Zweiten Weltkrieg zerstört wurde.

The original of "George Washington Crossing the Delaware" by Leutze. This painting hung in the Kunsthalle in Bremen until a bomb attack in World War II destroyed it.

„Bahnstation in Sacramento", gemalt von William Hahn.

"Sacramento Railroad Station" by the German-born American artist William Hahn.

„Sonntagmorgen in den Minen": Genreszene des deutschstämmigen Charles Nahl.

"Sunday Morning in the Mines" by Charles Nahl, the scion of an old German artist family.

Das berühmte Gemälde von Washingtons Überquerung des Delaware am Weihnachtsabend 1776 vor seinem Überraschungssieg bei Trenton wurde von dem in Gmünd/ Württemberg geborenen Emanuel Leutze gemalt. Das Idealporträt des Generals, dessen heroische, aber unseemännische Haltung das Boot in Wirklichkeit wohl zum Kentern brächte, inspirierte Generationen amerikanischer Schulkinder zu dem respektlosen Kommentar: „Warum setzen Sie sich nicht, Herr General?" (Metropolitan Museum of Art, New York).

The famous painting of Washington crossing the Delaware on Christmas Eve of 1776 prior to the battle of Trenton was painted by Emanuel Leutze, born in Gmünd in Württemberg. The idealistic portrayal of the General and his more important subordinates standing in the small boat would indicate that the artist was fairly unfamiliar with the elements of seamanship. For years, American schoolchildren have irreverently subtitled the painting "General, sit down, you're rocking the boat." (Metropolitan Museum, New York).

Er gehörte zum Kreis K. F. Lessings und hatte dem sentimentalen, erzählenden Gemälde in Amerika zu größter Verbreitung verholfen. „Westward the Course of Empire takes its Way": Dieser Titel des Leutze 1860 in Auftrag gegebenen Freskos im südwestlichen Treppenhaus des Capitols ist – wie die Gemälde Bierstadts – bezeichnend für das amerikanische Nationalgefühl zur Zeit der Eroberung des Westens.

In die Reihe der Amerikaner, die sich von der Düsseldorfer Schule stark beeinflussen ließen, gehören vor allem drei in Deutschland geborene „Frontier"-Maler, die die Besitznahme des Landes in vorderster Linie dokumentierten: Charles Wimar (1829–1863), Charles Christian Nahl (1818–1897), der aus einer traditionsreichen deutschen Künstlerfamilie stammte und William Hahn (1840–1906). Bekannter sind Eastman Johnson (1824–1906), Richard Caton Woodville (1825–1855) oder George Caleb Bingham (1811–1879), die zwar alle die Düsseldorfer Schule besuchten, dort aber allenfalls ein vertieftes Sehen der Natur oder der von ihnen häufig dargestellten häuslichen Genrebilder oder Volksszenen lernten. Ob Eastmans „In the Fields" in seinem objektiven Realismus auf Achenbachs Einfluß zurückzuführen ist, muß dahingestellt bleiben; die Art jedoch, wie hier das Licht wiedergegeben wird, ist typisch amerikanisch – man hat ihr den Namen Luminismus gegeben. Auch wenn die Düsseldorfer Schule auf die amerikanische Malerei nur einen begrenzten Einfluß ausgeübt hat, so zeigt sich ihr zeitweiliger Erfolg doch in der Gründung einer der ersten Gemäldehandlungen der USA überhaupt, die der preußische Konsul John G. Baker 1849 in New York ins Leben rief. Hatten sich amerikanische Maler zwischen 1840 und 1860 vielfach nach Düsseldorf begeben, so war es für die in den vierziger Jahren geborene Generation München, wo sie vor allem das Studium bei dem Historienmaler Karl von Piloty anzog. Bei ihm erlernte eine Reihe amerikanischer Künstler erstmals das Malen ohne Vorzeichnung,

Bierstadt's paintings, is characteristic of the American national spirit at the time the West was won.

Outstanding among the many American painters who were strongly influenced by the Düsseldorf School, were three German-born "frontier" painters who concentrated on documenting the pioneer expansion: Charles Wimar (1829–1863), Charles Christian Nahl (1818–1897), stemming from an old family line of German artists, and William Hahn (1840–1906). Perhaps even better known are Eastman Johnson (1824–1906), Richard Caton Woodville (1825–1855), or George Caleb Bingham (1811–1879), who, although they all attended the Düsseldorf School, at the most acquired a profounder way of seeing nature there, or picked up deeper insights for their many later genre – paintings of domestic or folk scenes. Perhaps the objective realism of Eastman's "In the Fields" shows the influence of Achenbach; however, the way he uses light is in the typically American manner which became known as "Luminism". As limited as the influence of the Düsseldorf School on American painting may have been, still its temporary success was reflected in the opening of one of the very first commercial galleries in the U. S. by the Prussian Consul John G. Baker (New York, 1849).

While Düsseldorf attracted American artists between 1840 and 1860, it was Munich which became the center of interest for the generation born in the 1840's. Here, a whole group of American artists flocked to study with the historical painter Karl von Piloty, who was the first to teach them painting without preparatory sketches, creating the form directly with brush and paints, in addition to passing on to them his masterful technical craftsmanship. Among the Americans who converged on Munich at that time were William Merritt Chase (1849–1916), Frank Duveneck (1848–1919), John W. Alexander (1856–1915), Joseph Rodefer du Camp (1858–1923), and Frederick P. Vinton (1846 to

„Das Urteil des Volkes": George Caleb Bingham malte diese Szene aus der Auseinandersetzung um die Einführung der Sklaverei in Kansas und Nebraska 1855.

George Caleb Bingham's "The Verdict of the People" (1855) illustrates the controversy over introduction of slavery in Kansas and Nebraska.

Ein frühes Beispiel des Luminismus: „Auf den Feldern" von Eastman Johnson, um 1875.

"In the Fields", an example of luminism, painted by Eastman Johnson, a Düsseldorf Academy graduate.

‚Realistische' Naturerfassung mit den Augen des Romantikers: „Forellenteich" von Worthington Whittredge, einem Schüler Andreas Achenbachs.

"The Trout Pool" by Worthington Whittredge who studied art under the German painter Andreas Achenbach.

In Düsseldorf wiederbelebte Genremalerei: „Die neuesten Meldungen" von Richard Caton Woodville.

"Reading the News" by Richard Caton Woodville, another artist who learned his craft at the noted Düsseldorf Art Academy.

„Der letzte Büffel", ein Gemälde Albert Bierstadts, der den fernen Westen Nordamerikas als erster auf großformatigen Ölbildern malte. Gegen Ende des 19. Jahrhunderts war dieser Titel schon fast Realität.

"Last of the Buffalo": Albert Bierstadt was the first to paint large oils of the far West. The title was almost a reality towards the end of the 19th Century.

das Herausmodellieren der zu erfassenden Form mit Pinsel und Farbe. Hier fanden sie zudem einen Lehrer, der ihnen solidestes technisches Können als Grundlage mitgab. In München trafen sich William Merritt Chase (1849–1916), Frank Duveneck (1848–1919), John W. Alexander (1856–1915), Joseph Rodefer du Camp (1858 bis 1923) und Frederick P. Vinton (1846–1911). Durch diese Maler, die später zum Teil Lehrer an amerikanischen Akademien wurden, verbreitete sich der sogenannte „Munich Style" rasch über die Vereinigten Staaten. Seine wesentlichen Kennzeichen sind eine betont realistische Figurenauffassung, verbunden mit einer spezifischen Art der Beleuchtung: ein Schlaglicht, das im Hintergrund in pastos aufgetragenen, dunklen und warmen Farben verdämmert.

1911). Since many of these painters later taught at American academies, the so-called "Munich Style" was soon introduced throughout the United States. It was characterized by an emphatically realistic portrayal of the human figure combined with a specific lighting-effect: a spotlight which fades away in the background in a twilight of warm, dim colors.

Auf nach Westen! Daniel Boone, Vorbild für Coopers ‚Lederstrumpf', führte 1775 die ersten weißen Siedler aus Virginia durch die Schlucht von Cumberland nach Kentucky. Als George Caleb Bingham diese Szene 1851 – zur Zeit des Goldrausches – malte, war sie bereits Geschichte.

*Westward Ho! Daniel Boone, model for Cooper's 'Leatherstocking', led the first white settlers from Virginia through the Cumberland Gap to Kentucky in 1775. When George Caleb Bingham painted this scene in 1851 – at the peak of the gold rush – it was **already** history.*

Goldwäscher haben ein ‚nugget‘ aus dem Flußsand gesiebt.

Gold prospectors find a nugget in the sieve.

Im Goldrausch

Während die meisten deutschen Staaten 1848 vom Revolutionsfieber geschüttelt wurden, brach in den USA eine Epidemie völlig anderer Art aus, die in kürzester Zeit die ganze übrige Welt erfaßte: der Goldrausch. Fast 100000 Besessene eilten innerhalb eines Jahres aus aller Herren Länder zu Wasser und zu Lande in den fernen Westen Amerikas. Zu den wenigen, die es verstanden, aus dem Gold Geld zu machen, gehörte der deutsche Kaufmann Heinrich Schliemann. Sein in Kalifornien erworbenes Vermögen verwandte er später dazu, noch weit wertvollere Schätze zu heben, als er die Überreste der antiken Festungen Trojas und Mykenes ausgrub und zum Begründer der wissenschaftlichen Archäologie wurde. Unter den Emigranten, die Deutschland 1849 verlassen mußten und von den Goldfunden vorübergehend nach Kalifornien gelockt wurden, befand sich auch Lola Montez, die Mätresse und „politische Beraterin" des Bayernkönigs Ludwig I., deren Affäre nicht wenig zum Ausbruch der Revolution in München beigetragen hatte. Neben unvorstellbarem Reichtum brachte das edle Metall manchem freilich auch jähes Verderben. Am vielleicht härtesten traf solches Unglück den Mann, auf dessen Grund der erste Fund gemacht worden war: Johann August Sutter. Im Badischen geboren, hatte er seine Jugend in der Schweiz verbracht und sich dann zur Auswanderung nach Amerika entschlossen. Nach vielen Irrfahrten überließ ihm schließlich 1839 der Gouverneur von Kalifornien 50000 Morgen Land am Fuß der Sierra Nevada, damals mitten in der Wildnis. Dort errichtete Sutter „New Helvetia", ein Musterländle mit großzügigen Weizenfeldern und riesigen Rinderherden. Doch all das wurde völlig ruiniert, als Sutters Angestellter James Marshall am 24. Januar 1848 den ersten Goldklumpen fand. Binnen weniger Monate hatten die Goldsucher unter Mißachtung aller Besitzrechte seine Herden geschlachtet und die Felder in Schürfparzellen aufgeteilt. Zwar bestätigte der Kongreß in Washington nachträglich Sutters Besitzansprüche, weigerte sich jedoch, ihm eine Entschädigung zu zahlen. Gänzlich gebrochen starb dieser einst so reiche Pionier als Opfer des Goldfiebers 1880 in völliger Armut.

The Gold Rush

While most of the German States were in the throes of revolutionary fever in 1848, a completely different kind of epidemic broke out in the United States, and infected all the rest of the world in no time at all: gold fever. Within the course of a single year, close to 100,000 prospectors bitten by the goldbug converged on the distant west coast of America, coming by land and by sea from a host of different countries. Among the very few of them who had the talent to make gold pay was the German merchant Heinrich Schliemann. He later used the fortune he made in California to dig for still more valuable treasures, and succeeded in excavating the remains of the legendary cities of Troy and Mycenae, thereby becoming the founder of modern scientific archaeology. Among the emigrants forced to leave Germany in 1849 who became lured by tales of gold in California, was Lola Montez herself, whose scandals as a mistress of King Ludwig I of Bavaria had contributed in no small way to the outbreak of the revolution in Munich.
While the precious metal brought unimagined wealth to some, it also plunged others into sudden ruination. Perhaps hardest hit of all was the very man on whose property the gold was first found: Johann (John) August Sutter. Born in Baden, he spent his youth in Switzerland before deciding to emigrate to America. After much aimless wandering, in 1839 he was finally granted 50,000 acres of land at the foot of the Sierra Nevada by the governor of California. In those days it was still a wilderness, but there Sutter built his "New Helvetia", an exemplary little "countree" with expansive wheat fields and enormous herds of cattle. But all his efforts came to ruin when his hired hand James Marshall found the first gold nugget on his land on January 24, 1848. Within a few months, gold-seekers – disregarding all property and trespassing laws – had slaughtered his herds and divided the fields into panning-areas. To be sure, the U. S. Congress later confirmed Sutter's property rights, but it refused to grant him compensation. This once successful pioneer died in 1880, completely impoverished and a totally broken man – a victim of gold fever.

Eine der schönsten Einwanderinnen war Lola Montez, die nach dem Ende ihrer Affäre mit dem Bayernkönig Ludwig I. in Amerika ihr Glück zu machen hoffte. Joseph Stielers Porträt ist noch heute die Attraktion von Ludwigs „Schönheitsgalerie" in Schloß Nymphenburg zu München.

The relationship between King Ludwig I of Bavaria and the dancer Lola Montez was a factor in the loss of his throne. Lola went off to seek her fortune in America. Joseph Stieler's portrait of her still hang's in Ludwig's "Gallery of Beauties" in Munich's Nymphenburg Castle.

Das deutsche Konsulat in Dawson, Alaska.

The German Consulate in Dawson, Alaska.

Sutters Sägemühle, wo 1848 das erste Gold gefunden wurde.

Sutter's Saw Mill, where gold was first found in 1848.

Oft war es lukrativer, nicht mit dem Gold, sondern mit den Goldsuchern Geschäfte zu machen: J. L. Niebergalls Kleiderbude in Colorado.

J. L. Niebergall – A German immigrant supplies the Colorado prospectors with their necessary haberdashery in the late 1850s.

Namenlose Gräber irgendwo in Alaska – nicht alle Träume gingen in Erfüllung. *Graves of nameless prospectors somewhere in Alaska – not everybody's dream came true.*

Eine wichtige Nebensache: Sport

An Important Incidental: Sports

Der Beginn des Sportunterrichts in den USA stand in den 20er Jahren des 19. Jahrhunderts im Zeichen einer engen Kooperation amerikanischer Pädagogen und deutscher Emigranten. Vor allem drei Schüler Friedrich Jahns – Carl Beck, Carl Follen und Franz Lieber – waren es, die das moderne Geräteturnen in den Vereinigten Staaten heimisch machten. Jahn (1778–1852), der Vater der deutschen Turnbewegung, hatte in den Leibesübungen ein politisches Kampfmittel in der Auseinandersetzung um die deutsche Einheit während und nach der Ära Napoleons gesehen. Wo erst einmal ein gesunder Körper war, würde sich, getreu der Maxime des Juvenal, der gesunde Geist schon einstellen – abgesehen davon, daß die Turnerei ohnehin als Sammelbecken politischer Freigeister fungierte. Es war abzusehen, daß Jahn damit in Preußen Schwierigkeiten bekommen mußte: 1819 wurde sein Turnplatz auf der Hasenheide bei Berlin geschlossen, Jahn selbst verhaftet. Einige seiner Schüler wanderten daraufhin nach Amerika aus.

Beck und Follen wurden Lehrer an der von George Bancroft begründeten Schule von Round Hill in Northhampton, Massachusetts. Dort richteten sie die erste Turnhalle in den Vereinigten Staaten ein, die mit den von Jahn entwickelten modernen Geräten – Barren, Pferd, Ringe, Reck – ausgestattet war. Beck war es auch, der die Jahn-Eiselens *Deutsche Turnkunst* ins Amerikanische übersetzte.

Weitere starke Impulse gingen von den Flüchtlingen der 48er Revolution in Deutschland aus. Als überzeugte Republikaner kamen sie in die Vereinigten Staaten und gründeten dort erste Turnvereine nach deutschem Muster, 1848 in Cincinnati und 1850 in Brooklyn. Entsprechend der steigenden deutschen Einwanderung nahmen diese Turnvereine in den folgenden Jahrzehnten stark zu, blieben dabei jedoch immer auf die Deutsch-Amerikaner beschränkt. Ihre soziale Funktion wurde wichtiger, als ihre sportliche, und mit vollzogener Integration der Einwanderer in die amerikanische Gesellschaft ging ihre Zahl wieder zurück.

Seit dem 19. Jahrhundert hat der Sport ständig an Bedeutung gewonnen. Die industrialisierte Umwelt hat unser aller Leben ungesünder gemacht: Mehr als zu Jahns Zeiten kommt es heute darauf an, Freizeitbeschäftigung zu finden, die nicht nur das körperliche, sondern auch das seelische Gleichgewicht wieder herstellen. Die USA liegen hier nicht nur mit den ursächlichen Problemen in Führung, sondern auch mit den Lösungsversuchen. Neue, attraktive Angebote für den Breitensport, wie Trimm-Dich-Pfade, Bowling-Hallen und Fitness-Center, haben mittlerweile – nach amerikanischem Vorbild – auch in der Bundesrepublik den Beweis angetreten, daß Sport nicht nur Schweiß sondern auch Spiel bedeutet.

Bis vor wenigen Jahren waren die deutsch-amerikanischen Sportbeziehungen auf einzelne Sternstunden beschränkt – etwa auf die Boxkämpfe zwischen Max Schmeling und Joe Louis in den 30er Jahren, oder die Starts von Jesse Owens bei den Olympischen Spielen 1936 in Berlin. Als Neger von Hitler mißachtet, war Owens dort der unumschränkte Liebling des Publikums. Sein sagenhafter Weitsprungweltrekord von 8,13 Metern blieb länger unüberboten, als irgendeine andere Bestleistung der Leichtathletik.

The first two decades of the 19th century saw the beginnings of physical education in the United States, which were marked by close cooperation between American pedagogues and German immigrants. It was primarily due to three students of Friedrich Ludwig Jahn – Carl Beck, Carl Follen, and Franz Lieber – that modern apparatus gymnastics took root in the United States. Jahn (1778–1852), the 'father of gymnastics', saw in physical training a political weapon to be used in the continuing struggle for German unification: he believed in Juvenal's maxim that a healthy body will produce a healthy mind. The gymnastics movement was a melting pot of "healthy minds" which happened to be politically unorthodox. It was thus to be expected that Jahn would run into difficulties in Prussia: in 1819, his training field on the "Hasenüder" near Berlin was closed down, and Jahn himself was arrested. Several of his students then emigrated to America.

Beck and Follen became teachers at the Round Hill School in Northampton, Massachusetts, which had been founded by George Bancroft. Through their efforts, the gymnasium became the first in the United States to be equipped with the modern apparatus developed by Jahn – parallel bars, the horse, rings, and horizontal bars. It was also Beck who translated the Jahn-Eiselen *German Gymnastics* into English.

The refugees from the German revolutions of 1848 also contributed to the spread of gymnastics. As convinced republicans, they came to the United States and founded the first athletic clubs to be organized along German lines – Cincinnati in 1848, Brooklyn in 1850. Due to increasing German immigration, the number of these clubs grew rapidly during the next decades, but they always remained restricted to German-Americans. The club's social function became more important than the athletic, and with complete integration of the immigrants into American society, their number decreased.

Since the 19th century, sports have continued to gain in importance. The industrialized environment we live in has not made us any healthier, less so in fact. It is much more necessary today than it was in Jahn's time to find forms of leisure activity which not only restore physical, but also mental equilibrium. The United States, which has the greatest problems in this area, has made the greatest attempts to solve them. Sport has been made available to the masses in the form of bowling alleys, physical fitness centers, and organized jogging. The American pattern has been copied in the Federal Republic, proving that sport can be as much play as it is perspiration.

Until recently, German-American sport relations consisted of scattered highpoints, such as the boxing matches between Max Schmeling and Joe Louis in the 1930's, or the performance of Jesse Owens at the 1936 Olympics in Berlin. Although disdained by Hitler because of his color, he was the undisputed favorite of the public. His fantastic world record in broad jump (8.13 meters) remained unsurpassed longer than any other track and field record.

Ausgangspunkt des modernen Geräteturnens: der erste Turnplatz des Turnvaters Jahn in der Berliner Hasenheide.

The "Gymnastics Father" Jahn first used modern gymnastic equipment in his exercise yard on the Rabbit Heath (Hasenheide) in Berlin in 1811.

Ausflug des „New Yorker Turnvereins" im Jahr 1854.   *"Excursion of the New York Turners" in 1854. The word Turner is based on the German word meaning "gymnast".*

Weitere sportliche Höhepunkte in den 30er Jahren setzte Gottfried Freiherr von Cramm, der „Tennisbaron", der als erster Deutscher im Wimbledon-Finale stand und als erster Spieler der deutschen Davispokalmannschaft den Amerikanern manchen harten Kampf lieferte. Gustav Rau, Chef der deutschen Reiterequipe, organisierte und leitete 1938 die erste umfassende Studienreise deutscher Reiter in den USA; an der Kavallerieschule der Militärakademie West Point hielt er einen vielbeachteten Vortrag über die Reiterei.

Heute findet zwischen den Vereinigten Staaten und der Bundesrepublik Deutschland ein regelmäßiger Austausch von Sportlern und Sportlehrern statt. Jedes Jahr nimmt eine Anzahl deutscher Spitzensportler Stipendien an amerikanischen Universitäten wahr. Schwimmer trainieren und studieren an der weltberühmten Schwimmschule von Long Beach; Leichtathleten finden an anderen Hochschulen der USA Arbeitsbedingungen vor, von denen die meisten europäischen Sportler – die des Ostblocks ausgenommen – nur träumen können. Die oft beschworene völkerverbindende Funktion des Sports bewährt sich im kleinen Rahmen dieser Stipendien mindestens ebenso, wie bei den großen internationalen Wettkämpfen – wo immer die Gefahr besteht, daß nationales Prestigedenken in den Vordergrund tritt.

Ein wesentlicher amerikanischer Beitrag zum deutschen Sport besteht in der Entwicklung und dem Export neuer Ballspiele. Zwar konnten sich Baseball und die amerikanische Art des Fußball in der Bundesrepublik nicht durchsetzen, während man in den USA langsam auf den europäischen Fußball („soccer") aufmerksam zu werden beginnt. Volley- und Basketball jedoch – beide gegen Ende des 19. Jahrhunderts

Other sport highlights of the 1930's were supplied by Gottfried Freiherr von Cramm, the "tennis baron", who was the first German to play in the Wimbledon finals, and who gave the Americans a run for their money as leading player of the German Davis Cup team. Gustav Rau, head of the German equestrian team, organized and led the first field trip of German equestrians to the United States; at the West Point cavalry school, he gave a much-admired lecture on horsemanship.

Today there is a constant exchange of athletes and teachers of physical education between the United States and the Federal Republic. Every year, a number of top German athletes take advantage of scholarships to American Universities. Swimmers train and study at the world-famous swimming school at Long Beach; track and field stars can find training conditions at American universities which most European athletes can only dream about, with the exception of those from Eastern Europe. On a small scale, these scholarships contribute just as much, if not more, to the idea that sports promote understanding between nations, as do international competitions – where there is always the danger that thoughts of national prestige will be uppermost.

A noticeable American contribution to German sports has been the development and export of new ball games. Baseball and American football have never really caught on in the Federal Republic, although the United States is becoming more aware of soccer (European "football"). But this is not the case with volleyball and basketball, both of which came into being in the United States towards the end of the 19th century. These games have become part of German athletic life, in schools and professionally. The Harlem

Basketball in höchster Perfektion: die Harlem Globetrotters. Hier 1971 in Düsseldorf.

A guest appearance of the Harlem Globetrotters in Düsseldorf in 1971.

in Amerika entstanden – sind aus dem heutigen deutschen Schul- und Leistungssport nicht mehr wegzudenken. Die Basketballkünstler der Harlem Globetrotters, die mehrfach auch in Deutschland gastierten, sind die besten Propagandisten für dieses Spiel, das sich auch in der Bundesrepublik ein Stammpublikum zu erobern beginnt. Spieler und Trainer aus den USA leisten hierbei tatkräftige Hilfe – kaum ein namhafter deutscher Basketballklub kommt heute noch ohne ‚seinen‘ Amerikaner aus.

Ein abschließendes Wort sei dem sportlichen Betätigungsdrang jener Minderheit gegönnt, der es in den USA gelungen ist, ein deutsches „Kulturgut" ersten Ranges zum Sportrequisit zu erhöhen: den Volkswagen. Er ist zum klassischen Austragungsort der Disziplin des „Car-Cramming" geworden, die sich die experimentelle Beantwortung der Frage zur Aufgabe gemacht hat, wie viele Menschen in und auf einem solchen Fahrzeug Platz haben. Die Rekordmarke – soweit wir wissen, wird sie derzeit in Amerika gehalten – steht auf 111.

Globetrotters, who have often appeared in Germany, are the best propagandists for basketball, which is starting to acquire a hard core of fans in the Federal Republic. American players and trainers are very much in demand – there is scarcely a German basketball team of any repute which does not have "its very own" American.

A closing word will be dedicated to the athletic endeavors of that American minority which has succeeded in transforming a highly-prized German cultural institution into sports equipment – the Volkswagen. It has become the classic training ground for the exacting discipline of "car cramming", the object of which is to establish how many people can fit into and on top of one. The latest American record stands at 111.

Ein Spaß amerikanischer Herkunft, der von deutschen Jungen begeistert aufgegriffen wurde: Seifenkistenrennen.

A soap box derby in Germany.

Auch 1972 noch von Autogrammjägern umlagert: Jesse Owens, der mehrfache Olympiasieger von 1936, bei den olympischen Spielen in München.

Jesse Owens, champion athlete of the 1936 Berlin Olympics, returned to Germany in 1972 where he visited the 20th Olympic Games in Munich.

Erziehung und Bildung

Education and Learning

Mit der poetischen Idee, Kinder wie Blumen erblühen zu lassen, schuf Friedrich Fröbel (1782 bis 1852) die „autodidaktische Anstalt" des „Kindergartens". Offenbar barg die Assoziation „Blumenkinder" schon damals politischen Zündstoff: Von 1851 bis 1860 waren die Kindergärten in Preußen wegen „destructiver Tendenzen auf dem Gebiet der Religion und Politik" verboten. Doch der Erfolg dieser frühen Vorläufer der Vorschulerziehung unserer Tage war nicht mehr aufzuhalten: Achtundvierziger, Flüchtlinge der deutschen Revolutionen, brachten das Konzept der Kindergärten erstmals in die Vereinigten Staaten. 1867 gründete Elizabeth Peabody (1804–1894) ein „American Froebel Institute" und noch heute trägt die inzwischen weltweit verbreitete Institution „Kindergarten" im amerikanischen Sprachbereich ihren alten deutschen Namen.

Auch am anderen Extrem des pädagogischen Spektrums, an den Universitäten, gab es im 19. Jahrhundert transatlantische Verbindungen: In Göttingen immatrikulierte sich 1815 der amerikanische Student Edward Everett, der es noch zum Präsidenten von Harvard bringen sollte. Ihm folgten George Bancroft, der Historiker, und der Dichter Henry Wadsworth Longfellow, der einem Freund schrieb, er solle keinesfalls versäumen, in Göttingen zu studieren: „Ich habe noch nie so große Vorteile für einen Studenten erlebt".

Die Vorzüge, durch die das deutsche Universitätssystem für Amerikaner attraktiv wurde, lagen nicht nur auf akademischem Gebiet: „Das deutsche Universitätsleben ist ein sehr freies Leben und scheint keine Beschränkungen zu kennen" beobachtete Mark Twain in Heidelberg, und rund 9000 amerikanische Studenten – für damals eine respektable Zahl – machten zwischen 1820 und 1920 die Probe aufs Exempel.

Neben enthusiastischem Lob gab es auch Tadel. Der Historiker Henry Adams (1838–1918) bemängelte das jahrhundertealte deutsche Vorlesungssystem, das ihm offenbar ebenso unzeitgemäß schien wie die Professoren selber. Nach seinem akademischen Gastspiel in Berlin mockierte er sich: „Die deutschen Studenten waren schon komische Viecher, aber ihre Professoren spotteten jeder Beschreibung". Im allgemeinen überwog jedoch die positive Einschätzung. So konnten die deutschen Hochschulen des 19. Jahrhunderts neben dem stolzen Bewußtsein ihrer langen Tradition das beruhigende Gefühl haben, dem so viel jüngeren amerikanischen Bildungswesen Beispiel und Vorbild zu sein.

Friedrich Froebel (1792–1852) had the poetic idea that children should be allowed to grow like flowers in a garden, and so he founded the "autodidactic institution" of the "Kindergarten". Even at that time the term "Flower-Children – Flower Power" apparently had politically explosive connotations: kindergartens were outlawed in Prussia between 1851 and 1860 because of "destructive tendencies in the areas of religion and politics". It was German refugees from the revolutions of 1848 who introduced the concept of the kindergarten to the United States. In 1867, Elizabeth Peabody (1804–1894) founded an "American Froebel Institute", and the "Kindergarten", now a worldwide institution, has to this day retained its old German name in the American language.

In the 19th century there were also transatlantic connections at the other end of the academic spectrum – the universities. The American student Edward Everett, who was later to become president of Harvard, matriculated at Göttingen in 1815. He was followed by the historian George Bancroft, and the poet Henry Wadsworth Longfellow, who said in a letter to a friend: "Do not on any account omit studying there . . . I never saw so great advantages for a student."

The attractions of the German university system for Americans were not only academic. As Mark Twain observed while in Heidelberg: "German university life is a very free life; it seems to have no restraints." Approximately 9,000 American students put this to the test between 1820 and 1920 – a very respectable quota for that time.

Along with enthusiastic praise there was also criticism. The historian Henry Adams (1838–1918) seemed to be of the opinion that the centuries-old German lecture system was just as antiquated as the professors themselves. After teaching in Berlin he made the wry comment that "the German students were strange animals, but their professors were beyond pay." But in general, the positive impression prevailed. So in addition to their pride in their long traditions, the German universities of the 19th century were able to enjoy the satisfaction of setting the example for the so much younger American educational system.

Even in 1930, according to a comparative study of American, English, and German universities, there were no signs of change in this complacent German attitude. It wasn't until after Hitler came to power that drastic changes occurred in education – and many other fields as well. The

Kinder aus aller Herren Länder spielen Fußball im internationalen Kindergarten in Bonn.

Children of all nations play soccer at the international kindergarten in Bonn.

Friedrich Fröbel – der Vater der Kindergartenidee. Das Bild zeigt ihn im Jahr 1840, als der erste Kindergarten eröffnet wurde.

Friedrich Fröbel – the father of the kindergarten – shown in 1840, the year the first kindergarten was established.

Amerikanische Schulkinder in York, im Staat Pennsylvanien, üben ein deutsches Lied. Das Jahr: 1805.

American school children learn a German song in a classroom in York, Pennsylvania, in 1805.

Dialog mit dem Computer – einer amerikanischen Erfindung, die inzwischen zunehmend auf allen Sektoren des Erziehungswesens eingesetzt wird.

Dialogue with the computer – an American invention now being applied on all levels of education in Germany.

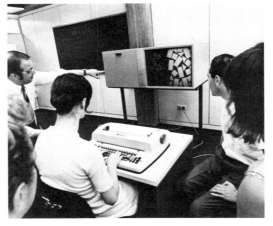

Die Gesamtschule, die alle Schultypen unter einem Dach vereint, ist in Deutschland eine relativ neue Einrichtung, die aber immer mehr an Boden gewinnt.

The type of public school, encompassing all levels of education in one building, is a relatively new idea in Germany, but it is gradually replacing the old segregated system.

Verkehrserziehung – ein Problem, das Fröbel sicher keine Sorgen machte.

Lessons in traffic safety – a problem that probably did not concern Friedrich Fröbel.

Noch 1930 bemerkt eine vergleichende Studie amerikanischer, englischer und deutscher Hochschulsysteme keine Anzeichen für eine Änderung dieser Selbstsicherheit. Erst die Machtübernahme Hitlers führte auf diesem wie auf so vielen anderen Gebieten zu einer drastischen Veränderung des Bildes. Die Emigration bedeutender Wissenschaftler, von denen viele auch nach dem Krieg in den USA blieben, hinterließ an den deutschen Universitäten Lücken, die nur langsam wieder aufgefüllt werden konnten. In geringerem Umfang und aus rein praktischen Gründen setzte sich diese Abwanderung in den 50er Jahren fort: Vor allem in naturwissenschaftlichen Fächern waren die Arbeitsbedingungen in den Vereinigten Staaten wesentlich großzügiger als in der Bundesrepublik Deutschland. Die Einbahnstraße der Einflüsse hatte sich, gegenüber dem 19. Jahrhundert, umgekehrt.

Auch in der pädagogischen Theoriediskussion, die heute eine entscheidende Rolle spielt, haben die USA einflußreiche Beiträge geleistet. Der Behaviorismus B. F. Skinners legte den Grundstein zu Theorien des programmierten Lernens, ohne die heute auch in Deutschland keine Lehrplangestaltung mehr denkbar ist. Die Diskussion über die Sprachbarrieren zwischen den sozialen Gruppen und ihre Überwindung ging von dem amerikanischen Soziologen Basil Bernstein aus und wird heute überall in Europa fortgesetzt. Auch Lehrerbildungsmethoden, wie das an der Universität Stanford entwickelte „Micro-Teaching" werden in der Bundesrepublik – im Zentrum für Neue Lernverfahren in Tübingen – weiterentwickelt. Das Konzept der Gesamtschulen, in denen Bildungswege verschiedener Niveaus gegeneinander durchlässig bleiben sollen, wurde ebenfalls unter dem Einfluß amerikanischer Vorbilder in Deutschland eingeführt. Allerdings ist die Durchsetzung solcher Neuerungen in der Bundesrepublik ein zeitraubendes Unterfangen, da die einzelnen Bundesländer eine in der Verfassung garantierte „Kulturhoheit" ausüben. Die Bonner Regierung kann auf dem Bildungssektor nur Rahmenrichtlinien erlassen, den Ländern jedoch kein einheitliches System vorschreiben. Ein praktischer Nachteil entsteht daraus, wenn Familien von, beispielsweise, Bayern nach Berlin umziehen und die Kinder dann einem völlig anderen Lehrplan oder sogar Schultyp konfrontiert sind.

emigration of prominent scientists, many of whom remained in the United States even after World War II, left vacancies in the German universities which it has taken a long time to fill. This emigration continued on into the Fifties on a smaller scale and for purely practical reasons – working conditions and pay (especially in the natural sciences) were considerably better than in the Federal Republic. The 19th century trend of influence was now reversed.

The United States has also made important contributions to the very current field of pedagogic theory. The Behaviorism of B. F. Skinner laid the cornerstone for the theory of programmed learning, without which present-day curriculum planning is unthinkable (also in Germany). The question of language barriers between different social groups and how to overcome them was introduced by the American sociologist Basil Bernstein, and is being discussed all over Europe today. Teacher education is also undergoing revision in the Federal Republic at the Center for the Study of New Learning Processes in Tübingen (somewhat along the lines of Stanford University's "Micro-Teaching").

The American concept of comprehensive secondary education, in which education proceeds on different levels at the same time in the same school, has also been introduced in Germany. However, the firm establishment of such a new and different school system in the Federal Republic is a time-consuming and extremely complicated operation, since each state is guaranteed absolute autonomy in education by its constitution. The Federal Government in Bonn can only offer guidelines in this matter – it is not empowered to prescribe one particular school system for the entire country. One obvious disadvantage of this system is that when a family moves from, let us say, Bavaria to Berlin, the children are confronted not only with a totally different curriculum, but perhaps even a different type of school.

But diversity can also be positive, in that it allows room for experimentation. Thirty thousand American high schools with almost ten million pupils are ample proof of this. The hotly disputed question of whether or not it is good to give grades (which shakes many teachers in Germany to their academic foundations) has been under discussion for a long time in the United States, and there

Vielfalt bringt freilich nicht nur Nachteile, sondern auch Gelegenheit zum Experiment. Dafür bieten die 30000 amerikanischen High Schools mit ihren knapp 10 Millionen Schülern das beste Beispiel. Die ketzerische Frage nach Sinn oder Unsinn der Notengebung – vielen deutschen Lehrern ein Rütteln an Grundfesten ihres Weltbildes – wird in den USA schon lange diskutiert und experimentell untersucht. An der John Adams High School in Portland, Oregon, zum Beispiel werden Noten nur noch auf ausdrücklichen Wunsch verteilt – zeugnisgeplagten deutschen Schülern muß dies vorkommen wie im Märchen.

Kindergarten und Märchentante haben heute in den Massenmedien Konkurrenten, von denen Fröbel sich nichts träumen ließ. Ernie, Bert, Bibo und Oskar aus der *Sesame Street* verdanken es deutsche Kinder, daß der Rolle des Fernsehens in der Vorschulerziehung endlich auch in der Bundesrepublik mehr Aufmerksamkeit geschenkt wird. Seit sie, via Mattscheibe, Spaß am Lernen und an sozialem Verhalten vermitteln, sind die Medien als pädagogisches Medium auch in Deutschlands Kinderzimmern salonfähig.

have been some experiments in this direction. One example is the John Adams High School in Portland, Oregon, which only gives grades if they are specifically requested – which must seem like a fairy tale to German school pupils, who are always under strong "grade pressure".

Kindergarten and the Fairy Godmother have competition today from the mass media that Friedrich Froebel could never have dreamed of. German kids can thank Ernie, Bert, Big Bird and Oscar from "Sesame Street" for the fact that the role of television in pre-school education has finally won more recognition in their country. Since they have shown, via the TV screen, that learning and good behavior can be fun, TV for toddlers is definitely "in" in Germany.

Sesamstraße – Ernie, Bert, das Krümelmonster und alle ihre Freunde sind in Deutschland genauso beliebt wie in ihrer Heimat. Das deutsche Fernsehen fügt noch zusätzliche Szenen ein, um die Kinder hier stärker mit den Figuren und ihren Problemen bekanntzumachen.

Sesame Street – Ernie, Bert, the Cookie Monster and all their friends are just as popular in Germany as they are at home. Special footage is added to the show to make the German children feel more at home with the characters and their problems.

Die internationale Schule in Bonn, wo neben deutschen und amerikanischen Schülern noch Kinder vieler anderer Nationen zusammen lernen und spielen.

The international school in Bonn, where besides German and American students children of many other nations study and play together.

Austausch und Begegnung

Unkenntnis ist der ideale Nährboden des Vorurteils: Um anderen Völkern gerecht zu werden, sie zu verstehen, zu akzeptieren und in ihrer Art zu schätzen, ist es eine elementare Voraussetzung, möglichst viel von ihnen zu wissen. Eigene Erfahrung, aktive Auseinandersetzung mit Lebensstil und Umwelt, Mentalität und Geschichte anderer Nationen ist hier unersetzlich.

Die Vereinigten Staaten von Amerika und die Bundesrepublik Deutschland unterhalten heute einen lebhaften Austausch von Schülern, Studenten und Wissenschaftlern. Nahezu 200 Organisationen, Stiftungen und Institutionen öffentlicher und privater Art bieten derzeit in beiden Ländern Stipendien, Seminare und Austauschprogramme an. Schon immer waren die USA für deutsche Austauschschüler und Studenten besonders attraktiv, und umgekehrt läßt sich für das amerikanische Interesse an Deutschland zumindest seit den 50er-Jahren sicher Ähnliches behaupten. In der jüngsten Vergangenheit hat sich dieser Trend auf beiden Seiten des Atlantik noch verstärkt.

Ohne nach ihrem Interesse gefragt worden zu sein, sind seit 1945 freilich schon immer junge Amerikaner nach Deutschland gekommen: als Soldaten der amerikanischen NATO-Streitkräfte. Die Eigenheiten ihres Berufes haben allerdings häufig zu ihrer Isolierung von der Bevölkerung beigetragen. Dennoch haben die meisten GI's auch außerdienstliche Eindrücke von der Bundesrepublik mit nach Hause genommen – wofür schon die Zahl derer spricht, die später nach Europa zurückkehrten, wo es sich mit den Geldern der „GI – Bill of Rights", einer finanziellen Starthilfe nach dem Austritt aus der Armee, billiger leben und studieren ließ. Seit einigen Jahren werden auch von Seiten deutscher Behörden entschiedene Versuche gemacht, die amerikanischen Soldaten stärker in den Alltag ihres Gastlandes zu integrieren.

Für das gegenseitige Kennenlernen und den Abbau von Vorurteilen ist zweifellos der Schüleraustausch von zentraler Bedeutung. Hier wirkt vor allem der „American Field Service" (AFS), der 1914 zur Betreuung Verwundeter aus dem ersten Weltkrieg gegründet wurde und seit 1947 auch den Austausch von Mädchen und Jungen im Alter von sechzehn bis achtzehn Jahren im Ausland organisiert. Über 3000 deutsche Schüler kommen auf diese Weise jährlich in die USA, über 1500 amerikanische Jugendliche in die Bundesrepublik. Die jungen amerikanischen Gäste haben hier Gelegenheit, für einige Zeit Anschluß an deutsche Familien zu finden und mit diesen zu leben. Aus eigener Anschauung lernen sie das tägliche Leben in ihrer Umgebung kennen, haben die Möglichkeit, sich die deutsche Sprache aus erster Hand anzueignen und vermitteln ihren Gastgebern gleichzeitig einen unmittelbaren Eindruck

Exchange and Encounter

Where ignorance is rife, prejudice thrives. In order to do justice to other peoples, understand and accept them, it is essential to know as much about them as possible. Personal experience, familiarity with the life style and environment, the mentality and history of other nations, are indispensable.

Today, there is a lively exchange of students, teachers and scientists between the U. S. A. and the Federal Republic of Germany. Close to 200 organizations, foundations and institutions in both countries, both public and private, offer scholarships, seminars and exchange programs. The United States has always been of particular interest to German exchange students, and the same may be said regarding American interest in postwar Germany, at least since the Fifties. Recently, the trend has grown even stronger on both sides of the Atlantic.

Of course since 1945 many young Americans have been coming to Germany regardless of whether or not they were personally interested; we are referring to the U. S. members of the NATO military forces. It is true that the peculiarities of their position have frequently resulted in isolating them from the German population as a whole. Nevertheless, most of the GI's have taken with them some off-duty impressions of the Federal Republic – as may be seen by the number of those who later returned to Germany, where both living and studying were cheaper on the GI Bill. In the last few years, even German municipalities have made some more determined efforts at drawing the American soldiers into the everyday life of the host country.

Student exchange doubtlessly is of primary importance for getting mutually acquainted and overcoming prejudice. This is the particular task of the "American Field Service" (AFS), which was founded in 1914 in order to care for the wounded of World War I, and since 1947 has also been organizing the international exchange of boys and girls between the ages of 16 and 18. More than 3000 German students visit the U. S. every year, while 1500 American teenagers come to Germany with the aid of this program. The young American guests have the opportunity to meet German families in their homes and live with them. They become familiar with the everyday life around them, have a chance to pick up the German language at first hand, and at the same time give their hosts an impression of American mentality and culture. The same opportunities are offered to the German teenagers who are given the opportunity to stay with an American family in the U. S. A. An AFS-student differs from a tourist in that he has a chance to get involved in the life of the country and the people.

In the field of university students' and teachers'

1954 im Landtagsgebäude von Düsseldorf: Austausch-Studenten aus allen Teilen Amerikas stellen sich der Kamera.

Exchange students from all over the United States pose in 1954 in the State Legislature building in Düsseldorf.

350 deutsche Austausch-Studenten treffen 1950 im Hafen von New York ein. Sie bildeten das erste Kontingent im Rahmen des Studenten-Austausches zwischen beiden Ländern nach dem Krieg.

350 German exchange students arriving in New York in 1950. This was the earliest exchange of students between the two countries after the war.

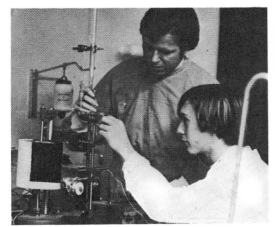

Die Universität von Maryland unterhält in Zusammenarbeit mit den amerikanischen Truppen eine Reihe von akademischen Institutionen in Europa. In München offeriert sie ein viersemestriges College-Programm.

The University of Maryland maintains a large operation in conjunction with the United States military in Europe, with headquarters in Heidelberg and a full-time junior college program in Munich.

Austauschstudenten des Verbandes der Deutsch-Amerikanischen Klubs berichten:

Exchange Students of the Federation of German-American Clubs Report:

HELEN HAMILTON, Oberlin College, Austauschstudentin in Marburg: . . . Ich kam nach Europa mit einigen Zielen im Kopf. Ich wollte meine Kenntnisse in der deutschen Sprache verbessern. Ich wollte die Vereinigten Staaten von einem anderen Blickpunkt sehen. Ich wollte die Bundesrepublik kennenlernen . . .

SUZY SMITH, Oberlin College, Austauschstudentin in Würzburg: . . . Was mir sehr gefallen hat, war die Behaglichkeit der Universitätsatmosphäre. Es gab hier keinen Druck. Der Mangel fester Regeln und bestimmter Forderungen zwingt einen dazu, wenn man ein sinnvolles Studium will, selbst Initiative und ein bißchen Originalität hervorzubringen . . .

CAROL HIGGINS, Ohio Wesleyan University, Austauschstudentin in Mainz: . . . Im Gegensatz zum amerikanischen System haben die Studenten hier die Möglichkeit, die Übungen und Kurse auszuwählen, die sie für die besten halten . . .

ED WESS, Bowling Green State University, Austauschstudent in Würzburg: . . . ist mir aufgefallen, daß es in Deutschland eine starke politische Aktivität und politisches Bewußtsein unter den Studenten gibt. Sie scheinen den aufrichtigen Wunsch zu haben, sich in internationaler Politik auszukennen . . .

ANN BEDELL, University of Arizona, Tucson, Austauschstudentin in Hamburg: . . . Seit ich in Deutschland bin, interessiert mich die Weltpolitik viel mehr als früher. Jetzt wohne ich im „Übersee-Kolleg", ein Studentenheim, wo fünfzig Prozent Deutsche sind und fünfzig Prozent Ausländer . . . Auch finde ich europäische Geschichte interessanter. Ich kann jetzt die Orte der bekannten Ereignisse sehen . . .

ERIKA ZUEHLKE, University of Arizona, Tucson, Austauschstudentin in Gießen: . . . Am wertvollsten für mich sind die Freundschaften, die ich mit deutschen Studenten und Familien bisher geschlossen habe. Ich habe mich auch besonders gefreut, meine Verwandten kennenzulernen . . .

JOHN T. WARREN, Florida Southern College, Austauschstudent in Freiburg: . . . Ich habe auch entdeckt, daß eine gute Flasche Wein, die man zusammen mit drei oder vier guten Freunden genießt, einen alle Sprachschwierigkeiten vergessen lassen kann . . .

MARY COLLINS, University of Texas, Austin, Austauschstudentin in Bonn: . . . Ich mache viele Ausflüge in die Wälder, in Wildlife-Parks usw. und lerne viele deutsche Familien kennen. Mir ist es äußerst interessant, deutsche Kinder zu kennen, da ich eines Tages Lehrerin werden will . . .

DAVID S. GOODMAN, Oberlin College, Austauschstudent in Heidelberg: . . . Meine Erfahrungen außerhalb des Akademischen sind für mich nicht weniger bedeutungsvoll. Ich kehre nach Amerika zurück mit teuren Erinnerungen an die Bekanntschaften, die ich hier gemacht habe, an viele erfreuliche Gespräche und an die Gastfreundlichkeit . . .

OLAF GATERMANN, Hamburg, Exchange Student at Oberlin College: . . . When I came here last summer I was really surprised: The U. S. is indeed the big "Melting Pot" I have heard of in school. It is a big – sometimes controversial – but always friendly and hospitable country . . .

BETTINA MICHAELIS, Bremerhaven, Exchange Student at Douglass College, New Brunswick, N. J.: . . . The exceptional friendliness of the Americans helped me through the first hectic days of registration. I made a lot of friends already during the first days. Up to that time in my life I never realized that one could meet people so easily and talk to them without any formalities . . .

CHRISTEL PERNACK, Wiesbaden, Exchange Student at Florida Southern College: . . . surprised when I arrived on campus. It reminded me much more of a huge park than of a college campus . . . the atmosphere is a very familiar one. This college appears to me like a big family. As the classes are rather small – in most of the classes I registered for, there are no more than fifteen students – the teacher is able to get more acquainted with the students, and so none of us gets lost in anonymity . . .

WOLFGANG MUNZINGER, Heidelberg, Exchange Student at the Rutgers University: . . . The campus system as a unit independent from the town, is very different from the more integrated version in Germany. At first, it felt very strange to be surrounded by only students . . .

PETER KOEPPEL, Karlsruhe, Exchange Student at Union College, Schenectady, N. Y.: . . . Most of the courses of the institute (Institute of Industrial Administration and Management) emphasize the practical side of theories. I have to admit that after three years of merely theoretical studies at the University of Karlsruhe I appreciate this . . .

SOLVEIGH KAEHLER, Hamburg, Exchange Student at the University of Arizona, Tucson: . . . University life is not only restricted to weekdays, but you will find many students there on Sundays too, going to the university cinema or theatre or studying in the libraries that are open all day long until 12 p. m. . . .

BRIGITTE SANDER, München, Exchange Student at Oberlin College: . . . I have noticed that the Americans are very hospitable and I experienced this quality during Christmas and New Year . . .

GÜNTER GÖTZ, München, Exchange Student at the University of Arizona, Tucson: . . . On my first trips around this country I was deeply impressed by its wideness and variety, by the fascinating, speedy life in Los Angeles or New York, by the endlessness of the desert in Arizona or New Mexico, by the greenness of Missouri. It is not just a country, it is a continent . . .

HANS-GEORG ENGELKEN, Hamburg, Exchange Student at the University of Delaware: . . . Having learned to understand and tolerate different patterns of thinking and different cultural values is, in my eyes, the most valuable experience of my stay . . .

*Gegenüber: Horst Schumann, Teilnehmer des Programms „Kaufleute und Techniker in die USA" der Carl-Duisberg-Gesellschaft (CDG), in seinem Reisebericht: „Ich kam als ,Kraut' nach Amerika. Aber ,sauer' bin ich nicht geworden." Um diesem etwas launigen Werbespruch gerecht zu werden, hat er sich in die entsprechende „Schale geworfen", die sämtliche Klischees vom „Keep-Smiling" bis zu den weißen Socken enthält, sozusagen als deutsches Gegengewicht für die wegen Sauerkrautgenusses (?) in Amerika manchmal als „Krauts" bezeichneten Deutschen. Diesen stereotypen Vorstellungen widerspricht er in seinem Bericht jedoch heftig: „Für mich bedeutete der CDG-Aufenthalt den Abschied von all den Klischeevorstellungen, die ich von Amerika hatte. Und ich bin sicher: Viele meiner amerikanischen Freunde und Bekannten haben sich nach den langen Gesprächen und Diskussionen ebenfalls von ihren Klischeevorstellungen über Deutschland getrennt.
Ich bin froh, daß ich die USA nicht aus der Touristen-Perspektive kennengelernt habe, sondern als Student und ganz normaler Mitarbeiter an einem ganz normalen Arbeitsplatz."*

Facing page: Horst Schumann, participant of a "Meet the People" program arranged by Carl-Duisberg-Gesellschaft (CDG), in an advertisement reporting his experiences states: "I came to America as a 'Kraut', but that didn't make me 'sour'." In accordance with this somewhat jocular slogan, he displays all of the clichés about America, from sweat shirt to tennis shoes as a kind of visual counterpoint to the American stereotyping of Germans as "Krauts" because of their alleged diet of sauerkraut. On the other hand, his report leaves no room for stereotypes: "The most important thing the CDG study program did was to destroy all the clichés I used to have about America. I am sure that the long discussions with my American friends did the same for their preconceptions about Germany. I'm glad I got to know the USA as a student and an ordinary worker in an ordinary job, rather than just as a tourist."

von amerikanischer Kultur und Mentalität. Gleiche Erfahrungen und Möglichkeiten bieten sich den deutschen Jugendlichen, die in den USA mit einer amerikanischen Familie leben dürfen. Ein AFS-Schüler unterscheidet sich von einem Touristen insofern, als er sich aktiv an den Problemen seiner Gastfamilie beteiligen, Eigeninitiative entwickeln und die Fülle der ihm gebotenen Möglichkeiten nützen sollte.

Auf dem Gebiet des Studenten- und Dozentenaustausches, bei dem neben dem Kennenlernen des fremden Landes die wissenschaftliche Fortbildung in den Mittelpunkt tritt, betätigt sich in den USA zum Beispiel die „Fulbright-Commission". Dieses nach seinem Initiator, Senator J. W. Fulbright aus Arkansas, benannte Programm existiert seit dem Jahr 1946; 1952 wurde im Rahmen des deutsch-amerikanischen Kulturabkommens auch die Bundesrepublik einbezogen. Seit 1953 werden jährlich etwa 200 Studenten, 50 Professoren und 20 Lehrer für ein Jahr als Stipendiaten aus den USA an eine deutsche Universität oder Schule vermittelt. Etwa die gleiche Anzahl deutscher Professoren, Lehrer und Studenten erhalten Reise- oder Vollstipendien für einen einjährigen Studien-, Lehr- oder Forschungsaufenthalt in den Vereinigten Staaten. Auf deutscher Seite liegt die Förderung der internationalen Hochschulbeziehungen vor allem in der Hand des aus staatlichen Geldern finanzierten „DAAD" („Deutscher Akademischer Austauschdienst"). Der DAAD unterhält in vielen Ländern Auslandsbüros und erhält Stipendien von den wichtigsten amerikanischen Universitäten zwischen Berkeley und Harvard.

Die bereits 1923 gegründete „Carl-Duisberg-Gesellschaft" wird teils aus öffentlichen Mitteln, teils von der deutschen Industrie gefördert. Dementsprechend unterstützt sie hauptsächlich die Weiterbildung auf wirtschaftlichen, technischen und landwirtschaftstechnischen Gebieten. Bis 1974 hat sie über 36 500 Studenten aus aller Welt zu Auslandsaufenthalten verholfen.

Die hier ausführlicher dargestellten Initiativen stehen als Beispiel für viele andere Programme: So bieten zum Beispiel die „Konrad-Adenauer-Stiftung", der „Verband der deutsch-amerikanischen Klubs", der „Lions Club" und die Rotarier ebenfalls Austauschprogramme für Studenten an. Die „Alexander von Humboldt-Stiftung", schon 1860 gegründet, ermöglicht seit 1953 qualifizierten jungen Akademikern aus den USA Forschungsaufenthalte an den Universitäten der Bundesrepublik. Anderer Art sind die Aktivitäten von Gesellschaften wie der „Atlantik-Brücke" und ihrer amerikanischen Schwester, dem „American Council on Germany": Sie organisieren Konferenzen und Seminare, beispielsweise für deutsche Politiker und Journalisten in den USA oder für amerikanische Offiziere in Deutschland.

Nicht nur Akademiker und Studenten haben heute die Möglichkeit, unmittelbare, persönliche Eindrücke an die Stelle von Klischees und Vorurteilen zu setzen. Durch die insgesamt 48 Städtepartnerschaften, die teilweise schon zur Zeit der Auswanderung, größtenteils aber nach dem Zweiten Weltkrieg eingerichtet wurden, erhält auch der „Normalbürger" Gelegenheit, genauer über die USA informiert zu werden. Neben Ausstellungen und der Entsendung von Delegationen wird auch auf dieser Ebene – oftmals unter großen finanziellen Opfern der beteiligten Gemeinden – ein regelmäßiger Schüleraustausch durchgeführt.

exchange, which provides academic and professional study programs beside the opportunity of getting acquainted with the country, the "Fulbright Commission" is particularly active in the U. S. A. This program, named after its founder, Senator J. W. Fulbright of Arkansas, has been in existence since 1946: in 1952 the Federal Republic of Germany was included in the program after the signing of the German-American Culture Agreement. Ever since 1953, approximately 200 university students, 50 professors and 20 instructors from the U. S. A. annually have received grants and been assigned for one year to a German university or academy. About the same number of German professors, instructors and students are granted travel or full scholarships for a one-year stay in the U. S. – to be used for study, teaching or research. The German end of promoting international relations between universities is handled by the "DAAD" ("Deutscher Akademischer Austauschdienst"), which is financed by the State. The DAAD maintains offices in many foreign countries, and distributes scholarships from all the most important universities, from Berkeley to Harvard.

The "Carl-Duisberg-Gesellschaft", founded as early as 1923, is supported partly by the State and partly by German Industry. For this reason, it principally supports graduate work in the field of economics, technology and agriculture. By 1974, it had arranged for more than 36,500 from all over the world to receive scholarship for study abroad.

The institutions described in more detail above led the way for many other projects. Thus the Konrad Adenauer Foundation, the Federation of German-American Clubs, the "Lions' Club" and the Rotarians also offer exchange programs for students. The Alexander von Humboldt-Stiftung, founded in 1860, has enabled qualified young scientists from the U. S. A. to do research work at the universities of the Federal Republic of Germany. Of another type are the activities of societies such as the Atlantik-Brücke and its U. S. A. counterpart, the American Council on Germany. They organize conferences and seminars, as for instance for German politicians and journalists in the U. S. A. or for U. S. Army officers in Germany.

Not only scholars and students nowadays have the opportunity to replace clichés and prejudices with personal and immediate impressions. By means of the 48 "sister cities" which were organized in some cases as early as in the days of the first emigrants, but mostly after World War II, the "ordinary citizen" is given the chance to find out more about the U. S. A. Besides exhibitions and the despatching of delegates, these "partner cities" – often at considerable expense to the communities in question – have also been carrying out a regular exchange of students.

Seit 1953 gewährt die Alexander von Humboldt-Stiftung amerikanischen Wissenschaftlern Forschungsstipendien in der Bundesrepublik.

Since 1953, the Alexander von Humboldt Foundation has provided opportunities for American scholars to do study and research at German universities.

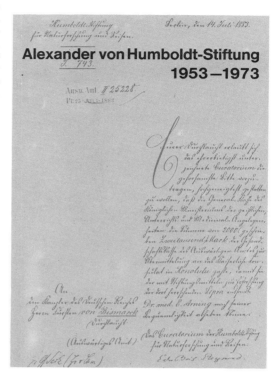

Unterzeichnung des deutsch-amerikanischen Fulbright-Abkommens durch John McCloy, den Hohen Kommissar in Deutschland, und Bundeskanzler Konrad Adenauer, 1952.

The signing of the German-American Fulbright Treaty by High Commissioner John J. McCloy and Chancellor Konrad Adenauer in 1952.

1975 – Die Bundesrepublik ehrt John McCloy durch die Errichtung einer nach ihm benannten Stiftung. Von rechts: Präsident Gerald Ford, John McCloy, U.S.-Außenminister Kissinger, Bundespräsident Scheel und der deutsche Außenminister Hans Dietrich Genscher.

In the name of the Federal Republic of Germany, President Scheel honors the former High Commissioner for Germany by establishing the John McCloy Fund in 1975. From the left to right: a military observer, German Federal Foreign Minister Hans Dietrich Genscher, President Scheel, Secretary of State Dr. Henry Kissinger, (Partly hidden) German parliament member Dr. Friedrich von Weizsäcker, Mr. McCloy and President Ford.

Die Verwaltungszentrale von Rotary International (Evanston, Ill.) und des Lions Club (Oak Brook, Ill.). Beide Vereinigungen sind auch in Deutschland durch örtliche Gruppen aktiv vertreten.

Headquarters of the service organizations, Rotary International (in Evanston, Ill.) and Lions Club, (Oak Brook, Ill.), both of which have active chapters throughout Germany.

Bürger von Rochester im Staat New York haben sich eingefunden, um deutsche Studenten aus Würzburg in ihrer Stadt willkommen zu heißen.

Welcoming committee greets students from Würzburg in Rochester, New York.

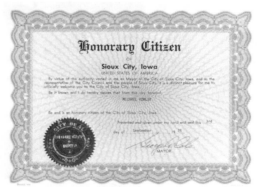

Ehrenbürger-Urkunde, die einem deutschen Besucher in Sioux City, im Staat Iowa verliehen wurde. Der Empfänger, Michael Köhler, ist Mitautor dieses Buches.

Certificate of Honorary Citizenship issued to a German visitor to Sioux City, Iowa. The recipient, Michael Köhler, is a co-author of this volume.

Ein Beitrag zur besseren Verständigung zwischen amerikanischen Soldaten und deutscher Bevölkerung: Captain Drew H. Brown mit dem ersten „Mitbürgerpaß" der Stadt Stuttgart.

Captain Drew H. Brown holding the first Honorary Citizen Pass to be issued by the City of Stuttgart.

No. 2/1974 - May   P 20007 F

„Gazette", die offizielle Zeitschrift des Verbandes der Deutsch-Amerikanischen Klubs e. V., die Austausch und Begegnung zwischen Deutschen und Amerikanern fördern.

"Gazette", the magazine of the Federation of German-American Clubs, which encourage exchange and encounter between German and Americans.

Eine Seite aus dem Gästetagebuch der Münchener Columbus-Gesellschaft.

A page from the visitor's book of the "Columbus-Gesellschaft", showing some of the society's social activities: Carnival ball, mountain hikes, ski outing, beer party, May dance in Castle Amerang.

Faschingsball am 8. 2. 1971 mit einigen bemerkenswerten "Columbuspaaren"

Bilder von unseren Bergwanderungen: Im Rotwandgebiet am 14. 3. 1971.

Skiausflug in die Wildschonau am 17. 1. 1971   und auf den Nockherberg am 18. 3. 1971

Maitanz auf Schloß Amerang am 8. 5. 1971

Die National Carl Schurz Association in Philadelphia will den kulturellen Austausch mit Deutschland fördern und zugleich in den USA das Verständnis für den Anteil der Amerikaner deutscher Abstammung an der geistigen und wirtschaftlichen Entwicklung Amerikas wecken und festigen. Ihre zweisprachige Zeitung „Rundschau" erscheint von September bis Mai monatlich in einer Auflage von über 100000 Exemplaren.

Die „Rundschau" berichtet – aus amerikanischer Sicht – über die verschiedenartigsten Aktivitäten im deutschsprachigen Raum.

The National Carl Schurz Association in Philadelphia promotes cultural exchange with Germany, and at the same time endeavors to awaken and strengthen America's awareness of the contribution made by citizens of German origin to the intellectual and economic development of the United States. The Association's bilingual periodical, "Rundschau", appears monthly from September to May, and has a circulation of over 100,000.

It is the purpose of "Rundschau" to provide for the student of the German language in the United States a report of activities in German-speaking areas as seen from an American point of view.

Botschafter ihrer Kultur: Goethe-Institute . . .

Neben den Institutionen, die dem Studenten- und Schüleraustausch auf breiter Ebene dienen, ist in der Bundesrepublik das Goethe-Institut von besonderer Bedeutung für die Pflege des kulturellen Kontakts mit anderen Ländern. Als größte nicht-staatliche Organisation auf diesem Gebiet ist es seit mehr als 20 Jahren auch am Kulturaustausch mit den USA maßgeblich beteiligt.

In Deutschland bestand das Goethe-Institut bereits seit dem Jahre 1932. 1952 wurde es, mit Zentralverwaltung in München, wiederbegründet und eröffnete 2 Jahre später seine ersten Zweigstellen im Ausland, die anfangs vor allem dem Sprachunterricht und der Erhaltung und Verbreitung deutschen Sprachguts im weitesten Sinne dienten. Schon die ersten Deutschkurse, mit denen 1953 in Bad Reichenhall (Bayern) die Tätigkeit nach dem Krieg wiederaufgenommen wurde, sahen Besucher aus den USA. Obwohl es seit Aufnahme der Spracharbeit kaum nennenswerte Werbung für diese Kurse gibt, ist die Zahl der amerikanischen Teilnehmer erstaunlich hoch: Bis Ende 1974 besuchten mehr als 26000 Amerikaner Deutschkurse an den 20 Goethe-Instituten, die inzwischen in der Bundesrepublik bestehen. Mit über 13% bilden sie die stärkste nationale Gruppe unter den Deutschlernenden. So ist es ein gerechter Zufall, daß im Juli 1975 eine Amerikanerin als 200000. Teilnehmerin der Deutschkurse im Inland gefeiert werden konnte: Die 25jährige Joy Heebinks aus St. Paul, Minnesota, die für ihr Glück der runden Zahl vom deutschen Bundespräsidenten Walter Scheel persönlich beglückwünscht wurde. Sie hatte sich im Goethe-Institut Schwäbisch-Hall eingeschrieben und beabsichtigt, in Heidelberg Theologie zu studieren.

Wie Joy sind die meisten Kursteilnehmer aus den Vereinigten Staaten Stipendiaten, die sich auf ihr Studium an einer deutschen Universität vorbereiten. Ihren Interessen und Erwartungen versucht das Goethe-Institut durch ein differenziertes Kursangebot – wie etwa spezielle Deutschkurse für Naturwissenschaftler – und ein breit gefächertes kulturelles Rahmenprogramm zu entsprechen. Die nostalgische Vorliebe vieler Amerikaner für mittelalterliche Städte läßt sich mit dem Wunsch nach einem möglichst rationellen Studiengang

Cultural Ambassadors: The Goethe Institute . . .

In addition to the organizations in the Federal Republic devoted primarily to student exchange programs, there is the Goethe Institute, whose special importance lies in the field of promoting cultural ties with other countries. As the largest publicly-sponsored, politically independent organization of its kind, it has played an instrumental part in cultural exchange with the United States for more than twenty years.

The Goethe Institute was already in existence in Germany since 1932. It was founded a second time in 1952, with its main office in Munich, and the first foreign branches were founded two years later. In the beginning, efforts were focused mainly on giving language lessons and on preserving and furthering the understanding of German. There were Americans in attendance at the very first postwar sessions of German courses, held in 1953 at Bad Reichenhall in Bavaria. Even though these language courses have never been widely advertised, the number of American participants is amazingly high: by the end of 1974, more than 26,000 Americans had studied German at the twenty Goethe Institutes now operating in the Federal Republic. Americans comprise more than 13 % of the total number of foreign students, making them the largest national group. So it wasn't at all surprising that the honor of being the 200,000th participant in these courses in the Federal Republic should fall to an American: Joy Heebinks, twenty-five years old, of St. Paul, Minnesota, who was personally congratulated by President Scheel. She had enrolled in the Goethe Institute at Schwäbisch-Hall, and planned to study theology at the University of Heidelberg.

Like Joy, most of the American course participants have scholarships or grants, and are planning to study at German universities. To satisfy their interests and expectations, the Goethe Institutes provide various courses, such as the specialized language of the natural sciences, and a diversified program of cultural activities. The fact that many Americans are attracted by the romantic atmosphere of the old German towns of the Middle Ages does not have to detract from their studies: Goethe Institutes are purposely established in

Amerikanischer Student beim Deutschunterricht im Sprachlabor eines Goethe-Instituts.

An American student learning German in the Goethe Institute's language lab.

Bundespräsident Walter Scheel beglückwünscht Joy Heebinks, die 200000. Sprachstudentin des Goethe-Instituts in der Bundesrepublik.

President Walter Scheel receives American student Joy Heebinks, the 200,000th foreign student to enter the Goethe Institute, in 1975.

Studenten aus aller Welt vor Schloß Comburg bei Schwäbisch-Hall.

Students from all countries pose in front of Castle Comburg near Schwäbisch-Hall.

Bei den Sprachkursen des Goethe-Instituts läßt sich das Angenehme mit dem Nützlichen verbinden: Wanderung in den Bayerischen Alpen.

A group of international scholars enjoys a stroll in the Bavarian Alps.

Nach einer Veranstaltung im New Yorker Goethe Haus 1973: Der Präsident des amerikanischen PEN-Clubs, Jerzy Kosinski (links) im Gespräch mit seinem schwedischen Kollegen Per Wästberg und Günter Grass rechts).

After a presentation at the New York Goethe House in 1973. The president of the American PEN-Club, Jerzy Kosinski (left) chatting with his Swedish colleague Per Wästberg and German novelist Günter Grass (right).

Aktion des deutschen Künstlers Otto Piene am Goethe-Institut in Boston.

"Action Sculpture" demonstrated by the artist Otto Piene at the Boston Goethe Institute.

vereinbaren: Bewußt wurden Goethe-Institute an einigen besonders reizvollen Orten eingerichtet, so in Schwäbisch-Hall oder Rothenburg ob der Tauber. Die Deutschkurse für amerikanische Studenten, die dort laufen, werden auf Grund einer Vereinbarung von der University of Connecticut anerkannt; bei erfolgreicher Teilnahme erhält der Student seine „credits".

Auch auf dem Sektor der Weiterbildung von Deutschlehrern und Germanisten sind die USA führend in der Statistik des Goethe-Instituts. Nicht nur zahlenmäßig sind die amerikanischen Germanisten hier die wichtigsten Partner. Auf ihre speziellen Erfordernisse zugeschnitten, wurde den dreiwöchigen Sommerkursen des Goethe-Instituts, die von Germanisten aus aller Welt besucht werden, ein ebenfalls dreiwöchiges Sonderprogramm für amerikanische Teilnehmer vorgeschaltet. 1320 Deutschlehrer und Germanisten aus den USA haben bisher an dem insgesamt siebenwöchigen Fortbildungsprogramm teilgenommen. Inhaltlich liegt das Hauptgewicht auf Deutschlandkunde, die Exkursionen innerhalb der Bundesrepublik, einen Berlinbesuch, Schulhospitationen, Werks- und Behördenbesuche sowie Gespräche mit Deutschen aller Altersgruppen und sozialen Schichten einschließt.

Die Fortbildung in der Bundesrepublik Deutschland ist nur ein Teil der kontinuierlichen Betreuung amerikanischer Deutschlehrer. Angesichts der Bedeutung dieses Berufes ist der ständige Kontakt und Erfahrungsaustausch mit ihnen auch eine der wesentlichen Aufgaben der Zweigstellen des Goethe-Instituts in New York, Boston und San Francisco. Bei Fachtagungen, Fortbildungsseminaren und Workshops, wie sie die drei amerikanischen Filialen seit Jahren veranstalten, erweist sich die enge und vertrauensvolle Zusammenarbeit mit dem amerikanischen Deutschlehrerverband (AATG) als besonders nützlich.

Das Goethe-Institut ist seit 1961 mit dem Aufbau und der Verwaltung der deutschen Kulturinstitute im Ausland betraut und unterhält heute 114 Zweigstellen außerhalb Deutschlands. Dabei ist die Spracharbeit eine zwar wesentliche, aber keineswegs die einzige Aufgabe der Institute. Die weiteren Funktionen – Informationstätigkeit und Vermittlung kultureller Programme – sind für die drei bislang in den USA tätigen Zweigstellen schon wegen der Größe des zu versorgenden Gebietes der schwierigere Teil der Arbeit. Eine Entlastung ist von der noch für 1975 vorgesehenen Eröffnung neuer Goethe-Institute in Atlanta und Chicago zu erwarten.

Seit der Einweihung der ersten amerikanischen Zweigstelle in Boston wurden zahlreiche wichtige Künstler aus der Bundesrepublik in den USA vorgestellt. Besonders erfolgreich war die Faßbinder-Filmwoche, die 1974 in Zusammenarbeit mit dem Filmverlag der Autoren durchgeführt wurde. Prominente Schriftsteller – wie Günter Grass, der 1973 in New York las – gehören ebenso zu den regelmäßigen Gästen des Goethe-Instituts, wie Musiker: 1976 und 1977 werden das Hamburger Ensemble Das Neue Werk und eine Tournee von Hans Werner Henzes *El Cimarrón* dem amerikanischen Publikum einen Eindruck von der Vielfalt der zeitgenössischen Musik geben. Auch die Entwürfe deutscher Bildungsplaner und die neuesten Ergebnisse linguistischer Untersuchungen an deutschen Universitäten finden durch die Tätigkeit des Goethe-Instituts ihren Weg in die Vereinigten Staaten.

such delightful surroundings as Schwäbisch-Hall and Rothenburg ob der Tauber. An agreement with the University of Connecticut enables the American students studying in these towns to receive college credits for successfully completed courses.

According to the Goethe Institute, the United States also leads statistically in enrollment in the Institute's program of advanced education for teachers of the German language and for specialists in Germanistics (the study of Germanic literature, culture, and philology). To meet specifically American requirements, the Goethe Institute now offers a special three-week session exclusively for Americans prior to its regular three-week summer session, whose attendance is international. So far, 1320 American German teachers and Germanists have taken part in this advanced program, which lasts a total of seven weeks, and features learning about Germany itself (customs, institutions, geography), excursions within the Federal Republic, a trip to Berlin, visits to schools, factories, governmental institutions, and provides the opportunity of engaging in conversation with Germans of all ages and social levels.

Advanced study in the Federal Republic is only part of what the Institute offers the American German teacher. In view of the significance of the teaching profession, one of the main tasks of the Goethe Institute branches in New York, Boston, and San Francisco is to enable teachers to stay in contact in order to exchange information and experiences. The way in which these Institutes have presented conferences, advanced seminars, and workshops over the years, owes a great deal to the close and friendly cooperation of the American Association of Teachers of German.

Since 1961, the Goethe Institute has been in charge of the establishment and administration of German Cultural Institutes in foreign countries, of which there are 114 today. The German language is an important, but by no means the only reason for their existence. The additional functions of distributing information and arranging cultural activities have so far constituted a greater challenge to the three branches operating in the United States, purely because of the size of the geographical areas to be covered. It is hoped that this burden will be more evenly divided once the new Goethe Institutes in Atlanta and Chicago have been opened (scheduled for 1975).

Since the dedication of the first American-based Goethe Institute in Boston, America has been introduced to many renowned artists of the Federal Republic. In 1974, a week devoted to the films of the young author-director-producer Rainer Werner Fassbinder, was particularly successful. Prominent writers such as Guenter Grass, who gave readings in New York in 1973, are frequent guests at the Institute. So are musicians: in 1976 and 1977, the Hamburg ensemble "Das Neue Werk", and a touring company of Hans Werner Henze's *El Cimarrón* will present to American audiences various aspects of contemporary music. The newest ideas of German educational planners and the latest publications on linguistic research are distributed in the United States by the Goethe Institute.

... und Amerika Häuser

Besser als jede Aufreihung von Zahlen und Fakten charakterisiert die populäre Wendung vom „geistigen CARE-Paket" die Verdienste der amerikanischen Kulturinstitute im Nachkriegsdeutschland. Boten sie doch zunächst vielfach die einzige Möglichkeit, den intellektuellen Nachholbedarf aus der Zeit des „Dritten Reichs" zu decken. Als früheste Einrichtung dieser Art wurde schon am 16. Januar 1948 in München die „American Library" eröffnet. Dort konnte man sich erstmals mit den Werken emigrierter deutscher Autoren bekanntmachen oder sich die Informationen beschaffen, die während der Nazizeit unzugänglich gewesen waren; und all das in geheizten Räumen, was damals einen zusätzlichen Anreiz bedeutete. Später stieg die Zahl der seit 1953 durch den „United States Information Service" betreuten „American Information Centers" auf über fünfzig. Dieser Umfang verringerte sich dann freilich im Lauf der Jahre wieder, als in den kleineren Städten die öffentlichen Bibliotheken und Volkshochschulen ihre Arbeit aufnahmen und die wesentlichsten Funktionen der Informationszentren übernehmen konnten. So gibt es heute Amerika-Häuser in sieben westdeutschen Großstädten (Berlin, Hamburg, Hannover, Köln, Frankfurt, Stuttgart und München) und daneben ebenfalls sieben „Deutsch-Amerikanische Institute" in Universitätsstädten wie Saarbrücken, Freiburg oder Kiel.

Mit der Zahl hat sich auch die Aufgabe dieser Häuser gewandelt: von der „re-education" zur sachlichen Informierung über die laufenden Ereignisse in den Vereinigten Staaten. Längst gibt es den moralisierenden (und propagandistischen) Zeigefinger „What is Democracy?" nicht mehr. Er wurde abgelöst vom deutsch-amerikanischen Dialog, der auch unbequeme Themen des beiderseitigen Verhältnissen nicht ausspart.

Zwar mußten inzwischen so ambitionierte Projekte wie eigene Orchester oder Theaterensembles – die es während der 50er Jahre wahrhaftig gegeben hatte – aus dem Budget gestrichen werden. Doch nach wie vor bieten die amerikanischen Kulturinstitute allmonatlich ein erstaunlich reiches Angebot an Ausstellungen, Konzerten, Theater- und Filmabenden, sowie Vorträge und Podiumsdiskussionen, zu denen nicht selten Prominenz aus allen Bereichen des kulturellen und politischen Lebens gewonnen werden kann. Als VIPs besonderer Art seien aus der umfangreichen Gästeliste der letzten Jahre nur die Raumfahrer genannt: John Glenn und die Mannschaften von

... and America Houses

Better than any enumeration of figures and facts, the colloquial expression "CARE packages for the mind" characterizes the role played by American cultural institutions in postwar Germany. After all, in some places and at least for some time, they provided the sole opportunity to "catch up" intellectually after the spiritual vacuum of the Third Reich. The earliest establishment of this kind was the "American Library", which opened in Munich in January 1948. Here, for the first time, one could find the recent works of German emigré authors, or get facts and information which had not been available during the period of National Socialism. And all this in well-heated rooms, which at that time was a considerable attraction in itself. Later on, the number of United States Information Centers sponsored by the United States Information Service since 1953, rose to more than fifty. Of course their number was reduced again later on, when the public libraries and adult education centers in the smaller towns took over some of the most important functions of these information centers.

Today there are America Houses in seven major West German cities (Berlin, Hamburg, Hannover, Cologne, Frankfort, Stuttgart, and Munich) as well as seven "German-American Institutes" in University towns such as Saarbrucken, Freiburg or Kiel.

Along with their number, the purpose of these houses has undergone a change: from "re-education" to objective information on current events in the U. S. The moralizing "What is Democracy" with its overtones of sometimes heavy-handed propaganda has given way to German-American discussions which make no attempt to avoid even somewhat touchy subjects pertaining to the mutual relationship. It is true that some ambitious projects such as orchestras and stock companies – which actually did exist during the Fifties – had to be cut from the budget. Nevertheless, the American cultural institutions offer a surprisingly varied monthly fare of exhibits, concerts, theatre and motion pictures, as well as lectures and round table discussions which frequently feature prominent personages from the world of culture as well as politics. Among the many VIP guests of recent years were John Glenn and the crews of Apollo 11 and 15. But the most vital part of all the information centers remains the library. Today, besides the traditional circulating library department (7,000 volumes) it includes a comprehensive collection of reference works, some

„ Ei, ei, wer hätte das gedacht!" – eine Karikatur von 1955.

"Good Heavens, who would have expected that?" – cartoon from 1955.

Eine Ausstellung von preisgekrönten Werbegraphiken, die der New Yorker „Art Director's Club" für das Amerika Haus in München organisiert hatte.

An exhibition of graphic arts and advertising put on by the Art Director's Club of New York at Munich Amerika Haus.

Eine Theater- und Filmausstellung im Münchner Amerika Haus.

A theatre and motion picture exhibition at Munich's Amerika Haus.

Die Bibliotheken der Amerika Häuser besitzen ein reiches Angebot an Büchern zum Studium und zur Unterhaltung in Englisch, wie auch auf Deutsch.

The America House libraries provide volumes for study and entertainment in both English and German.

Das Amerika Haus in München – eines von sieben solchen Häusern in der Bundesrepublik.

The Munich America House – one of seven such U. S. cultural centers in the Federal Republic.

Apollo 11 und 15. Herzstück der Informationszentren ist jedoch die Bibliothek geblieben. Sie umfaßt heute neben der traditionellen Ausleih-Abteilung eine umfangreiche Sammlung von zum Teil höchst spezialisierten Nachschlagewerken und in jüngster Zeit auch audiovisuelle Informationsmittel wie Video- und Mikrofilmgeräte. Das Schwergewicht liegt aber neuerdings auf den rund 500 Zeitschriften, die es dem regelmäßigen Leser erlauben, mit den neuesten Erkenntnissen auf nahezu jedem Berufs- oder Interessengebiet Schritt zu halten.

of them highly specialized, and more recently audiovisual teaching aids using video and microfilm.

However, the emphasis has lately been on the periodicals, about 500 in number, which enable the regular visitor to keep abreast of the latest discoveries and information in every field of professional and human interest.

Wissenschaft und Forschung

Wenn nach den Schlagworten gefragt wird, die die kulturelle Leistung Deutschlands am prägnantesten umreißen sollen, so ist entweder vom „Land der Musik" die Rede oder von dem der „Dichter und Denker". In der Tat hatte Deutschland zur Zeit Beethovens, Goethes oder Kants in den Naturwissenschaften nicht allzu viel zu bestellen: Zwar begann der deutsch-amerikanische Wissenschaftsaustausch 1766 mit einem Besuch Benjamin Franklins bei der „Königlichen Gesellschaft der Wissenschaften" zu Göttingen; seine ersten Höhepunkte erreichte er jedoch in den philologischen und philosophischen Fächern. Hier wären etwa die Amerikaner zu nennen, die Anfang des 19. Jahrhunderts in Deutschland studierten: Der Historiker George Bancroft und der Philosoph Ralph Waldo Emerson sind die bekanntesten. Etwas außerhalb der streng wissenschaftlichen Gefilde ist der Einfluß des deutschen Idealismus auf die amerikanische Literatur bemerkenswert. *Moby Dick*, Herman Melvilles Parabel vom Weißen Wal, ist das großartigste Beispiel für diese transatlantische Ausstrahlung Immanuel Kants.

Georg Wilhelm Friedrich Hegel (1770–1831), der einflußreichste deutsche Denker nach Kant und vor Marx, fand seinen amerikanischen Sachwalter in der schillernden Figur Henry Brokmeyers (1828–1906). Er stammte aus Preußen, wanderte mit 16 Jahren, völlig mittellos und ohne ein Wort Englisch zu können, nach Amerika aus und brachte sich dort zunächst als Gerber durch. Später folgten Studium, Verweis vom College, Einsiedelei in der Wildnis, ein Versuch als Farmer und endlich, im Januar 1866, Gründung und erste Präsidentschaft der Philosophischen Gesellschaft von St. Louis. Aus ihr ging der Kreis der „St. Louis Hegelians" hervor, die in dem Hegel-

Science and Humanities

When asked for the cliché which best describes German cultural achievements, one usually hears something like "land of music" or "poets and philosophers". It is true that at the time of Beethoven, Goethe, and Kant, Germany did not have all that much to offer in the natural sciences: the first German-American exchanges in scientific fields took place in 1766, when Benjamin Franklin visited the Royal College of Sciences at Göttingen, but the greatest activity was in philology and philosophy. At this point, some Americans studying in Germany at the beginning of the 19th century should be mentioned, the most famous of whom were the historian George Bancroft and the philosopher Ralph Waldo Emerson. Outside of the purely scientific sphere there was the strong influence of German Idealism upon American literature. *Moby Dick*, Herman Melville's parable of the white whale, is the best example of the transatlantic 'crossing' of Immanuel Kant.

Georg Wilhelm Friedrich Hegel (1770–1831), the most influential German thinker after Kant and before Marx, found his American spokesman in the unconventional figure of Henry Brokmeyer (1828–1906). He was a native of Prussia, who emigrated to America at the age of sixteen with no money and without knowing a word of English. First he worked as a tanner, then he studied and was expelled from college. This was followed by the attempt at a farmer's life in the wilderness, and finally, in January of 1866, by the founding of the Philosophical Society of St. Louis, of which he was the first president. This group then gave birth to the St. Louis Hegelians. It cannot be said of the Hegel-enthusiast Brokmeyer that he was a systematic thinker; on the contrary, he was apparently capable of being magnificently

Hermann von Helmholtz war einer der vielseitigsten und bedeutendsten Naturwissenschaftler des 19. Jahrhunderts. Er formulierte bereits den Begriff des Elementarteilchens. (Gemälde von Ludwig Knaus, 1881).

Hermann von Helmholtz, one of the most important scientists of the 19th Century, made significant contributions to a vast area of learning from philosophy to physiology. (Painting by Ludwig Knaus, 1881).

Max Planck, der Begründer der Quantentheorie.

Max Planck, whose quantum theory laid the groundwork for the whole field of nuclear physics.

Der deutschstämmige amerikanische Physiker Albert Abraham Michelson, Nobelpreisträger 1907. Seine Messungen der Lichtgeschwindigkeit schufen die Voraussetzungen für Einsteins spezielle Relativitätstheorie.

Albert Abraham Michelson, a German-born Californian who won the Nobel Prize in Physics in 1907. His measuring of the speed of light made possible Einstein's Theory of Relativity.

Hahns Notiz über die Kernspaltung auf einer Gedenkmünze.

Hahn's note on the results of the experiment.

Der Arbeitstisch, an dem Otto Hahn und F. Straßmann die erste Kernspaltung gelang.

The work table on which Otto Hahn and F. Straßmann first split the atom.

Enthusiasten Brokmeyer zwar keinen besonders systematischen Denker, aber ein höchst anregendes Orakel hatten. Keine der englischen Übersetzungen, die er von seinem Lieblingsphilosophen anfertigte, ist je veröffentlicht worden – angeblich sollen sie amerikanischen Lesern ebenso schwer verständlich sein, wie es wohl Hegels deutsches Original wäre. Dennoch war Brokmeyer – auch als Herausgeber der *Zeitschrift für spekulative Philosophie* – ein großer Anreger und wichtiger kultureller Mittler zwischen Deutschland und Amerika.

Von der spekulativen Philosophie zur exakten Wissenschaft: Gegen Ende des 19. Jahrhunderts brachte die Wissensexplosion in den Naturwissenschaften auch in Deutschland eine Reihe von bedeutenden Forschern hervor, z. B. den Physiologen Emil du Bois-Reymond, den Chemiker Emil Fischer (Nobelpreis 1902) oder den Physiker Max Planck (Nobelpreis 1918). Zusammen mit ihren Schülern begründeten sie den Weltruhm der deutschen Forschung zu Anfang unseres Jahrhunderts. Deutsche Universitäten wurden damals zum Mekka der jungen Wissenschaftler, die aus aller Herren Länder nach Heidelberg, München oder Berlin strömten, um dort bei einem der 'Großen' zu studieren. Eine besonders hohe Zahl von Gaststudenten kam aus den Vereinigten Staaten von Amerika.

Während die deutsche Grundlagenforschung in den USA einen guten Ruf genoß, war Europa von den Leistungen der angewandten Technik in der Neuen Welt beeindruckt. So kam es nach den Weltausstellungen in Chicago (1893) und St. Louis (1904) zur Vereinbarung eines Professorenaustausches zwischen dem preußischen Unterrichtsministerium und den Universitäten Harvard und Columbia. Dort lehrte fortan ein „Kaiser-Wilhelm-Professor", während in Berlin ein „Roosevelt-Professor" Gastvorlesungen hielt.

ambiguous. None of the English translations he made of the works of his favorite philosopher have ever been published. It seems likely that they would have been just as incomprehensible to American readers as Hegel in German would have been. But Brokmeyer was still a stimulating and important cultural contract between Germany and America, also as publisher of the *Magazine of Speculative Philosophy*.

And now back to pure sciences: during the great breakthrough in knowledge of the natural sciences towards the end of the 19th century, a number of prominent researchers emerged in Germany: the physiologist Emil du Bois-Reymond, the chemist Emil Fischer (Nobel Prize 1902), and the physicist Max Planck (Nobel Prize 1918), among others. Along with their students, they were responsible for the worldwide reputation which German research enjoyed at the beginning of the 20th century. German universities were then the 'mecca' for young scientists from all over the world, who came to Heidelberg, Munich, or Berlin to study with one of the 'Greats'. A large number of these foreign students came from the United States of America.

America was impressed by German experimental research and Europe was in turn impressed by American achievements in the field of applied science. This mutual admiration bore fruit after the World's Fairs in Chicago (1893) and St. Louis (1904): the Prussian Ministry of Education and the universities of Harvard and Columbia made an agreement to exchange lecturers. After that, there was a "Kaiser-Wilhelm professor" in America, and a "Roosevelt professor" in Berlin.

World War I put a stop to this exchange, but Germany's leading role in the field of basic research was not yet endangered: great personalities like Arnold Sommerfeld and Albert Einstein continued to work in the universities of the

Der Erste Weltkrieg unterbrach diesen offiziellen Austausch, gefährdete Deutschlands Führungsrolle in der Grundlagenforschung jedoch noch nicht: Große Forscherpersönlichkeiten wie Arnold Sommerfeld und Albert Einstein wirkten weiter an den Universitäten der Weimarer Republik; jüngere, kongeniale Kräfte wie die Atomphysiker Max Born (Nobelpreis 1954), Werner Heisenberg (1932), James Franck (1925) und Otto Hahn (Nobelpreis für Chemie, 1944) traten ihnen zur Seite. Schon drei Jahre nach Kriegsende wurde Sommerfeld wieder an die Universität von Wisconsin eingeladen, von wo ihm später ein Großteil seiner Studenten nach München folgte, um dort die begonnenen Studien fortzusetzen. Auch Werner Heisenberg und Max Born lasen in den Vereinigten Staaten und brachten bei ihrer Rückkehr amerikanische Studenten mit.

Mit der nationalsozialistischen Machtergreifung 1933 fand die wissenschaftliche Hochblüte in Deutschland ein abruptes Ende. In den Jahren bis zum Kriegsbeginn flohen viele Wissenschaftler von Rang – ein Großteil in die USA (eine Liste, die keinen Anspruch auf Vollständigkeit erhebt, findet sich auf Seite 53 dieses Buches). Freie Forschung war unter Hitler nicht mehr möglich: Selbst etwas so Abstraktes, wie Einsteins Relativitätstheorie, wurde im „Dritten Reich" als „jüdische Physik" und ergo „undeutsch" diffamiert. Beispielhaft verdeutlicht die Emigration Einsteins, des ‚Papstes der Physik', die Talfahrt der deutschen Wissenschaft während des Hitler-Regimes.

Wie die meisten anderen prominenten Forscher konnte Einstein seine Arbeit in den USA sofort wieder aufnehmen: von 1933 bis zu seinem Tod im Jahr 1955 war er Mitglied des „Institute for Advanced Study" in Princeton. Er war es auch, der auf Drängen seiner besorgten Kollegen Präsident Franklin D. Roosevelt jenen berühmten

Weimar Republic, supported by congenial younger colleagues, such as the atomic physicist Max Born (Nobel Prize 1954), Werner Heisenberg (1932), James Franck (1925), and Otto Hahn (Nobel Prize for Chemistry, 1944). Only three years after the war, Sommerfeld received another invitation to lecture at the University of Wisconsin. A large number of his students later followed him to Munich to continue their studies. Werner Heisenberg and Max Born also lectured in the United States, and were also followed back across the Atlantic by American students.

Genuine scientific research in Germany came to an abrupt halt when the National Socialists came to power in 1933. In the few remaining years before the outbreak of World War II, most of the prominent scientists fled the country – a large number to the United States. (A list, which does not pretend to be complete, can be found on page 53 of this book.) When war finally did come, an emigration of brilliant minds took place throughout Europe. Any research which was not specifically war-oriented was impossible under Hitler: even something as abstract as Einstein's theory of relativity was condemned by the Third Reich as being "Jewish physics", and ergo, "non-Aryan". With the emigration of Einstein, the 'Pope of Physics', the international consequences of what Hitler had done to science became obvious: Europe's leading role in science was assumed by the United States. If Europe had not been deprived of her intellectuals, this would not have happened so soon, nor would it have been so final.

Like most other prominent researchers, Einstein was able to resume work immediately in the United States: from 1933 until his death in 1955, he was a member of the Institute for Advanced Study in Princeton. At the urging of his uneasy colleagues, he wrote the famous letter to President

Der Nobelpreisträger im Kinderzimmer: Neben den Kritzeleien der Jüngsten löst Einstein ein mathematisches Problem. Der Schweizer Hans Erni malte diese Anekdote 1957, zwei Jahre nach Einsteins Tod.

Dr. Albert Einstein, painted in 1957 by the Swiss artist Hans Erni. The Nobel Prize winner in a playroom: Next to the children's scrawl he solved a math problem.

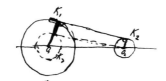

Einsteins Antwort für ein amerikanisches Schulmädchen, das ihn um Hilfe bei den Hausaufgaben gebeten hatte.

Einstein's reply to an American schoolgirl who wrote to him asking for help on her homework.

Albert Einstein bei der Verleihung der Ehrendoktorwürde der Harvard Universität am 20. Juni 1935. Neben ihm James Bryant Conant, später Präsident von Harvard und von 1953 bis 1955 Hoher Kommissar der USA in Deutschland.

Albert Einstein received an honorary doctorate from Harvard University in June of 1935. The picture shows Einstein with Professor James B. Conant who subsequently served as President of Harvard and High Commissioner of Germany.

Brief schrieb, in dem er vor der Möglichkeit einer deutschen Atomrüstung warnte und der zur Entwicklung der amerikanischen Atombombe führte. Seine Weltanschauung faßte er, ebenso sympathisch wie naiv, in den Satz: „Raffiniert ist der Herrgott, aber boshaft ist er nicht."

Der Exodus der Wissenschaften betraf nicht nur die Physik: Das Institut für Sozialforschung der Universität Frankfurt emigrierte mit seinen wichtigsten Protagonisten, Max Horkheimer und Theodor W. Adorno, an die Columbia University in New York. Ebenfalls in New York wurde, mit Hilfe der Rockefeller Stiftung, eine Exiluniversität gegründet: die „New School for Social Research". An ihr sammelten sich Flüchtlinge aller Fakultäten, Theaterleute wie Erwin Piscator ebenso wie die Berliner Gestaltpsychologen Max Wertheimer, Wolfgang Köhler und Kurt Koffka. Ihre experimentelle Psychologie, die besonders auf dem Gebiet der Kreativitätsforschung Pionierarbeit leistete, gewann in den Vereinigten Staaten größeren Einfluß, als ihr in ihrem Ursprungsland bis heute beschieden ist.

Vollzog sich der materielle Wiederaufbau Deutschlands nach dem Zweiten Weltkrieg überraschend schnell, so trat das Ausmaß der geistigen Verödung, die der Nationalsozialismus hinterlassen hatte, erst nach und nach zu Tage. Neben der Vertreibung der Wissenschaftler wirkten sich auch die Dezimierung der Generation, die den Krieg hatte führen müssen, und die Zerstörung der Universitäten verzögernd auf die Wiederaufnahme der Forschung aus. Auch hier sprangen die Vereinigten Staaten helfend ein: In Berlin unterstützte die Ford Foundation die 1948 in studentischer Selbsthilfe gegründete „Freie Universität" (die im Ostsektor der Stadt gelegene „Alexander von Humboldt Universität" war den Bewohnern der Westsektoren während und nach der Blockade von 1949 nicht mehr zugänglich). Wichtiger noch wurden die Forschungsstipendien, mit denen nun deutsche Wissenschaftler in den USA versuchten, Anschluß an die Entwicklungen innerhalb ihrer Fächer zu finden.

Franklin D. Roosevelt, in which he warned of the possibility of German atomic mobilization, and which then led to the development of the American atomic bomb. He summed up his philosophy of life, as appealing as it was naive, in a few words: "God is clever, but He is not cruel."

The scientific exodus was not restricted to physics: The Institute for Social Research of the University of Frankfort moved, along with its most important protagonists, Max Horkheimer and Theodor W. Adorno, to Columbia University in New York. With the help of the Rockefeller Foundation, a university in exile was also founded in New York: the New School for Social Research. Refugees of all academic disciplines gathered here – theater people such as Erwin Piscator, the Berlin Gestalt psychologists Max Wertheimer, Wolfgang Köhler, and Kurt Koffka. Their experimental psychology – especially their pioneer research into the creative process – won them a larger following in the United States than they'd had in their homeland, and this is still so today.

Germany's physical recovery after World War II was astonishingly fast. But the healing of the mind and spirit, which had been deadened by National Socialism, took considerably longer. In addition to the vacuum left by the scientists who had fled, an entire generation – the one which fought the war – had been virtually wiped out; the universities had been destroyed – these factors all hampered the resumption of research. The United States did not stand idly by: The Free University of Berlin, founded by students in 1948, received aid from the Ford Foundation; Alexander von Humboldt University, which is in East Berlin, had been inaccessible to West Berlin students during and after the Blockade. Still more important were the research grants which enabled German scientists to study in the United States and catch up on the latest developments in their fields.

Dieser Urahn der modernen Teilchenbeschleuniger wurde 1930 von E.O. Lawrence und N.E. Edlefsen an der Universität Berkeley gebaut.

The ancestor of the modern cyclotron was built in 1930 by E.O. Lawrence and N.E. Edlefsen at the University of California in Berkeley.

DESY, das Deutsche Elektronensynchrotron in Hamburg.

DESY, the German electron synchrotron in Hamburg, is based on Lawrence and Edlefsen's principles.

Die Verhaltensforschung, die von Deutschland ausging, liefert heute selbst Kybernetikern und Nachrichtentechnikern wichtige Anregungen. Hier werden Bienen, die sich an einer Zuckerlösung gütlich tun, hinterrücks für Experimente markiert.

Behavioral research was initially a German idea. In this experiment bees are fed sugar water which distracts their attention so that they can be marked with colored dots for further study.

Auch die Vereinigten Staaten selbst, deren historische Entwicklung zunehmend zum Testfall für Europa wird, sind in der Bundesrepublik endlich als Objekt akademischer Forschung institutionalisiert. War die amerikanische Literatur früher der „Blinddarm" der Anglistik, so wurden nach dem Krieg an immer mehr Universitäten eigene Institute für Amerikastudien eingerichtet. Deren Größe und finanzielle Ausstattung entspricht zwar meistens noch nicht der Bedeutung des Gegenstandes – doch sind die Geisteswissenschaften ja in der glücklichen Lage, mit ihren Resultaten nicht proportional von der investierten Summe abzuhängen.

Gerade das finanzielle Problem trug zusätzlich zur Verlagerung des Schwergewichts der naturwissenschaftlichen Forschung in die USA bei. Die Hochenergiephysik, die in den 50er Jahren aktuell zu werden begann, läßt sich nicht mehr an Arbeitstischen wie dem Otto Hahns betreiben. Sie erfordert Großforschungsanlagen, deren materiellen Aufwand fast nur noch Staaten von der Größe der USA tragen können. In Europa hat man sich mit der Gemeinschaftgründung des „Conseil Européen pour la Recherche Nucléare" (CERN) beholfen; die Bundesrepublik Deutschland nahm ein Elektronensynchrotron erst in Angriff, als amerikanische Erfahrungen vorlagen und es überdies gelungen war, einen abgewanderten Spezialisten nach Deutschland zurückzuholen. Dem internationalen Wissenschaftlerteam, das am „Desy", dem Deutschen Elektronen-Synchrotron in Hamburg arbeitet, gelang 1975 innerhalb eines Monats die Entdeckung zweier bis dahin unbekannter Elementarteilchen – jeweils wenige Wochen danach konnten amerikanische Forscher den Fund bestätigen.

Auch in der Organisation der universitären Forschung beginnt man, orientiert an amerikanischen Beispielen, ehrwürdigen deutschen Traditionen den Zopf abzuschneiden: Bisher etwa pflegte – und pflegt es zum Teil auch noch – es zur Würde eines deutschen Hochschulprofessors zu gehören, daß er Institutsleiter und dadurch mit ablenkendsten Verwaltungsarbeiten belastet war; in den USA können sich die Professoren auf ihre Forschungsarbeiten konzentrieren. Nur unter der Bedingung, daß dieses amerikanische ‚Department-System' übernommen werde, kehrte Rudolf Mößbauer 1961 vom California Institute of Technology an die Technische Universität in München zurück. Das Prestige seines Nobelpreises (für Physik, 1961) half, die Forderung durchzusetzen – ein Ereignis, das unter deutschen Forschern als „zweiter Mößbauer-Effekt" sprichwörtlich geworden ist.

The United States itself, whose historical development is regarded more and more as a test-case for Europe, has finally become an object of institutionalized academic research. American literature used to be considered a useless appendage of Anglistics, but after the war, more and more universities established their own institutes for American Studies. Their size and financial resources are seldom commensurate with the importance of the subject – but the field of Humanities is in a fortunate position, in that findings are not inextricably linked to the amount of money invested.

Finance was also a reason for shifting the bulk of research activity to the United States. Experiments in high energy physics, which accelerated in the 1950's, can no longer be carried out at a work table like that of Otto Hahn. They require enormous research centers, which only a country the size of the United States can afford. Europeans helped each other with the mutual founding of the "Conseil Européen pour la Recherche Nucléaire" (CERN), but the Federal Republic did not attempt the construction of an electron-synchrotron before having access to American findings, and winning back an emigrated German specialist in this field. In 1975, the international team working on "Desy", the German electron-synchrotron, discovered two previously unknown particles within a month's time, and the findings were verified by American researchers shortly afterwards.

American methods are also challenging time-honored German traditions in the organization of university research: until recently, the 'image' of a German university professor demanded that he also be the chief administrator of his institute. In the United States, a professor can concentrate strictly on his research work. When Rudolf Mössbauer left the California Institute of Technology in 1961 to return to the Technical University in Munich, he did so only on the condition that the American department-system be introduced. His Nobel Prize was a help in pushing this demand through – an event which German researchers have christened the "second Mössbauer-effect".

Mainau Statement

We who sign this appeal are scientists from many countries,
of several races, of different creeds, of different political
convictions. Our association is that we have all been privileged
to be awarded Nobel Prizes.

We have given freely a life-time to the service of science.
Science, we think, is a way to a fuller life for mankind. But
we are alarmed at realising that this same science is providing
man with the instruments for self-destruction.

In a full scale war the earth can be so infested with radio-
activity as to destroy whole nations. This destruction can
strike down neutrals as well as combatants.

If the major powers engage in war who can guaranty that it
will not develop into such a deadly struggle? Thus a nation
that engages in an all-out war invites its own destruction
and endangers the whole world.

We do not deny that today the peace of the world may be
maintained by the fear of these deadly weapons. Yet we feel
that it would be self-deception if governments should believe
that over a long period the fear of these weapons will prevent
war from occurring. Fear and tension have too frequently
produced war. Likewise, it would be self-deception to
believe that minor conflicts could always be settled by
the use of traditional weapons. In extreme need, no warring
nation will deny itself the use of any weapon that scientific
techniques can supply.

All nations must bring themselves to the decision by which

./.

*The Mainau Statement of July 15, 1955, a protest against
the atomic bomb, was initiated by Otto Hahn.*

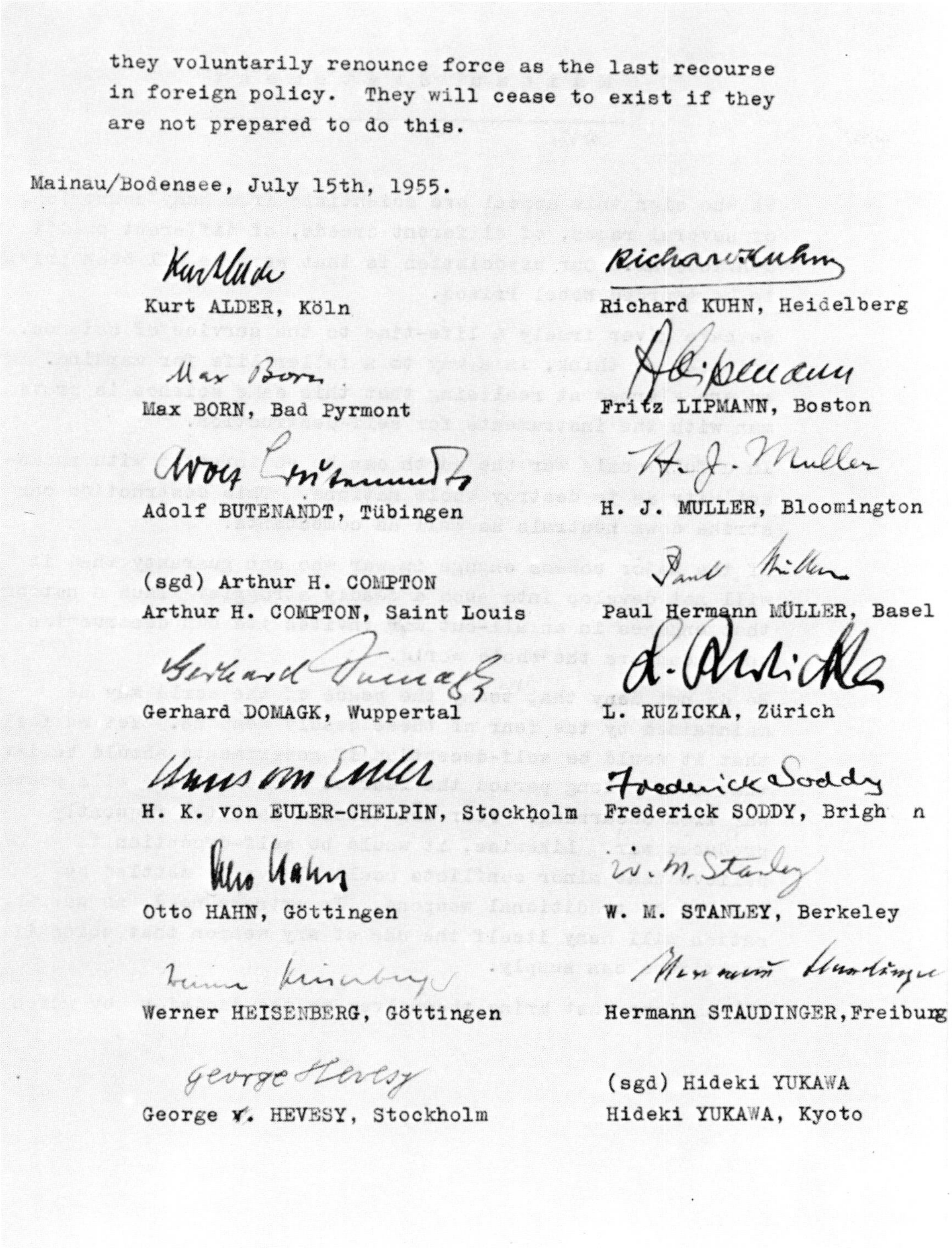

they voluntarily renounce force as the last recourse in foreign policy. They will cease to exist if they are not prepared to do this.

Mainau/Bodensee, July 15th, 1955.

Kurt ALDER, Köln	Richard KUHN, Heidelberg
Max BORN, Bad Pyrmont	Fritz LIPMANN, Boston
Adolf BUTENANDT, Tübingen	H. J. MULLER, Bloomington
(sgd) Arthur H. COMPTON Arthur H. COMPTON, Saint Louis	Paul Hermann MÜLLER, Basel
Gerhard DOMAGK, Wuppertal	L. RUZICKA, Zürich
H. K. von EULER-CHELPIN, Stockholm	Frederick SODDY, Brigh n
Otto HAHN, Göttingen	W. M. STANLEY, Berkeley
Werner HEISENBERG, Göttingen	Hermann STAUDINGER, Freiburg
George v. HEVESY, Stockholm	(sgd) Hideki YUKAWA Hideki YUKAWA, Kyoto

Die „Mainauer Kundgebung" vom 15. Juli 1955. Otto Hahns Initiative führte zu diesem Protest gegen die Atombombe, die Nobelpreisträger aus den USA, der Bundesrepublik, Schweden, der Schweiz und Japan unterzeichneten. Der deutsche Text lautete:

Wir, die Unterzeichneten, sind Naturforscher aus verschiedenen Ländern, verschiedener Rasse, verschiedenen Glaubens, verschiedener politischer Überzeugung. Äußerlich verbindet uns nur der Nobelpreis, den wir haben entgegennehmen dürfen.
Mit Freuden haben wir unser Leben in den Dienst der Wissenschaft gestellt. Sie ist, so glauben wir, ein Weg zu einem glücklicheren Leben der Menschen. Wir sehen mit Entsetzen, daß eben diese Wissenschaft der Menschheit Mittel in die Hand gibt, sich selbst zu zerstören.
Voller kriegerischer Einsatz der heute möglichen Waffen kann die Erde so sehr radioaktiv verseuchen, daß ganze Völker vernichtet würden. Dieser Tod kann die Neutralen ebenso treffen wie die Kriegführenden.
Wenn ein Krieg zwischen den Großmächten entstünde, wer könnte garantieren, daß er sich nicht zu einem solchen tödlichen Kampf entwickelte? So ruft eine Nation, die sich auf einen totalen Krieg einläßt, ihren eigenen Untergang herbei und gefährdet die ganze Welt.
Wir leugnen nicht, daß vielleicht heute der Friede gerade durch die Furcht vor diesen tödlichen Waffen aufrechterhalten wird. Trotzdem halten wir es für eine Selbsttäuschung, wenn Regierungen glauben sollten, sie könnten auf lange Zeit gerade durch die Angst vor diesen Waffen den Krieg vermeiden. Angst und Spannung haben so oft Krieg erzeugt. Ebenso scheint es uns eine Selbsttäuschung, zu glauben, kleinere Konflikte könnten weiterhin stets durch die traditionellen Waffen entschieden werden. In äußerster Gefahr wird keine Nation sich den Gebrauch irgendeiner Waffe versagen, die die wissenschaftliche Technik erzeugen kann.
Alle Nationen müssen zu der Entscheidung kommen, freiwillig auf die Gewalt als letztes Mittel der Politik zu verzichten. Sind sie dazu nicht bereit, so werden sie aufhören, zu existieren.
Mainau/Bodensee, 15. Juli 1955

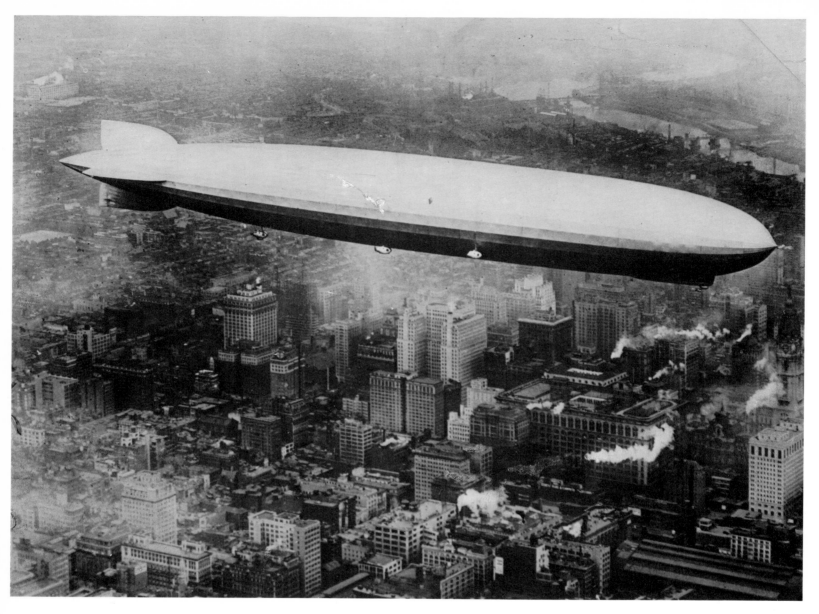

GRAF ZEPPELIN
EUROPE-PAN AMERICA FLIGHT
65¢   65¢
UNITED STATES POSTAGE

Sonderbriefmarke der amerikanischen Post anläßlich des Amerika-Rundflugs des „Graf Zeppelin" 1930.

A special issue of the U.S. Post Office commemorating the dirigible's round-trip flight over America in 1930.

Lilienthals „Vogelflugzeug", mit dem er seit 1891 über 2000 erfolgreiche Flugversuche unternahm; heute im Deutschen Museum in München. Bei der Erprobung eines Eindeckers stürzte Lilienthal 1896 tödlich ab.

Lilienthal with his "Gliderbird", an early experiment in heavier than air flight. The apparatus is currently in the German Museum in Munich. The inventor subsequently died in a crash landing during experimentation on a single decker.

Das Luftschiff „Graf Zeppelin" im Oktober 1928 über Manhattan. Den Kommandanten, Dr. Hugo Eckener, nannte eine amerikanische Zeitung überschwenglich einen ‚zweiten Kolumbus' – denn wie Kolumbus hatte der „Graf Zeppelin" seine Atlantiküberquerung in Palos begonnen.

The airship "Graf Zeppelin" over the Manhattan sky-line in October of 1928. An American newspaper enthusiastically hailed the commander, Dr. Hugo Eckener, as a 'second Columbus', because Eckener too started his journey over the Atlantic from Cape Palos in Spain.

Flugvorführung Orville Wrights in Berlin-Johannisthal, 1909.

Orville Wright in Berlin, 1909.

Von den Rhinower Bergen bis Cape Canaveral

Drei Jahrtausende brauchte die Menschheit vom Traum des Ikarus zu Leonardos erster Skizze eines vogelähnlichen Flugapparates; noch einmal vier Jahrhunderte vergingen, bis Otto Lilienthal 1891 in Rhinow bei Berlin seinen ersten Luftsprung wagte: stolze 25 Meter weit. Wenig mehr als ein halbes Jahrhundert genügte schließlich, um dieses Abenteuer in die Routine der fliegenden Kinosessel unserer Tage zu verwandeln: 12 Kilometer über dem Atlantik schallschnell und beschaulich zwischen New York und Frankfurt unterwegs, während die Stewardess einen Drink serviert und auf der Leinwand womöglich Hollywoods Breitwandtribut an die ‚tollkühnen Männer in ihren fliegenden Kisten' zu sehen ist.

Die Geschichte dieser tollkühnen Männer ist die einer Jagd nach Rekorden – höher, weiter, oder schneller. Konkurrenzdenken kennzeichnet sie jedoch erst in zweiter Linie: Ausschlaggebend war immer das Unerhörte, an dessen Verwirklichung man gemeinsam arbeitete: der Traum vom Fliegen. Die Pioniere, die sich ihm verschrieben hatten, fühlten sich als Glieder einer Kette: Sie wußten, daß hier mehr als in jedem anderen Bereich der Technik Zusammenarbeit, ständiges Geben und Nehmen, Voraussetzung des Erfolges ist.

Der erste freie Motorflug der Gebrüder Wright am 17. Dezember 1903 in Kitty Hawk war auch ein Erfolg des 1896 tödlich abgestürzten Otto von Lilienthal, der als erster den starren Tragflügel benützt hatte. Ohne Orville und Wilbur Wright wiederum wäre der deutsche Motorflug am Boden geblieben: Sie gründeten in Johannisthal, nahe Berlin, die erste Fliegerschule und Flugzeugfabrik Deutschlands.

Nach dem ersten Weltkrieg – Zeit des Roten Barons, von dem Snoopy noch heute naiv träumt – wurde die Überquerung des atlantischen Ozeans, der Brückenschlag zwischen den Kontinenten, zu einem der lohnendsten Ziele der jungen Fliegerei. Die Engländer Alcock und Brown waren 1919 die ersten, denen der Flug in der windbegünstigten West-Ost Richtung gelang; sie erreichten mit knapper Not Irland und überließen dadurch Charles Lindbergh den Ruhm, 1927 erstmals von Kontinent zu Kontinent, von New York nach Paris geflogen zu sein. Der deutsche Dichter Bertolt Brecht hat dieses Ereignis in seiner von Kurt Weill vertonten Kantate *Der Ozeanflug* behandelt. Noch im selben Jahr gelang Chamberlaine und Levine der erste Direktflug von New York nach Berlin; sie wurden in Tempelhof nicht weniger stürmisch gefeiert als Lindbergh auf dem Pariser Flughafen Le Bourget. Im April 1928

From the Rhinow Mountains to Cape Canaveral

Three thousand years went by between Icarus' dream of flying and da Vinci's first sketch of a bird-like flight-contraption; another four centuries passed till Otto von Lilienthal went airborne in Rhinow near Berlin in 1891 – for all of 82 feet. But then it took only a little more than half a century for this adventure to leave the realm of the spectacular and become the flying movie-seats we know today. Supersonic serenity 7 miles over the Atlantic as the stewardess serves you dinner and a drink between New York and Frankfort, while you might even be watching Hollywood's wide-screen homage to *Those Magnificent Men in their Flying Machines.*

The tale of those daring men is one of a record-breaking race: higher, farther, and faster. Yet the idea of competition was subordinate to the primary goal of attaining the unheard-of. And it took teamwork to make the dream of flying come true. The pioneers who devoted themselves to that dream knew they were but links in a great chain: they knew that here, more than in any other technological field, mutual cooperation was the key to success.

The Wright Brothers' first motorized free flight in Kitty Hawk on December 17, 1903, was also a posthumous triumph for Otto von Lilienthal, who was the first to use rigid wing structure and who fatally crashed in 1896. On the other hand, motorized flight in Germany got helped off the ground by Orville and Wilbur Wright, who promoted the founding of the first German flying school and aircraft factory in Johannisthal near Berlin.

After the First World War – the heyday of the Red Baron, about whom Snoopy still wistfully dreams – crossing the Atlantic and creating an air-bridge between the continents became one of the most auspicious prospects of fledgling aviation. The first successful flight from west to east (the direction favored by the wind) was accomplished in 1919 by the Englishmen Alcock and Brown. They barely managed to land in Ireland, thus leaving Charles Lindbergh to take the honors of being the first to make it from continent to continent, from New York to Paris in 1927. This event was celebrated by the German author Bertolt Brecht in his radio-cantata *The Lindbergh Flight*, with music by Kurt Weill. Before 1927 was over, Chamberlaine and Levine had made the first direct flight from New York to Berlin, where their reception at Tempelhof Airport was no less exuberant than Lindbergh's had been at the Paris airport Le Bourget. The first transatlantic flight from east to west was piloted by the Germans von Hünefeld and Köhl and the Irishman Fitzmaurice in April 1928, from Berlin's Tempelhof via Baldonnel, Ire-

Atlantiküberquerer Charles Lindbergh vor seinem Ryan-Eindecker „Spirit of St. Louis".

Charles A. Lindbergh poses in front of the "Spirit of St. Louis".

Köhl, von Hünefeld und Fitzmaurice, die den Atlantik als erste von Ost nach West überquerten.

The first men to fly the Atlantic east to west – Köhl, von Hünefeld, and Fitzmaurice.

überquerten dann die deutschen Piloten von Hünefeld und Köhl zusammen mit dem Iren Fitzmaurice den Atlantik erstmals von Ost nach West, von Berlin Tempelhof über Baldonnel in Irland nach Labrador. New York bereitete ihnen einen begeisterten Empfang, ebenso der Besatzung des Luftschiffes ‚Graf Zeppelin‘, das ebenfalls 1928 über der Skyline Manhattans auftauchte.

Mit der Fahrt des ‚Graf Zeppelin‘ und der Ozeanüberquerung des zwölfmotorigen deutschen Riesenflugbootes Do X, das 1931 bereits 70 Passagiere nach New York beförderte, stehen wir schon an der Schwelle des modernen Linienflugverkehrs, der auf der Nordatlantikstrecke 1937 von dem Luftschiff ‚Hindenburg‘ eröffnet wurde. Die tragische Katastrophe der ‚Hindenburg‘ während der Landung in Lakehurst (New Jersey) am 6. Mai beendete jedoch die Ära des Zeppelins, kaum daß sie begonnen hatte, zivile Früchte zu tragen. Im gleichen Jahr 1937 nahmen auch die amerikanischen Gesellschaften Imperial Airways und Pan American Airways den planmäßigen Flugverkehr zwischen den USA und Europa auf.

Spätestens hier endet die Geschichte der ‚tollkühnen Männer‘; es beginnt die Phase des modernen Massenflugverkehrs, dessen Jumbo Jets mit ‚fliegenden Kisten‘ nichts mehr gemein haben. 1958 wurden erstmals ebensoviele Menschen mit Flugzeugen über den Atlantik befördert wie mit Schiffen: jeweils eine Million. 1972 lautete das Verhältnis bereits 13 Millionen zu 200000. Das Flugzeug hat die Menschen einander näher gebracht – es steht zu hoffen, daß dies nicht nur im geographischen Sinne gilt.

Die Faszination, die die selbstverständlich gewordene Fliegerei eingebüßt hat, geht heute von der Raumfahrt aus. Auch ihre Frühgeschichte ist mit deutschen Namen, vor allem dem Wernher von Brauns, verbunden – gleichzeitig freilich von der Erinnerung an Hitlers unselige ‚Wunderwaffe‘ V 2 überschattet. Dreißig Jahre später steht die Bundesrepublik am Beginn einer intensiven Zusammenarbeit mit den Vereinigten Staaten: Der deutsch-niederländische Konzern VFW-Fokker ist Hauptauftragnehmer der European Space Agency (ESA) beim Bau des bemannten Raumlabors, das erstmals 1980 von der ‚Space-Shuttle‘, dem wiederverwendbaren Raumtransporter der NASA, in eine Umlaufbahn gebracht werden soll. Vielleicht wird es eines Tages Schauplatz eines weiteren historischen Händedrucks im All sein – diesmal unter Beteiligung europäischer Astronauten. Bis dahin bleiben gemeinsame Forschungsprojekte wie die in München gebaute, in Cape Canaveral gestartete Sonnensonde ‚Helios‘ oder der Nachrichtensatellit ‚Symphonie‘ wichtige Zeugen jener internationalen Kooperation, ohne die sich Raumfahrt auf lange Sicht wahrscheinlich nicht mehr betreiben lassen wird.

land, to Labrador. New York gave them an enthusiastic reception, as it also did the crew of the airship "Graf Zeppelin", which appeared over the skyline of Manhattan that year too.

With the transatlantic crossings of the "Graf Zeppelin" and the twelve-engined giant German aircraft "Do X", which carried 70 passengers to New York as early as 1931, we are on the threshold of modern passenger transport. The North Atlantic route was opened in 1937 by the airship "Hindenburg", but the era of the zeppelin as a commercial carrier was cut short by the tragic landing catastrophe of the "Hindenburg" at Lakehurst, N. J., on May 6. That same year Imperial Airways and Pan American Airways, both American companies, introduced regular passenger service between the United States and Europe.

That completed the transition from the days of "those magnificent men" to the age of modern mass air transit, whose Jumbo Jets have little in common with those early "flying machines". In 1958, for the first time, as many passengers (one million) crossed the Atlantic by air as by ship. By 1972, the proportion was already 13 million to 200,000. The airplane has brought people closer to each other; one may hope in more ways than just geographically.

The spectacular fascination which diminished when flying became matter-of-course, has been rekindled by today's space flight. Even the early days of rocketry were associated with German names, particularly with that of Wernher von Braun, although the memory of Hitler's unholy "Wonder Weapon", the V-2, still lingers. Now, thirty years later, the Federal Republic is entering a period of intense cooperation with the United States. The Dutch-German concern VFW-Fokker is the main contractual supplier of the European Space Agency (ESA) in building the manned Space Lab, which will be sent into orbit in 1980 by the Space Shuttle, NASA's reusable space transporter. Perhaps some day it will be the scene of another historical handshake in space – this time including European astronauts. Until then we must be content with cooperative research projects such as the solar probe "Helios" (built in Munich and launched from Cape Canaveral), or the communications satellite "Symphony", as proof of the mutual cooperation necessary for the development of long-term space projects.

Das zwölfmotorige deutsche Riesenflugboot „Do X" 1931 im New Yorker Hafen.

The twelve-engined German seaplane "Do X" moored in New York harbor, 1931.

Ein Zeiss Planetarium, wie es auch im Astronautentraining Verwendung fand. Das „Einstein Spacearium", das am 4. Juli 1976 als Geschenk der Bundesregierung an die USA im neuen Nationalen Luft- und Raumfahrtmuseum in Washington, D. C., eröffnet wird, ist das modernste Gerät dieser Art.

A Zeiss Planetarium, used by the astronauts during training. The most modern construction of this type is the "Einstein Spacearium", a gift of the Federal Republic to the United States – to be opened to the public on July 4, 1976 in the new National Air and Space Museum in Washington, D. C.

Die bescheidenen Anfänge der Raumfahrt in Reinickendorf bei Berlin 1930. Zweiter von rechts: Wernher von Braun.

Beginnings of rocket technology in Reinickendorf near Berlin – the young Wernher von Braun is the second from right.

Thomas O. Paine, Vorsitzender der amerikanischen Weltraumbehörde NASA, vereidigt Dr. Wernher von Braun im März 1970 als seinen Stellvertreter.

Dr. Wernher von Braun is sworn in as Vice Chairman of the National Aeronautics and Space Administration (NASA) by Chairman Dr. Thomas O. Paine in Washington in 1970.

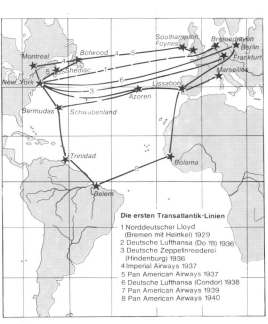

A map of the earliest trans-oceanic flight routes.
1 The Norddeutscher Lloyd ship "Bremen" carried a small plane on board which preceeded her into port carrying the mail (1929).
2 Lufthansa seaplane route via the Azores (1936).
3 German Zeppelin company's transatlantic route for the dirigible "Hindenburg" (1936/37).
4 Imperial Airways (1937).
5 Pan American Airways (1937).
6 Lufthansa (1938).
7 Pan American Airways (1939).
8 Pan American Airways (1940).

Die ersten Transatlantik-Linien

1 Norddeutscher Lloyd
  (Bremen mit Heinkel) 1929
2 Deutsche Lufthansa (Do 18) 1936
3 Deutsche Zeppelinreederei
  (Hindenburg) 1936
4 Imperial Airways 1937
5 Pan American Airways 1937
6 Deutsche Lufthansa (Condor) 1938
7 Pan American Airways 1939
8 Pan American Airways 1940

Begegnung durch Reisen

„Reisen bildet" meint ein deutsches Sprichwort, und ein anderes schwingt sich gar zu der gewagten Behauptung auf, wer eine Reise tue, der könne was erzählen. Selbst hinter solch massiver Banalität steckt ein wahrer Kern. Was für einen Anteil die technischen und finanziellen Reiseerleichterungen des 20. Jahrhunderts am – zugegeben zähen – Abbau nationaler Engstirnigkeit haben, würde uns deutlich bewußt, wenn wir uns in die Postkutschenzeit zurückversetzen lassen könnten: wahrscheinlich hätten wir nur geringe Chancen, je weiter zu blicken, als bis zum nächsten Kirchturm. Allenfalls ein gedruckter Reisebericht könnte uns den Horizont erweitern helfen – aber wo sollen wir in unserem Dorf einen herbekommen?

Zu den ersten Reiseberichterstattern, die den Einwohnern Nordamerikas Kunde aus Deutschland brachten, gehört Thomas Jefferson, der 1788 von Holland rhein- und mainaufwärts nach Frankfurt reiste. Er fühlte sich an seine Heimat erinnert, und nicht zuletzt auch an die Emigranten, die in den pfälzischen Kriegen Ludwigs XIV. nach Amerika ausgewandert waren. „Viel schönes Land", so schrieb er, „habe ich am Rhein gesehen, und schlechtes, sobald ich mich vom Rhein entfernte. Die Gegend hier ist wie ein zweites Heimatland für uns: Aus der Pfalz kamen all die Deutschen, die, nach den Abkömmlingen der Engländer, den größten Teil unseres Volkes ausmachen. Oft kam ich mir vor, wie im Norden von Maryland und Pennsylvanien . . .". Auch das damals bereits zerstörte Schloß zu Heidelberg erregte Jeffersons Bewunderung – wie die zahlloser Generationen amerikanischer Touristen nach ihm: „Dies Schloß ist die edelste Ruine, die ich jemals sah". Vielleicht war es die Zerstörung, die

Mutual Understanding Through Travel

German proverbs such as "Travel broadens the mind" or "He who takes a trip will have many a tale to tell", banal though they may be, contain a basic truth. The 20th century's technological advances have made travel economically possible for the average man. This has been an undeniable factor in the – albeit gradual – breaking-down of nationalistic prejudices; consider how narrow our horizon might have been, had we lived in the days of the stagecoach: chances are we might never have got past the next village. Possibly reading about someone's travels could have helped us widen our horizon, but would such a book have been available in our town?

One of the first to publish accounts of his travels in Germany for North American readers was Thomas Jefferson, who journeyed up the rivers Rhine and Main from Holland to Frankfort in 1788. The landscape reminded him of his homeland, and he wrote, thinking of the emigrants who came to America when Louis XIV invaded the Rhenish Palatinate in 1688 and began the War of the League of Augsburg: "I have seen much good country on the Rhine, and bad whenever I got a little off of it. The neighborhood of this place has been to us a second mother country. It is from the Palatinate on this part of the Rhine that those swarms of Germans have gone who next to the descendants of the English, form the greatest body of our people. I have fancied myself often in the upper parts of Maryland and Pennsylvania." Like generations of countless American tourists after him, Jefferson admired the fortress on the hill at Heidelberg, already a ruin at that time: "This chateau is the most noble ruin I have ever seen." But as for the classicistic palace gardens at Schwetzingen, where every angle reflects the will

Der Naturforscher Alexander von Humboldt schlug schon 1804 bei seinem Besuch in Washington Präsident Jefferson den Bau des Panamakanals vor. Eröffnet wurde der Kanal erst gut hundert Jahre später, 1914.

Alexander von Humboldt suggested the building of the Panama Canal on a visit to President Jefferson in Washington in 1804.

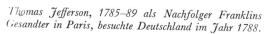

Thomas Jefferson, 1785–89 als Nachfolger Franklins Gesandter in Paris, besuchte Deutschland im Jahr 1788.

Thomas Jefferson visited Germany in 1788.

Karl Bodmer auf den Spuren von Lewis und Clark: Die Mündung des Fox River, gemalt 1833.

Karl Bodmer painted this remarkable landscape of the mouth of the Fox River on an exploration following the trail blazed by Lewis and Clark.

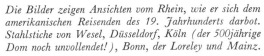

Die Bilder zeigen Ansichten vom Rhein, wie er sich dem amerikanischen Reisenden des 19. Jahrhunderts darbot. Stahlstiche von Wesel, Düsseldorf, Köln (der 500jährige Dom noch unvollendet!), Bonn, der Loreley und Mainz.

Views of a journey down the Rhine as seen by Cooper, Longfellow and a number of other visitors from across the sea. Steel etchings of Wesel, Düsseldorf, Cologne (with the 500 year old cathedral still uncompleted), Bonn, the Loreley and Mainz.

das Schloß für die Augen dieses Demokraten so edel machte. Über die klassizistischen Gärten Schwetzingens, in denen jeder rechte Winkel vom Willen des Herrschers kündet, befand er jedenfalls trocken: „Da sieht man, wieviel Geld für eine häßliche Sache ausgegeben werden kann."

Heidelberg und der Rhein waren auch im 19. Jahrhundert Fixpunkte auf den europäischen Reiserouten amerikanischer Schriftsteller-Touristen. Longfellow beschrieb Bonn 1829 als „das ‚ultima Thule' der rheinischen Schönheiten" – ein doppelsinniges Kompliment für die heutige Bundeshauptstadt. James Fenimore Cooper besuchte Deutschland während seines siebenjährigen Europa-Aufenthaltes zweimal, 1830 und 1831. Seine rund zweitausend Seiten füllenden Reisejournale enthalten manche subtile Beobachtung, etwa die, daß man am meisten Gefühl für Musik bei „unseren amerikanischen Negern und den Deutschen" finde. Mark Twain teilt diese Ansicht in *A Tramp Abroad*, der Beschreibung seiner 1878 bequemlichkeitshalber per Eisenbahn unternommenen Fußwanderung durch Deutschland und die Schweiz, offenbar nicht, wenn er Richard Wagner mit „Zahnweh in der Magengegend" vergleicht. Trotz seiner sarkastischen Ironie, die nichts und niemanden ungeschoren läßt, dokumentiert Twains Reisebericht jene Europasehnsucht, die etwa zur selben Zeit amerikanische Touristenschwärme in die Heimat ihrer Vorfahren zu treiben beginnt. Mit dem Massentourismus unserer Tage hat dies freilich noch nichts gemein: Nur die Arrivierten des „Gilded Age", des vergoldeten Wirtschaftswunders nach dem Bürgerkrieg, konnten sich damals das Statussymbol „Europareise" leisten.

Bret Harte, Henry Adams, Teddy Roosevelt gehören ebenfalls zu den Deutschlandbesuchern aus den Vereinigten Staaten, die ihre Eindrücke und Erfahrungen in Buchform brachten. Thomas Wolfe besuchte Deutschland, die Heimat seines Vaters, dreimal. Auf dem Münchener Oktoberfest trug er aus einer Schlägerei ein gebrochenes Nasenbein davon – auch das sind unvergeßliche Reiseeindrücke! Denkwürdiger ist der Niederschlag, den Wolfes Erlebnisse bei den Berliner Olympischen Spielen von 1936 in *Es führt kein Weg zurück* gefunden haben: Hunderte von winzigen Details, wie sie nur dem unbefangenen Blick des Besuchers auffallen konnten, vermitteln ein klareres Bild vom Deutschland Adolf Hitlers, des „kleinen dunklen Mannes mit dem Operettenschnurrbart", als es die Deutschen wohl selbst hatten.

Auch unter den deutschen Besuchern Nordamerikas finden sich berühmte Namen, wie der des Naturforschers Alexander von Humboldt (1769 bis 1859). Auf der Rückkehr von seinen Expeditionen durch Süd- und Mittelamerika machte er 1804 auch in Philadelphia und Washington Station, wo er in Präsident Jefferson eine Persönlichkeit von ähnlich universaler Bildung kennen und schätzen lernte. Bei ihren Gesprächen soll erstmals der Gedanke aufgetaucht sein, Atlantik und Pazifik mit einem Kanal durch die Landenge von Panama zu verbinden.

of the ruler, he caustically noted: ". . . they show how much money may be laid out to make an ugly thing."

In the 19th century as well, Heidelberg and the Rhine remained obligatory stopping-points on the European itineraries of American writer-tourists. Longfellow described Bonn in 1829 as "the 'ultimate Thule' of (the Rhine's) beauties" – an equivocal compliment for the town that is today the capital of the Federal Republic. James Fenimore Cooper visited Germany twice during his seven-year sojourn in Europe, in 1830 and again in 1831. The two thousand pages of his travel journals contain many a subtle observation, for instance, that one finds the most feeling for music among "our American Negroes and the Germans". Mark Twain doesn't exactly share this opinion when he compares Richard Wagner with a "toothache in the pit of (the) stomach" in *A Tramp Abroad*, a description of his tramping comfortably by train through Germany and Switzerland in 1878. Despite his sarcastic irony, which stops at no one and nothing, Twain's travel report documents the nostalgia for Europe which at that time already began to drive hordes of American tourists to the homelands of their forefathers. Of course that was nothing compared to today's mass tourism; in those days, only the arrivé of the "gilded age" of economic recovery following the Civil War could afford the status symbol of that "trip to Europe".

Among the visitors to Germany from the United States who wrote books about their impressions and experiences are Bret Harte, Henry Adams, and Teddy Roosevelt. Thomas Wolfe went to Germany, the birthplace of his father, three times. He once had his nose broken during a brawl at the Munich *Oktoberfest*, indeed an "unforgettable impression"! But even more memorable for us is Wolfe's description of the Olympic Games in Berlin in 1936, in *You Can't Go Home Again*. Only the impartial eye of a visitor could be struck by the hundreds of tiny details which give a clearer picture of the Germany of Adolf Hitler, "a little dark man with a comic-opera moustache", than the Germans had themselves.

Among the German visitors to North America, there are illustrious names as well, as that of the naturalist Alexander von Humboldt (1769–1859). On the way back from his expeditions through South and Central America, in 1804 he made stops in Philadelphia and Washington, where he met President Jefferson, a personality of similar universal learning, whom he held in high esteem. It is said that during their conversations, the thought of connecting the Atlantic and the Pacific by means of a canal through the Isthmus of Panama came up for the first time.

In welcher Kneipe er ein Bier trinkt: Das teilt Thomas Wolfe seinem deutschen Verleger Heinrich Maria Ledig-Rowohlt auf diesem Notizzettel mit.

A memorandum from Thomas Wolfe to his German publisher, Heinrich Maria Ledig-Rowohlt. The note was written in the 1930s.

Zeitgenössische Karikatur von Mark Twain als „Tramp Abroad".

A contemporary caricature of Mark Twain at work on his "A Tramp Abroad".

Ein anderer deutscher Forscher, Maximilian Prinz zu Wied, machte sich 1833 in St. Louis auf, den Spuren von Lewis und Clark zu folgen. In Begleitung des schweizerischen Malers Karl Bodmer reiste er missouriaufwärts bis an den Fuß der Rocky Mountains. Die Skizzen, Zeichnungen und Aquarelle, die Bodmer auf dieser Reise von Indianern der verschiedenen Sioux-Stämme anfertigte, sind heute kulturgeschichtliche Dokumente ersten Ranges. Den Indianern galt es übrigens als glückbringende Medizin, von dem weißen Mann mit Pinsel und Papier gemalt zu werden: sie glaubten sich dadurch unverwundbar!

Attraktionen dieses Kalibers können auch die „Erlebnisreisen" nicht mehr bieten, mit denen geschäftstüchtige Touristikmanager heute in Marktlücken stochern. Das nötige Kleingeld vorausgesetzt, hat nun jeder Gelegenheit, fremde Länder mit fertig abgepackten Sehenswürdigkeiten im Jet-Tempo zu besichtigen. Wahrscheinlich waren die Reisenden der Postkutschenzeit gerade deshalb so viel bessere Beobachter, weil sie so viel langsamer vom Fleck kamen.

Another German, the explorer Maximilian Prinz zu Wied, set off in St. Louis in 1833 to follow in the tracks of Lewis and Clark. Accompanied by the Swiss artist Karl Bodmer, he traveled up the Missouri to the foothills of the Rocky Mountains. The sketches, drawings, and watercolors, which Bodmer made of various types of Sioux Indians on the journey, are today cultural and historical documents of the highest value. And the Indians themselves were delighted to have their portraits made by the white man with the brushes and paper: they believed it made them invulnerable.

Attractions of this caliber are rarely encountered in the "adventure trips" which tourist agencies offer today. Yet now, anybody with a bit of spare cash has the possibility of whizzing in jet-tempo through foreign countries with prepackaged points of interest. Still, it might be that travelers in the days of the stagecoach were better observers just because they went so much slower.

Internationaler Touristenblick: Früher wurden viele potentielle Sehenswürdigkeiten unbedachterweise über der Augenhöhe angebracht – heute ist Genickstarre deshalb das Berufsrisiko eines jeden Touristen.

With all the baroque splendor above their heads, let us hope the ladies included plenty of liniment in their luggage.

Vor dem Aufbruch studieren amerikanische Rucksack-Reisende den Stadtplan vor der Frankfurter Jugendherberge.

American back-packers study the map in front of the youth hostel in Frankfurt.

quãdo inter se dicutur. Nã in octauo
z tricesimo anno teporibz ptolomei
euergetis regis postqz prueni i egiptu:
et cum multu teporis ibi fuisse inueni
ibi libros relictos nõ parue neqz conte
mnede doctrine. Itaqz bonu et necessa
riu putaui et ipse aliqua addere dili
gentia z labore interptandi libru istu:
z multa vigilia attuli doctrinã i spa
tio teporis ad illa q ad fine ducunt li
brum istu dare: et illis q volut animu
intendere et discere queadmodu opor
teat instituere mores qui secudum le
gem domini pposuerint vitam agere.

Explicit plog9 Incipit liber ecclesiastic9.

Mnis sapientia a do
mino deo e: z cu illo
fuit semper: z est an
te euum: Arenam
maris z pluuie gut
tas z dies seculi: qs di
numerauit: altitudine celi z latitu
dine terre z pfudu abissi: qs dimesus
est sapientiam dei precedentem omnia:
qs inuestigauit prior omniu creata
est sapietia: et intellctus prudentie ab
euo. Fons sapientie verbu dei inexcel
sis: et ingressus illius mãdata eterna.
Radix sapientie cui reuelata e: et astu
tias illi9 qs agnouit? Disciplina sa
pientie cui reuelata est z manifestata:
et multiplicationem ingressus illius
quis intellexit? Vnus est altissimus
creator omniu oiipotes z rex potes.
et metuendus nimis: sedens sup thro
num illius: z dominas deus: Ipse cre
auit illã in spiritu sancto: z vidit z di
numerauit et mesus e. Et effudit illã
sup omnia opera sua: et sup omnem
carne secudum datu suu: z pbet illam
diligentibz se. Timor domini gloria
z glatio: z leticia z corona exultatiois.

Timor domini delectabit cor: et dabit
leticiã z gaudiu in longitudine dies.
Timenti deu bene erit in extremis: z in
die defunctionis sue benedicet. Dilecto
dei honorabilis sapietia: quibz aute
apparuerit i visu: diligut eã: i visione
z i agnitone magnaliu suo. Initiu
sapientie timor domini: z cu fidelibz
in vulua concreatus est: z cum electis
feminis graditr z cum iustis z fidelibz
agnoscitur: Timor domini scientie
religiositas. Religiositas custodiet et
iustificabit cor: iocunditate atqz gaudi
um dabit: Timenti deu bene erit inex
tremis et in diebz cosolationis illius
benedicet. Plenitudo sapientie timere
deum: et plenitudo a fructibus illius.
Omne domu illi9 implebit a generati
onibus: et receptacula a thesauris illi
us. Corona sapientie timor domini:
replens pacem et salutis fructum: z vi
dit et dinumerauit eam. Vtraque
aute suut dona dei: Scientiã et intel
lectu prudentie: sapientia cõparcietur:
et gloriã tenentiu se exaltat: Radix sa
pietie e timere deu: rami eni illi9 longe
ui. In thesauris sapientie intellect9 et
scietie religiositas: execratio aute pecca
toribz sapientia. Timor domini expel
lit peccatu: Nam qui sine timore est
non poterit iustificari: iracundia enim
animositatis illius subuersio eius e
Vsqz in tempus sustinebit patiens: z
postea reddicio iocunditatis. Bon9 sen
sus. usqz i temp9 abscondet verba illi9:
et labia multoru enarrabut sensu illi9.
In thesauris sapientie significatio di
scipline: execratio aute peccatori cultu
ra dei: Fili cocupiscens sapientiã cõser
ua iusticiã: z deus pbebit illã tibi. Sa
pietia eni et disciplina timor domini:
z qp beneplacitu e illi fides z mãsuetudo:

Von der „Schwarzen Kunst" und der Freiheit der Presse

1452: Nach zwanzigjährigen Vorarbeiten beginnt Johannes Gensfleisch, der sich Gutenberg nennt, in der alten deutschen Bischofstadt Mainz mit dem Druck der Bibel. Das erste mit beweglichen Lettern – Gutenbergs Erfindung – hergestellte Buch soll auch das schönste werden: Drei Jahre lang arbeiten an die 20 Setzer und Drucker an einer Auflage von nur 200 Exemplaren. Dann ist das Ziel erreicht, der Erfinder jedoch ruiniert: Obwohl die gedruckte Bibel mit 40 Gulden – dem vierfachen Jahresverdienst eines Schreibers! – fast so viel kostet wie die üblichen handgeschriebenen, kann Gutenberg die – umgerechnet – halbe Million Mark, die er zur Finanzierung seines Prestige-Projektes geliehen hatte, nicht zurückzahlen: Er verliert seine Druckerei, mit ihr das Monopol auf seine Erfindung, und verbringt den Rest seines Lebens als Almosenempfänger am Hof des Landesfürsten. Für spätere Generationen verkörpern er und Christoph Kolumbus, die Erfindung des Buchdrucks und die Entdeckung Amerikas, das Ende des Mittelalters und den Beginn der Neuzeit.

500 Jahre später ist die 42zeilige, lateinische Bibel von 1456 das teuerste Buch der Welt: Bereits 1930 erwarb die Kongreßbibliothek in Washington ein Exemplar für über eine Million Mark – heute dürfte der Wert ein Vielfaches betragen. Von den 48 Bibeln, die ganz oder teilweise erhalten sind, befinden sich zur Zeit 14 in den USA, davon allein 7 in New York.

Keine fünfzig Kilometer von Mainz entfernt treffen sich Gutenbergs späte Nutznießer seit 1949 jeden Herbst zur Frankfurter Buchmesse. Wer diesen größten Buchmarkt der Welt einmal besucht hat, wird Marshall McLuhans Prophezeiung vom bevorstehenden Ende des Buchzeitalters mit Gelassenheit zur Kenntnis nehmen. Auch die amerikanischen Verlage, für die Frankfurt der wichtigste internationale Umschlagplatz ist, sehen zu Recht keinen Anlaß zur Panik: Ihre Teilnehmerzahl (1975 rund 280) nimmt nach wie vor zu.

The Art of Printing and Freedom of the Press

In the year 1452, after twenty years of preparation, Johannes Gensfleisch, who called himself Gutenberg, began to print the Bible in the old German episcopal city of Mainz. The first book ever printed with movable type, Gutenberg's invention, was also to be the most beautiful: it took twenty type-setters and printers three long years to produce an edition of a mere two hundred copies. The goal was achieved, but the inventor was ruined. Although the printed Bible cost forty guilders (four times the yearly wages of a scribe), making it almost as expensive as the traditional handwritten version, Gutenberg did not earn enough money to repay the equivalent of the $ 200,000 he had borrowed to finance his prestigious project. He lost his printing shop, and along with it the exclusive rights to his invention. And so he spent the rest of his life as a charity case on the estate of his territorial prince. His invention of the printing press, along with Columbus' discovery of America, marks the dividing line, historically speaking, between the end of the Middle Ages and the beginning of modern times.

Five hundred years later, the forty-two-line Latin Bible is the most expensive book in the world. Even in 1930, the Library of Congress had to pay more than $ 200,000 for a copy – it is difficult even to imagine what it would cost today. Of the forty-eight Bibles still extant, either partially or in their entirety, fourteen are in the United States, seven in New York alone.

Less than thirty miles from Mainz, Gutenberg's present-day beneficiaries have met every autumn since 1949 at the Frankfort Book Fair. Anyone who has visited this Book Fair – the largest in the world – will be inclined to chuckle at Marshall McLuhan's prophecy that we are approaching the end of the Age of Books. Even the American publishing houses, for whom Frankfort is the most important international market, see no reason for panic – in fact, the number of American participants (approximately 280 in 1975) still continues to increase.

Eine der 1282 Seiten der lateinischen Bibel, die Johannes Gutenberg um die Mitte des 15. Jahrhunderts in Mainz druckte. Sie enthält den Beginn des Buches Jesus Sirach aus den Apokryphen. Die farbigen Initialen und Ranken wurden nachträglich von Hand eingemalt.

One of the 1,282 pages of the Gutenberg Bible, printed in Mainz in the middle of the 15th century. The Latin text of this illustration is that of the Apocryphal Ecclesiasticus. The illumination was done by hand.

Eine Titelseite von Johann Peter Zengers „New York Weekly Journal". Der mit „Cato" gezeichnete Artikel stammt vermutlich von James Alexander.

Front page of John Peter Zenger's "New York Weekly Journal" with a text by the American "Cato", believed to be James Alexander.

Die erste deutschsprachige Zeitung Amerikas, „gedruckt bey B. Francklin".

The first German language paper in the United States, printed by Benjamin Franklin.

Was sich heute in Frankfurt als papierverschlingende Großindustrie präsentiert, begann für Nordamerika 1638 in Cambridge, Massachusetts. Zusammen mit dem im folgenden Jahr nach John Harvard benannten College (der heutigen Universität) wurde dort die erste Druckerei und Verlagsbuchhandlung der Kolonien gegründet. Der erste Bibliothekskatalog von Harvard, 1723 veröffentlicht, zeigt, daß die geistig interessierten Kreise Neuenglands schon damals regen Anteil am wissenschaftlichen Leben Deutschlands nahmen: Unter den fremdsprachigen Büchern der Bibliothek hielten sich deutsche und französische die Waage. Etwa zur selben Zeit erschienen in Pennsylvanien auch die ersten Publikationen für deutsche Einwanderer. Kein geringerer als Benjamin Franklin, der seine Karriere als Drucker begann, verlegte 1730 das erste in Nordamerika veröffentlichte deutschsprachige Buch, dem schon 1732, ebenfalls aus Franklins Druckerei, die *Philadelphische Zeitung* folgte.

Zusammen mit dem deutschen Einwanderer Johann Peter Zenger (1697–1746) spielt Benjamin Franklin auch eine wichtige Rolle in der frühen amerikanischen Diskussion über die Freiheit der Presse. Franklin war mit dieser Materie aus eigener Erfahrung vertraut: Erst durch ein politisch motiviertes Berufsverbot für seinen Bruder James war er zum Herausgeber einer Zeitung geworden. Zu seinen ersten Initiativen gehörte der Nachdruck von „Catos" Essay „Of Freedom of Speech" im *New England Courant* vom 11. September 1721. „Cato" war das Pseudonym zweier englischer Publizisten (Trenchard und Gordon), deren aufklärerische politische Theorie vor allem auf der Freiheit der Rede aufbaute. Diese war im frühen 18. Jahrhundert weder in Europa noch in Amerika eine Selbstverständlichkeit. Das bekam auch Zenger zu spüren, dessen *New York Weekly Journal* heute als erste politisch oppositionelle Zeitung der Kolonien gilt. Auch er bemühte „Catos" berühmten Essay, um sich vor seinen Gegnern abzusichern, veröffentlichte 1733 jedoch zusätzlich einen Aufsatz, der als erste ausführliche Theorie der Pressefreiheit in den Vereinigten

The big paper-consuming industry we see in Frankfort today had its North American beginnings in 1638 in Cambridge, Massachusetts. It was here that the first printing business and the first publishing house and book store in the colonies were established. In the following year, the college named after John Harvard (today's Harvard University) was founded here. The first library catalogue of this college (1723) shows that New England intellectual circles were curious even then about what was going on in Germany. Books in German and in French were equally popular. At about the same time, the first publications for German immigrants appeared in Pennsylvania. In 1730, the first German-language book to be published in North America was brought out by no less a personage than Benjamin Franklin, who began his career as a printer. Two years later, his press also produced the German-language periodical, the *Philadelphische Zeitung*.

Along with German-born Johann Peter Zenger (1697–1746), Franklin played an important role in the early controversy over freedom of the press in America. Franklin had first-hand knowledge of this argument: he had become a newpaper publisher by virtue of a printing and publishing ban placed upon his brother James. One of his initial endeavors was the reproduction of the "Cato" essay, "Of Freedom of Speech", in the *New England Courant* of September 11, 1721. "Cato" was the pseudonym of two English journalists (Trenchard and Gordon), whose enlightened political theory was built primarily upon freedom of speech – which was not taken for granted in the early 18th century, either in Europe or in America. This was also driven home to Zenger, whose *New York Weekly Journal* is today regarded as the first colonial newspaper of the political opposition. He too made use of the famous "Cato" essay as a weapon against his opponents. In addition, he published another essay in 1733, which has since gone down in history as the first detailed theory of the freedom of the press in the United States. The author of this essay was James Alexander, Zenger's attorney,

Die erste Nummer der ersten Zeitung, die in der amerikanischen Besatzungszone Deutschlands nach dem Krieg eine Lizenz erhielt. Das kleine Bild zeigt Brigade-General Robert A. McClure bei der Überreichung der Lizenz-Urkunde am 31. Juli 1945.

The first edition of the first newspaper to receive a license in the American occupation zone after the war. Lead stories include Clement Richard Atlee's election as British Prime Minister, progress of the war in Japan, the U. S. Senate's ratification of the United Nations bylaws and the three power conference in Potsdam. Brigadier General Robert A. McClure (below) is shown here granting the license on July 31, 1945.

Frankfurter Rundschau

Veröffentlicht unter Lizenz Nr. 2 der Nachrichtenkontrolle der Militärregierung

Jahrgang 1, Nummer 1   Mittwoch, den 1. August 1945   Einzelpreis: RM 0.20

Das Ergebnis der englischen Unterhauswahlen

Absolute Mehrheit der Arbeiterpartei
Attlee — der neue Premierminister

Clement Richard Attlee

Ehrenvolle Begrüßung
der „Frankfurter Rundschau" durch die Militärregierung

Alle Kraft gegen Japan

Der neuen Zeitung zum Geleit!

Zählung der Stimmen

Der Eindruck in England

Ueberwältigende Mehrheit
Senat in Amerika ratifiziert Weltfriedenssatzungen der Vereinten Nationen

Unterhaus tagt am 15. August

Präsident Harry S. Truman

Der Krieg gegen Japan
Elf Städte wurden gewarnt, sechs davon brennen bereits

Unsterbliche Opfer . . .

Dreimächte-Konferenz tagt weiter

Alliierter Kontrollrat

Laval verläßt Spanien

Staaten in die Geschichte eingegangen ist. Autor war Zengers Anwalt James Alexander, der, ebenfalls unter dem Pseudonym seiner englischen Kollegen, die Ungeheuerlichkeit zu behaupten wagte, daß die Herrschenden „Laster haben wie ihre Mitmenschen auch". Durch die Veröffentlichung solch freizügiger Anschauungen, mehr aber noch durch das Aufdecken konkreter politischer Mißstände, machte Zenger sich bei dem damaligen New Yorker Gouverneur Cosby nachhaltig unbeliebt: 1734 wurde er wegen angeblicher übler Nachrede festgenommen und leitete sein Blatt 9 Monate lang aus der Zelle weiter, bis ein Gericht ihn am 4. August 1735 freisprach. Von diesem Tag datiert die Tradition der freien Presse, die noch und gerade heute der berechtigte Stolz der Vereinigten Staaten ist. Einige ihrer Exponenten waren auch später von deutscher Herkunft, beispielsweise Arthur Simon Ochs, der von 1896 bis 1935 die *New York Times* herausgab und dessen Nachfahre Arthur Ochs Sulzberger dieselbe Funktion noch heute ausübt. Der Ungar Joseph Pulitzer (1847–1911), an den seit 1917 die nach ihm benannten Preise für Journalisten und Künstler erinnern, begann seine Laufbahn bei der deutschsprachigen *Westlichen Post* in St. Louis. Er war wohl das bedeutendste – nach mancher Meinung auch das einzige – Genie, das aus der deutschamerikanischen Presse hervorgegangen ist. Deren Bedeutung stieg und fiel mit den Einwanderungsziffern: Gab es 1890, auf dem Höhepunkt der deutschen Immigration in die USA, noch 727 deutschsprachige Zeitungen, so erscheinen heute, da aus den Einwanderern von einst längst Amerikaner geworden sind, nur noch wenige, meist regional beschränkte Blätter.

Ihre seit zwei Jahrhunderten ununterbrochene Tradition der Pressefreiheit prädestinierte die USA, 1945 die Neuorganisation des von Hitler gleichgeschalteten deutschen Journalismus einzuleiten. Mit der am 31. Juli 1945 als erste Nachkriegszeitung lizensierten *Frankfurter Rundschau* beginnt diese Tradition auch für den Raum der späteren Bundesrepublik. Unter dem Einfluß amerikanischer und britischer Presseoffiziere übernahmen die deutschen Zeitungen auch das anglo-amerikanische Prinzip, Nachrichten und Kommentare deutlich voneinander zu trennen – eine Praxis, die im deutschen Journalismus selbst vor 1933 nicht üblich gewesen war.

who, likewise under the pseudonym of "Cato", dared to make a preposterous assumption – that those who are in power "have just as many vices as those who are not". The publication of such liberal views, coupled with the embarassing exposure of instances of political misconduct, served to make Zenger persona non grata in the eyes of New York Governor Cosby. In 1734, Zenger was arrested, ostensibly on grounds of slander. He ran his newspaper from his prison cell for nine months, until he was acquitted by a court on August 4, 1735. On this day, the tradition of a free press was born, a tradition of which the United States is still proud (especially today). Some of this tradition's later exponents were also of German extraction: Arthur Simon Ochs, publisher of the *New York Times* from 1896 until 1935, as well as his successor, Arthur Ochs Sulzberger, who still holds this position today. The Hungarian Joseph Pulitzer began his career with the German-language newspaper *Westliche Post* in St. Louis. The prize which bears his name has been awarded every year since 1917 to outstanding artists and journalists. He was one of the geniuses of German-American journalism. The importance of the German-American press increased or declined according to the number of immigrants. In 1890, when German immigration to the United States reached its highest peak, there were 727 German-language newspapers. Now that yesterday's immigrants are today's American citizens, those papers which remain are few in number and predominantly regional in character.

Two hundred years of uninterrupted freedom of the press predestined the Americans for the task of "de-Hitlerizing" and reorganizing German journalism in 1945. The first post-war newspaper, the *Frankfurter Rundschau*, was licensed on July 31, 1945, and a new tradition was established in the country which was to become the Federal Republic of Germany. Following the American and British example, German newspapers adopted the principle of clearly differentiating between news reporting and news commentary – a practice which had not been common in Germany even before 1933.

So entscheidend der Geist, in dem eine Zeitung gemacht wird, auch sein mag – ebenso wichtig sind die technischen Mittel der Herstellung. Die 1846 von dem Amerikaner Richard M. Hoe erfundene „Revolving Press", eine Rotationsdruckmaschine, trug ebensoviel zur Entstehung des modernen Zeitungstyps bei wie die Setzmaschine „Linotype" des Deutschen Ottmar Mergenthaler, die erstmals am 3. Juli 1886 in der Druckerei der New Yorker *Tribune* ihre Bewährungsprobe bestand. In der Gutenbergschen Offizin hätte die Herstellung einer Sonntagausgabe der *New York Times* wohl Jahre gedauert – moderne Maschinen schaffen es am Samstag.

As important as the spirit behind a newspaper may be, the technical aspects of its production are no less important. The revolving press, invented by the American Richard M. Hoe, has contributed just as much to the newspaper as we know it today as has the Linotype typesetting machine, invented by the German Ottmar Mergenthaler. The latter machine passed its first test in the printing offices of the *New York Tribune* on July 2, 1886. It would have taken years to put out a Sunday edition of the *New York Times* in Johannes Gutenberg's printing shop – modern machines do it every Saturday.

**Frankfurter Buchmesse
Frankfurt Book Fair
Foire du Livre de Francfort
9.-14. Oktober 1975**

Die Frankfurter Buchmesse kann auf eine lange Tradition zurückschauen. Ihre Ursprünge reichen bis ins 15. Jahrhundert zurück. Heute ist sie die größte und spektakulärste Veranstaltung ihrer Art auf der Welt.

The Frankfurt Book Fair has been a regular event since the second third of the 15th century. Re-established after the War in 1949, it is today the most important publishing trade fair in the world.

Wilhelm Busch und die Comics

Unter den zahlreichen „amerikanischen" Erfindungen gelten die Comics vielleicht als die amerikanischste. Doch schon eine der ersten „echten" Comicserien verweist mit dem Titel „Katzenjammer Kids" auf Deutschland. In der Tat sind deutsche und europäische Einflüsse nicht ganz unbeteiligt an der Entstehung der Comics.
Der Schweizer Rodolphe Toepffer (1799–1846), dessen „Bilderromane" schon Goethe lobte, und Wilhelm Busch (1832–1908), dessen „Max und Moritz" anfangs von Pädagogen ebenso attackiert wurde wie hundert Jahre später die Comic-Hefte, waren Mitte des 19. Jahrhunderts Geburtshelfer des neuen Mediums. Busch und viele Autoren der zahllosen europäischen Bilderbogen benutzten schon manche der zeichnerischen Mittel, die auch für die ,komischen Streifen' unserer Tage noch charakteristisch sind: Zerlegung der Handlung in eine „filmische" Folge von Einzelbildern, Überzeichnung der Mimik, dynamische Bildgestaltung, unmittelbare Zuordnung von Bild zu Text, wenn auch noch ohne die typischen Sprechblasen. Selbst humoristische Wochenendbeilagen, die Wiege der Comics, waren nicht auf amerikanische Zeitungen beschränkt. So hatte zum Beispiel das *Neue Münchener Tagblatt* schon um 1890 jede Woche die mit Witzen und Bildgeschichten gefüllte achtseitige Beilage „Münchener Humoristische Blätter". In einer ähnlichen Zeitungsbeilage des *New York Journal* von William Randolph Hearst (1863 bis 1951) erschienen am 12. Dezember 1897 auch erstmals die „Katzenjammer Kids", die in zweierlei Hinsicht deutsche Eltern haben: Zum einen entstanden sie, weil Hearst eine Übersetzung von „Max und Moritz" gelesen hatte und etwas Ähnliches als Attraktion im harten Konkurrenzkampf mit Joseph Pulitzers (1847–1911) *New York World* suchte. Zum anderen war Rudolph Dirks, der die Erlebnisse von Hans und Fritz zeichnete, 1877 in Deutschland geboren worden und 1884 mit seiner Familie in die USA gekommen. Seit 1912 gibt es die mit starkem deutschen Akzent sprechenden „Katzenjammer Kids" doppelt, weil Dirks von der Konkurrenz abgeworben wurde.

Wilhelm Busch and the Comics

Of all the countless American "inventions", the comics are probably looked upon as the most truly American. And yet one of the very first comic strips has a title with a strong German accent – the "Katzenjammer Kids". As a matter of fact, German and other European influences did play a part in the early history of the comics.
The Swiss Rodolphe Toepffer (1799–1846), whose "picture romances" were already praised by Goethe, and Wilhelm Busch (1832–1908), whose "Max and Moritz" was originally attacked by educators with the same fury as were the comic books by their great-grandsons a hundred years later, helped to popularize the new medium toward the middle of the 19th century. Busch, as well as many other artists turning out the innumerable European "picture sheets" of the time, already made use of many of the artistic methods still characteristic of the comic strips of our day: telling the story by means of a motion-picture-like sequence of individual pictures, exaggeration of facial expressions, stressing of action, close relationship between pictures and captions (although without the "balloons" typical nowadays). Even Sunday supplements, where the comics originated, were not confined to American newspapers. The *Neue Münchener Tageblatt*, for example, published an 8-page weekly supplement devoted to jokes and picture stories as early as 1890. It was called "Münchener Humoristische Blätter". In a similar Sunday supplement of the *New York Journal* published by William Randolph Hearst (1863–1951), the "Katzenjammer Kids" made their first appearance on December 12, 1897. The Katzenjammer Kids may be said to be of German parentage twice over: to begin with, they owed their existence to the fact that Hearst had read "Max and Moritz", and was looking for something of the sort to use in his hard battle with his principal competitor Joseph Pulitzer (1847–1911), publisher of the *New York World*. Moreover, Rudolph Dirks, who was commissioned to draw the adventures of Hans and Fritz, had been born in Germany in 1877, and came to America with

Der letzte Streich und das traurige Ende von Max und Moritz, gezeichnet und getextet von Wilhelm Busch (1865).

The last prank and the sad end of Max and Moritz by Wilhelm Busch (1865).

Vorläufer heutiger Comic-Serien: ein Neuruppiner Bilderbogen („Aschenbrödel oder die Geschichte vom gläsernen Pantöffelchen") um 1835.

A predecessor of the comic strip was the Neuruppin Illustrated Journal. The story is "Cinderella or the story of the Glass Slipper", published in 1835.

Ein bekannter Maler als Comic-Zeichner: Entwürfe Lyonel Feiningers für „The Kin-der-Kids", 1909.

First Sketches for "The Kin-der-Kids" drawn by Lyonel Feininger in 1909.

Moritz! what fate led you and Max,
To cut holes in the miller's sacks?

See! Peasant Meck is coming round
To lift his maltsacks from the ground;

Scarce has he got one on his back,
When out the corn runs from the sack.

The rustic cries in wondering plight —
'Why! bless my soul, the bag grows light.'

Ah! now he spies with gladdened face,
Our Max and Moritz' hiding place;

Quick, pops them into his great bags,
Just like two bundles of old rags.

And Max and Moritz both feel ill,
For Meck is going to the mill.

'Hi! master miller, come this way!
Grind this for me without delay!'

The miller says — 'come give it here'
And down the funnel shoots the pair.

Rick-rickserackey! rickserack!
Round goes the mill with measured crack;

And here you can the urchins see,
Ground down as fine, as fine can be.

And all the pieces quickly were
Devoured by the poultry there.

Hearst durfte laut Gerichtsbeschluß die Serie unter dem ursprünglichen Titel mit einem anderen Zeichner weiterproduzieren, während Dirks die Figuren unter dem Titel „The Captain and the Kids" ebenfalls weiterzeichnete.

Amerikanische Zeitungsverleger hatten in den Comics ein Mittel entdeckt, neue Leser anzulocken. Doch um die Jahrhundertwende waren in den Vereinigten Staaten noch nicht genügend Zeichner verfügbar, die das neue Medium beherrschten. So suchte James Keely von der *Chicago Tribune* 1905 in Berlin Mitarbeiter für die sonntägliche Comicsbeilage. Anfang 1906 stieß er auf einen in Amerika aufgewachsenen Sohn deutschstämmiger Eltern, der eigentlich Musiker werden sollte, nun aber in Hamburg und Berlin als Zeichner lebte: Lyonel Feininger (1871–1956). Von März bis Spätsommer 1906 zeichnete Feininger für die *Chicago Tribune* insgesamt 47 Seiten der Serien „The Kin-der-Kids" und „Wee Willie Winkie's World". In den „Kin-der-Kids" arbeitete er comic-üblich mit Sprechblasen, bei „Wee Willie Winkie" in der eher europäischen Tradition einer Trennung von Bild und Text. Feiningers Comics sind Vorboten seines künstlerischen Werkes. Sie verdeutlichen, was man in Europa erst langsam zu erkennen beginnt: Daß Comics von Künstlern und auch – wenn nicht sogar in erster Linie – für Erwachsene gemacht werden. Noch auf der großen Feininger-Retrospektive 1973 in München wurden seine Comics völlig übergangen, während das New Yorker Museum of Modern Art schon 1963 auf diesen Bereich seines Wirkens hinwies. Feininger selbst hat sich von seinen Karikaturen und Comics nie distanziert.

Feininger und Dirks waren nur zwei von zahlreichen Zeichnern, die deutsche und europäische Illustratorentradition zur amerikanischen Comics-Tradition umformten. In Deutschland wurde diese Zeichnertradition zwischen den beiden Weltkriegen zwar aufrechterhalten, mit Ausnahme von E. O. Plauens „Vater und Sohn" blieb sie auf dem Comic-Sektor jedoch international ohne Bedeutung. Vereinzelt gab es in dieser Zeit schon Comic-Importe wie „Winnie Winkle", „Micky Maus" und „Prinz Eisenherz".

Nach dem zweiten Weltkrieg wurde zunächst versucht, mit deutschen Themen („Rumpelstilzchen") an die durch den Krieg unterbrochene Tradition anzuknüpfen. Doch es überwogen sehr bald deutsche Ausgaben amerikanischer Reihen wie die heute immer noch führende Heftserie „Micky Maus". Diese Importe behinderten eine eigenständige deutsche Comic-Produktion sehr stark und erweckten den Eindruck, daß es sich bei Comics um ein rein amerikanisches Phänomen handele.

Nach einer Anti-Comics-Welle in den 50er Jahren erfreuen sich heute in der Bundesrepublik die Comics auch im akademischen Bereich lebhaften Interesses. Eine Flut von Büchern beschäftigt sich mit ihnen, zahlreiche Studenten bestreiten ihre Prüfungen mit diesem Thema. Selbst Lehrpläne und Schulbücher umgehen den einst heiklen Gegenstand nicht mehr: Comics sind nicht nur zum Unterrichtsthema, sondern sogar schon zu einem didaktischen Hilfsmittel avanciert.

his family in 1884. Since 1912, there have been *two* strips featuring the "Katzenjammer Kids" who speak with a strong German accent. When Dirks was lured away by the competition, Hearst was given permission by the Courts to continue the strip under its original name, using another artist; while Dirks also continued to draw the same characters, now called "The Captain and the Kids".

In the comics, American editors had found a way to attract new readers. However, around the turn of the century there were not enough artists in the United States versed in the new medium. Thus it happened that James Keely of the *Chicago Tribune* went to Berlin in 1905 to look for new talent to work on the Sunday supplement. Early in 1906, he ran into a man of German ancestry who had grown up in the U. S.; he was to have been a musician but worked as an artist and cartoonist in Hamburg and Berlin. His name was Lyonel Feininger (1871–1956). From March until late summer 1906, Feininger drew a total of 47 pages of "The Kin-der-Kids" and "Wee Willie Winkie's World" for the *Chicago Tribune*. In the case of the Kin-der-Kids he used the customary "balloons"; "Wee Willie Winkie" adhered to the predominantly European separation of pictures and captions. Feininger's comics foreshadowed his later work as an artist. They made clear something which Europeans are only now beginning to realize: that comics are created by artists, and also – if not primarily – for adult readers. As late as on the occasion of the great Feininger retrospective in Munich in 1973, his comics were disregarded completely. The New York Museum of Modern Art, on the other hand, had already called attention to that phase of his work in 1963. As for Feininger himself, he never felt that his cartoons and comics were beneath his dignity.

Feininger and Dirks were only two of the numerous artists who were instrumental in re-shaping the German and European tradition of illustrating to create the American comics. In Germany, this tradition was preserved in the period between the two World Wars; with the possible exception of E. O. Plauen's "Father and Son", however, it did not influence the comics on an international scale. A few comics were already imported to Germany at that time, such as "Winnie Winkle", "Mickey Mouse" and "Prince Valiant".

After World War II, some attempts were made to revive the tradition interrupted by the war – this time using German themes ("Rumpelstiltskin"). But the German adaptations of American strips soon predominated, as for example the comic book series of "Mickey Mouse", which still holds first place. These imports constituted an almost insuperable obstacle to the development of any independent production of German comics, also giving the impression that comics were a purely American phenomenon.

After a wave of anti-comic feeling in the Fifties, the "funnies" today are the object of considerable interest on the part of even academic circles in the Federal Republic of Germany. A large number of books have been written about them and many students are writing theses on the subject. Even school curricula and textbooks no longer avoid mentioning this formerly controversial matter. The comics nowadays are not only a subject to be taught, but have even advanced to the point where they are being utilized themselves as an aid to teaching.

Ein exemplarisches Beispiel für Bildgeschichten ohne Worte: „Vater und Sohn" von E. O. Plauen (um 1935).

E. O. Plauen's "Father ond Son" was the only internationally known German comic strip between the two world wars.

Zur selben Zeit erfreuten sich die Fortsetzungen von Harold R. Forsters „Prinz Eisenherz" in deutschen Zeitungen großer Beliebtheit.

At the same time Harold R. Forster's "Prince Valiant" was a popular strip in German newspapers.

„The Katzenjammer Kids" von dem deutschstämmigen Zeichner Rudolph Dirks war einer der ersten echten Comic Strips. Er erscheint seit 1897. Dieses frühe Beispiel der Serie ist zugleich die erste 1908 in Europa nachgedruckte Folge.

"The Katzenjammer Kids" by German-born artist Rudolph Dirks is counted among the first genuine comic strips. It has been appearing since 1897. This early sample of the strip is the first one to have been reprinted in Europe in 1908.

1958 besuchte Walt Disney das Berliner Film-Festival. Deutsche Kinder ziehen seine Micky-Maus-Geschichten noch immer allen anderen Comic-Serien vor.

In 1958 Walt Disney paid a visit to the Berlin Film Festival. German children still buy more Mickey Mouse comics than any other comic book.

133

Poesie und Prosa

Nordamerika eröffnet seine literarische Selbstdarstellung vor dem deutschen Publikum mit den Romanen James Fenimore Coopers (1789–1851), die ab 1826 in mehreren Parallelausgaben zu erscheinen beginnen. Vom alten Goethe respektvoll bewundert, den Verlegern als exotisches Lesefutter willkommen, wurden sie von der breiten Öffentlichkeit förmlich verschlungen – was man zur selben Zeit wohl von keinem Werk der deutschen Literatur in den Vereinigten Staaten behaupten kann. Allerdings war es hauptsächlich „Lederstrumpf", der, bis heute als Jugendbuch verkannt, Auflagenehren einheimste. Diese einseitige Bevorzugung der Indianerromane tat nicht nur dem Autor Cooper Unrecht, sondern dürfte auch an mancher noch heute spürbaren romantischen Verzerrung des deutschen Amerikabildes mitschuldig sein.

Größeren Schaden hat in dieser Hinsicht jedoch zweifellos Karl May (1842–1912) angerichtet, der mit seinem Indianerhäuptling Winnetou einen „edlen Wilden" schuf, neben dem Coopers Chingachgook als Ausgeburt rüdesten Realismus wirken muß. Generationen deutscher Jugendlicher haben die May'sche Fantasielandschaft seitdem zu der ihren gemacht und sind wohl nicht immer der Gefahr entgangen, sie mit Amerika zu verwechseln ...

Wenigstens diesen Vorwurf, ein Land zu beschreiben, ohne es je betreten zu haben, kann man Mays Kollegen Friedrich Gerstäcker (1816–1872) nicht machen; er lebte sechs Jahre an der „frontier", ehe er nach Deutschland zurückkehrte und seine populären Reise- und Abenteuerromane zu schreiben begann.

Poetry and Prose

The first literary self-portrait of North America to reach a German audience was drawn in the novels of James Fenimore Cooper (1789–1851) which, beginning in 1826, started appearing in several different and simultaneous editions. Respectfully admired by the old Goethe, and welcomed by the publishers as light reading with an exotic flavor, they were hungrily consumed by the German readership, and their circulation was immense – which is more than can be said of any work of German literature in the United States. It is true that it was mostly the *Leatherstocking Tales*, which, even today erroneously looked upon as a book for young readers, went through edition after edition. This one-sided partiality for the "frontier novels" not only failed to do justice to their author, Cooper, but is probably partly responsible for the romantic distortion of the German idea of America which, to some extent, persists to this day.

Much greater harm in this respect, however, was undoubtedly done by Karl May (1842–1912), who, in the person of Winnetou the Indian Chief created a "noble savage" next to whom Cooper's Chingachgook would have appeared as the acme of uncompromising realism. Generations of German boys have been as familiar with the country painted for them by the imagination of Karl May as with their own back yards, and probably not a few of them have actually mistaken that landscape for the real America.

At least it could not be said of Karl May's fellow writer, Friedrich Gerstäcker (1816–1872), that he was describing a country he had never seen; he actually lived on the frontier for six years before he returned to Germany and began to write his popular books on travel and adventure.

Atelieraufnahme von Karl May als „Old Shatterhand" mit Winnetous „Silberbüchse".

Karl May posing as "Old Shatterhand" with Winnetou's "Silver Rifle".

Edgar Allan Poe, Schmidts amerikanischer Hausgeist, Held von „Zettels Traum".

Edgar Allan Poe, hero of Schmidt's giant novel, "Zettels Traum".

Arno Schmidt, hier vor seiner Bargfelder Einsiedelei, entlarvte Karl Mays Wilden Westen als Traumgebilde.

Arno Schmidt, here in front of his hermitage in Bargfeld, originally exposed May's Wild West as a figment of the imagination.

James Fenimore Cooper; seine „Littlepage-Chronik" wird zur Zeit von Arno Schmidt übersetzt.

James Fenimore Cooper; his "Littlepage Papers" are presently being translated by Arno Schmidt.

Gegenüber: Buchillustration von Jürgen Seuss zu Hermanns Hesses „Steppenwolf", nach dem sich auch eine amerikanische Beat-Band nannte.

"For lunatics only": Illustration for Hesse's novel "Steppenwolf" by J. Seuss. A well known American beat band named itself after this book.

Nur für Verrückte!

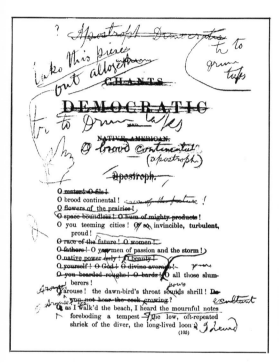

Ähnlich wie Cooper erging es jenem Buch, das der anderen ethnischen Minderheit der USA gewidmet war und eine der meistverbreiteten Schriften des 19. Jahrhunderts wurde: Harriet Beecher Stowes (1811–1896) Sklavenmelodram *Uncle Tom's Cabin.* Von Heinrich Heine enthusiastisch mit der Bibel verglichen, erlebte es schon im Jahr seines Erscheinens – 1852 – vier gleichzeitige deutsche Übersetzungen in 14 verschiedenen Ausgaben! Die Vielzahl freier Bühnenbearbeitungen und simplifizierender Kurzfassungen, die folgte, verfestigte noch das im Original schon zwiespältig angelegte Bild des zwar grausam mißhandelten, dabei aber naiv-demütigen, ja kindlichen Negers, und von der ursprünglich sehr konkreten sozialen Anklage blieb in dem Jugendbuch, zu dem *Onkel Toms Hütte* in Deutschland letztlich geworden ist, nur ein unverbindlicher Appell an die Humanität. Noch eine deutsche Verfilmung aus dem Jahre 1964 legt Zeugnis ab von dieser Verharmlosung, die heute glücklicherweise nicht mehr meinungsbildend ist: Seit 1945 vertritt das schwarze Amerika auch in Deutschland seine Sache selbst. Gerade in jüngster Zeit werden die Publikationen prominenter Vertreter der Black Power Bewegung – z. B. Eldridge Cleaver, Angela Davis, Malcolm X – von deutschen Verlagen fast ohne Verzögerung nachgedruckt.

Another book dealing with an ethnic minority group of the U. S. had a fate similar to that of Cooper's novels, and actually became one of the most widely-read books of the 19th century: Harriet Beecher Stowe's (1811–1896) slave melodrama *Uncle Tom's Cabin.* Enthusiastically compared to the Bible by Heinrich Heine, it appeared during the year of its first publication (1852) in four simultaneous German translations and in fourteen different editions! The numerous stage adaptations and simplified condensed versions which followed only served to solidify the original, schismatic image of the Negro slave – cruelly mistreated, it is true, but at the same time naive, humble, even childlike. And all that remained of the originally very direct accusations against the system of slavery in the original, when it had dwindled to a children's book in Germany, was a noncommittal appeal to human mercy and kindness. A German motion picture version made as recently as 1964 still shows how the hard facts were prettified. Today, of course, its influence is negligible. Ever since 1945, Black America has been pleading its own cause, in Germany too. Particularly in recent years, the works of prominent spokesmen of the Black Power movement – as, for instance, Eldridge Cleaver, Angela Davis and Malcolm X – are published in Germany without delay.

Jack London und sein „Seewolf", wie das deutsche Fernsehen ihn sich 1971 vorstellte. Raimund Harmstorf spielte Wolf Larsen in dem vierteiligen Fernsehfilm.

Jack London and his "Sea Wolf", as the German TV-audience viewed him in 1971. Raimund Harmstorf was Wolf Larsen in the four-part television film.

Dorothy Thompson lernte ihren Mann Sinclair Lewis, Nobelpreisträger 1930, im Jahr 1927 in Berlin kennen. Nach der Veröffentlichung ihres Augenzeugenberichtes „Ich sah Hitler" wurde sie 1934 als erste Auslandskorrespondentin aus dem nationalsozialistischen Deutschland ausgewiesen.

Dorothy Thompson first met her husband Sinclair Lewis in Berlin in 1927. After the publication of her eyewitness report "I Saw Hitler" (1934), she was to become the first foreign correspondent to be expelled from Nazi Germany.

Von den amerikanischen Klassikern, denen der exotische Reiz des Indianer- oder Negermilieus fehlte, ist nur Mark Twain (1835–1910) noch zu seinen Lebzeiten in Deutschland populär geworden – freilich unter dem einschränkenden Markenzeichen des Humoristen: sein pessimistisch philosophierendes Spätwerk ist außerhalb Amerikas lange unerkannt geblieben.

Thoreau, Emerson, Melville, Hawthorne und Whitman dagegen wurden erst in unserem Jahrhundert langsam auch in Deutschland bekannt. Als Initiatoren und Wegbereiter wirkten dabei häufig nicht Verleger oder Kritiker, sondern Schriftsteller, Verschworene auf der Suche nach Bundesgenossen: Im Fall Whitmans beispielsweise so gegensätzliche Temperamente wie der Naturalist Johannes Schlaf und, in seiner Rede „Von deutscher Republik" (1922), Thomas Mann.

Wie es ihm gebührt, fällt Edgar Allan Poe (1809–1849), der abgründige Rationalist des Grauens und der Groteske, auch hier aus dem Rahmen: Nachdem seine literarische Einbürgerung um die Jahrhundertwende durch Hanns Heinz Ewers, Gustav Meyrink und den kongenialen Illustrator Alfred Kubin begonnen hatte, wurde er 1970 unversehens zu einer Zentralfigur der deutschen Gegenwartsliteratur. Arno Schmidt (geb. 1914), auch als Übersetzer um ihn verdient, stellte sein Werk und seine Person in den Mittelpunkt eines 1352seitigen Romanmonstrums *Zettels Traum*. Mag Poe dort auch vornehmlich als Folie für die Selbstanalyse des Autors Schmidt dienen, so enthüllt das Buch doch ein Detailwissen, das in der deutschen Rezeption des amerikanischen 19. Jahrhunderts einzigartig ist.

Of the great American authors whose writings lacked the exotic appeal of the Indian or the Negro, only Mark Twain (1835–1910) became known in Germany during his lifetime, although only as a humorist. The pessimistically philosophical works of his later period long remained undiscovered outside the United States.

As for Thoreau, Emerson, Melville, Hawthorne and Whitman, they only gradually became known in Germany during the course of this century. Instrumental in this were frequently not so much publishers or critics, but rather other writers, partisans who were looking for allies to help their cause. In the case of Whitman, for example, his advocates included such opposite personalities as Johannes Schlaf, the naturalist, and, in his address "Von deutscher Republik" (1922), Thomas Mann. As was to be expected, Edgar Allan Poe (1809 to 1849), the profound protagonist of the horrible and the grotesque, once more refuses to fit the pattern: originally introduced to Germany about the turn of the century by Hanns Heinz Ewers, Gustav Meyrink and his congenial German illustrator, Alfred Kubin, he suddenly became a central figure of contemporary German literature in 1970. Arno Schmidt (b. 1914), who had already done very well by Poe as his translator, made his life and work the focal point of his outsize 1352-page novel *Zettels Traum*. Even though in this instance Poe is used merely as a foil to set off the self-analysis of the author, the book still reveals a familiarity with detail unique in the German reception of the literature of 19th century America.

Das zwanzigste Jahrhundert, von dem eine Redensart will, daß es die Kontinente einander näherrückt, hebt auch die räumlich/zeitlichen Distanzen zwischen den Nationalliteraturen weitgehend auf. Von Jack London über den Auflagenriesen Hemingway bis zu William Faulkner, Joseph Heller oder William Burroughs ist dem deutschen Leser kaum ein interessanter amerikanischer Autor unbekannt geblieben – ganz zu schweigen von den *Love Stories, Liebesmaschinen* und *Honigsaugern*, deren ebenso clevere wie gefährliche Schreibe den Sektor der Unterhaltungsliteratur zu dominieren droht. Klappt es aus unerfindlichen Gründen einmal gar nicht, so erbarmt sich Hollywood, und Fitzgeralds *Großer Gatsby* erscheint als „Buch zum Film".

Gerade angesichts der sich hier abzeichnenden Entwicklung von einer Weltliteratur zu einem Weltmarkt der Literatur dürfen die Versuche zweier Einzelgänger nicht vergessen werden, die deutsche Nachkriegslyrik mit amerikanischer Hilfe aus den Fesseln ihrer eigenen Tradition zu befreien: Der Dichter und Übersetzer Rainer M. Gerhardt versuchte in seiner, zusammen mit Robert Creeley (geb. 1926) edierten Zeitschrift *fragmente* die neue amerikanische Dichtung Pounds, W. C. Williams' und Charles Olsons für Deutschland stilbildend zu machen. Er starb 1954, mit erst 27 Jahren. Inzwischen ist das Gedichteschreiben in den USA zu einem Volkssport geworden – in der Bundesrepublik dagegen zur beargwöhnten Beschäftigung rechtfertigungsbedürftiger Außenseiter. Diese Schere schließen zu helfen mag die geheime Hoffnung Rolf Dieter Brinkmanns gewesen sein, der als Herausgeber der Anthologie *Acid* (1969) mit den von ihm übersetzten Texten wohl auch etwas von der Unbefangenheit übertragen wollte, mit der amerikanische Lyriker sich – im Gegensatz zu ihren deutschen Kollegen – auszudrücken wagen. Noch im Titel seines letzten Gedichtbandes, der erst nach seinem Tod erschien, klingt ein amerikanischer Mythos nach: *Westwärts*. Fünfunddreißigjährig wurde Brinkmann 1975 in London von einem Auto überfahren.

The twentieth century, of which it has been said that it has brought the Continents closer together, also largely eliminates the distances in time and space between the literary works of the nations. From Jack London and the best-selling Hemingway to William Faulkner, Joseph Heller or William Burroughs, there is hardly an interesting American author who has remained unfamiliar to German readers – not to mention phenomena such as *Love Story, The Love Machine* or *The Honey Badger*, a style of writing which, as clever as it is dangerous, threatens to dominate the sector of light reading. If, for some imponderable reason, success does fail to materialize, there are always the movies, and Fitzgerald's *The Great Gatsby* is reissued as the "book the picture was based on".

Precisely because of this development, which tends to turn World Literature into a World Market of Literature, the attempts of two loners should not be forgotten who tried to free German postwar lyric poetry from the fetters of its own past through American aid: the poet and translator Rainer M. Gerhardt, through his periodical *fragmente*, which he edited with Robert Creeley (b. 1926), attempted to influence German literature through the new American poetry of Pound, W. C. Williams and Charles Olson. He died in 1954, only 27 years of age. In the meantime, the writing of poetry has become a form of national recreation in the U. S. while, in the Federal Republic of Germany, it is the rather suspect occupation of outsiders attempting to justify their views. To close this gap may have been the secret hope of Rolf Dieter Brinkmann, who, as editor of the anthology *Acid* (1969), along with verses he translated, was probably trying to convey something of the ease and freedom with which American poets – in contrast to their German colleagues – dare to express themselves. In the title of his last, posthumously published volume of poetry, there lies the echo of an American myth: *Westward*. At 35, Brinkmann was run over and killed by a car in London in 1975.

Deutsche Schriftsteller, die während des „Dritten Reiches" in die USA emigrierten (von links):

Heinrich und Thomas Mann, 1930 in Berlin.

Erich Maria Remarque, 1929 mit „Im Westen nichts Neues" Bestsellerautor in den USA, heiratete 1958 die amerikanische Schauspielerin Paulette Goddard.

Carl Zuckmayer (rechts), hier 1952 mit Erich Kästner in der internationalen Jugendbibliothek, München.

German writers who emigrated to the USA during the "Third Reich" (from the left):

Heinrich and Thomas Mann in 1930 Berlin.

Erich Maria Remarque, author of the 1929 bestseller "All Quiet on the Western Front"; here with his wife, American actress Paulette Goddard, in 1958.

Carl Zuckmayer (right), with Erich Kästner ("Emil and the Detectives") in the International Youth Library, Munich.

William Faulkner (links) in Hamburg mit Sohn und Nachfolger Rowohlts, Heinrich Maria Ledig-Rowohlt.

William Faulkner (left) in Hamburg with Rowohlt's son and successor, Heinrich Maria Ledig-Rowohlt.

Im amerikanischen Exil: Franz Werfel („Das Lied von Bernadette") und seine Frau Alma, Witwe Gustav Mahlers, geschieden von Walter Gropius und Modell Oskar Kokoschkas für die „Windsbraut" (Gemälde im Hintergrund).

Emigré Franz Werfel (" The Song of Bernadette") and his wife Alma, widow of Gustav Mahler, divorced wife of Walter Gropius and model for her lover Oskar Kokoschka in his painting "Die Windsbraut" (on wall).

Wand in Henry Millers Arbeitszimmer in Pacific Palisades, Kalifornien, 1963; unter Millers Aquarellen ein Foto Hermann Hesses, eines seiner Lieblingsautoren.

Wall in Henry Miller's workshop at Pacific Palisades, Cal., 1963. Beneath his watercolors, a photo of Hermann Hesse, one of his favorite writers.

Gerhart Hauptmann in New York, 1932 porträtiert von dem amerikanischen Fotografen Edward Steichen.

On a visit to New York in 1932, Gerhart Hauptmann posed for this impressive portrait by Manhattan photographer Edward Steichen.

December 18, 1946

Mr. Ernst Rowohlt
c/o Rowohlt Verlag GMBH
Rathausstrasse 2TII
(24) Hamburg 1, Germany

My dear Ernst:

I was delighted to receive your letter which reached me in translation after some delay, and was glad to know that you are well and back in business again. You certainly had a hell of a war and I am delighted that you were not one of the numerous Krauts that we killed in Schnee Eifel or Hurtgen Forest. Do not think that this is the language of the oppressive victor as you certainly killed many more of our boys at both of these places than we killed of you. (glad we never killed each other)

Please write to Anne Marie Horschitz for me and tell her I look forward to having her translate my works again. She was the finest translator I ever had in any language.

Please keep in touch with me through my lawyer, Maurice J. Speiser, 630 Fifth Avenue, New York 20, N.Y., and let me know what conditions are and when you think it will be feasible to publish in Germany again. Then we can discuss making a deal. In the meantime I will not make any other deals with German publishers without getting in touch with you first.

However, please try to dig up a little money so that I will not have to be at the Kaiserhof again waiting while you chase money all over Berlin.

With warmest affection,

Your old counter-comrade,

Ernest Hemingway

Ernest Hemingway, und sein erster Nachkriegsbrief an seinen deutschen Verleger Ernst Rowohlt.

Ernest Hemingway, and his first post-war letter to his German publisher, Ernst Rowohlt.

Obwohl die Vereinigten Staaten in John Quincy Adams (1767–1848) einen Präsidenten aufzuweisen haben, der als Übersetzer deutscher Dichtung (Gellert und Wieland) hervorgetreten ist, kann man ebenfalls erst im 20. Jahrhundert von einer wirklichen Präsenz deutscher Literatur in Amerika sprechen. Dies gilt nicht nur für einige jener Autoren, die wie Bert Brecht, Thomas und Heinrich Mann, Franz Werfel, Erich Maria Remarque oder Lion Feuchtwanger im amerikanischen Exil der Bedrohung durch den Nationalsozialismus entgingen. Auch Klassiker wie Goethe oder Heinrich Heine (1797–1856) sind jener Minderheit, die sich überhaupt für Literatur interessiert, wenigstens mit ihren Hauptwerken ein Begriff. Von den Universitäten, an denen sich das Nachleben klassischer Autoren hüben wie drüben hauptsächlich abspielt, ging auch die amerikanische Renaissance Hermann Hesses (1877–1962) aus, die in den 60er Jahren viele Jugendliche der späten Beat- und frühen Hippie-Generation in einsame „Steppenwölfe" verwandelte: Wie Harry Haller, ihr Vorbild aus dem Jahr 1927, flüchteten sie aus der Leistungsgesellschaft in den Irrationalismus der Droge und glaubten dabei, in Hermann Hesse einen Guru zu finden.

Unter den zeitgenössischen deutschen Schriftstellern, die sich in den USA einen breiteren Leserkreis erobern konnten, sind Heinrich Böll (geb. 1917), „Blechtrommler" Günter Grass (geb. 1927) und Uwe Johnson (geb. 1934) am bekanntesten. Johnson hat seine Romantetralogie *Jahrestage* in New York angesiedelt, wo er zur Zeit, Material für den letzten Band sammelnd, auch lebt.

Wohl in der doppelten Absicht, solche engen literarischen Beziehungen hervorzuheben und noch weiter zu intensivieren, veranstaltete die inzwischen aufgelöste deutsche Schriftstellervereinigung „Gruppe 47" ihre Jahrestagung 1966 in Princeton. Dort machte der österreichische Autor Peter Handke (geb. 1942) zum ersten Mal von sich reden, dessen *Wunschloses Unglück*, einen Bericht vom sinnleeren Leben und Sterben seiner Mutter, Michael Wood im *New York Times Book Review* 1975 als „das beste Stück Neuer Literatur seit Jahren" rezensierte.

Ähnliche Superlative hat 1973 *Gravity's Rainbow* geerntet, Thomas Pynchons (geb. 1937) Abrechnung mit der Geschichte, dargestellt am Beispiel von Deutschland und Amerika. Die österreichische Schriftstellerin Elfriede Jelinek arbeitet zur Zeit an der fast unlösbaren Aufgabe, dieses Buch ins Deutsche zu übertragen: Erst die oft unterschätzte Arbeit der Übersetzer macht literarische Beziehungen zwischen den Nationen zu einem konkreten Angebot für Leser. Der Übersetzer hat das letzte Wort.

Although in John Quincy Adams (1767–1848) America had a president who became known as the translator of German poetry (Gellert and Wieland), it is again not until the 20th century that we can speak of any actual presence of German literature in America. This is true not only for authors such as Bert Brecht, Thomas and Heinrich Mann, Franz Werfel, Erich Maria Remarque or Lion Feuchtwanger, who had escaped the threat of National Socialism by exile in the United States. Even classics such as Goethe (1749–1832) or Heinrich Heine (1797 to 1856) are well known to that section of America interested in literature at all, at least through their major works. The American renaissance of Hermann Hesse (1877–1962) also originated at the universities which, on both sides of the Atlantic, have remained the guardians of the legacy of classical authors. In the 60's, many teenagers of the late "beat" and early "hippie" generation turned into lonely "Steppenwolves": like Harry Haller, their 1927 model, they fled from the pressures of everyday living into the irrational world of drugs, claiming Hermann Hesse as their Guru.

Among the contemporary German writers who have been able to establish themselves with the U. S. reading public, the most widely known are Heinrich Böll (b. 1917), the "Tin Drummer" Günter Grass (b. 1927) and Uwe Johnson (b. 1934). The scene of Johnson's tetralogical novel *Anniversaries* is New York, where he is also living at present, gathering material for the final volume.

Obviously with the intention of emphasizing such close literary relationships and of intensifying them even further, the German writer's association "Group 47" (now disbanded) held their yearly meeting of 1966 in Princeton, New Jersey. There, the Austrian writer Peter Handke (b. 1942) first attracted attention. His *A Sorrow Beyond Dreams*, a report on the meaningless life and death of his mother, was described by Peter Wood in the *New York Times Book Review* in 1975 as "the best piece of new writing I have seen in several years".

In 1973, similar superlatives were lavished on *Gravity's Rainbow*, Thomas Pynchon's (b. 1937) view of history, shown through the example of America and Germany. At the present time, the Austrian writer Elfriede Jelinek is struggling with the well-nigh insuperable task of translating the book into German. It is the frequently underestimated work of the translators which opens the doors to true literary intercommunication between nations. The translator has the last word.

*Taschenbuchausgaben sorgen für die internationale Ver-
breitung zeitgenössischer Literatur: Vonneguts "God
Bless You, Mr. Rosewater" in Deutschland, Bölls
"Gruppenbild mit Dame" in Amerika.*

*Paperbacks provide international distribution of con-
temporary works; Kurt Vonnegut's "God Bless You,
Mr. Rosewater" in Germany, Heinrich Böll's "Group
Portrait With Lady" in the United States.*

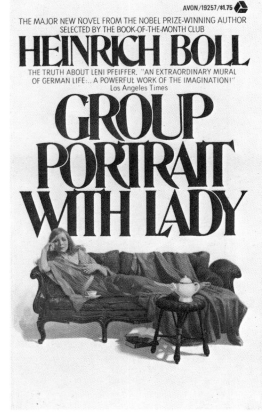

*Der amerikanische Lyriker Robert Lowell (geb. 1917),
der in "Imitations" und "History" Gedichte von Heinrich
Heine und Rainer Maria Rilke nachempfunden hat.*

*American poet Robert Lowell adapted poems by Heinrich
Heine and Rainer Maria Rilke in his "Imitations" and
"History".*

*Die deutsche Romanautorin Barbara König war im Früh-
jahr 1975 Gast der Universität Austin, Texas.*

*German novelist Barbara König was poet in residence at
the University of Texas in Austin in the spring semester
of 1975.*

*Tagung der "Gruppe 47" in Princeton 1966. Von rechts:
Literaturwissenschaftler Hans Mayer, Lyriker Erich
Fried.*

*Meeting of the "Group 47" in Princeton, 1966. From the
right: literary critic Hans Mayer, poet Erich Fried.*

Theater und Musical

Das Theater ist keine Kunstform für Einzelkämpfer und Dachkammerpoeten; es blüht nicht voraussetzungslos im Verborgenen, sondern reflektiert die äußeren Bedingungen, unter denen es gemacht wird. Bei Ländern, die eine so unterschiedliche Geschichte, und damit auch eine so unterschiedliche Theaterstruktur haben wie die Vereinigten Staaten und Deutschland, fällt auch das allabendlich auf der Bühne bejubelte oder ausgepfiffene Ergebnis entsprechend unterschiedlich aus.

Das junge Amerika des frühen 19. Jahrhunderts wäre nicht Schritt für Schritt mühsam der Wildnis abgerungen worden, hätten seine Bewohner sich allabendlich im Theater vergnügt. Zur selben Zeit glaubte keiner der zahllosen fürstlichen Kleinstaaten Deutschlands, ohne eigenes Hoftheater auskommen zu können. Die Fürsten sind mittlerweile verschwunden – aber ihre Hoftheater hat die Bundesrepublik noch heute: in jeder größeren oder mittleren Stadt, von wirtschaftlichen Zwängen dank öffentlicher Subventionen fürstlich frei. Amerika, das Land des freien Unternehmertums, bekam währenddessen, was ihm gebührte: In wenigen Metropolen zentralisierte Theater, die als wirtschaftliche Unternehmungen geführt werden, sich also rentieren müssen. Mehr Chancen für Nachwuchs und Experiment daher in Deutschland (wo es so viele ständig spielende Opernhäuser geben soll, wie in der gesamten übrigen Welt); Perfektion und höherer handwerklicher Standard dagegen in den USA. Mögliche Nachteile: das deutsche System braucht weniger Rücksicht auf das Publikum zu nehmen, das amerikanische nimmt eher zu viel.

In seiner drastischen Vereinfachung ist dieses Bild ein wenig schief – entspricht darin jedoch dem, was in der Bundesrepublik vom amerikanischen Theater wahrgenommen wird. Die wichtige Theaterszene Off- und Off-Off-Broadway oder an den Universitäten ist so schwer verpflanzbar, daß sie außerhalb der USA nur durch Gastspiele und vom Hörensagen bekannt werden konnte. Vor allem das „Living Theatre", das von 1964 bis zu seiner Auflösung 1970 fast nur in Europa auftrat, hat

Musicals and Drama

If the theater is like a plant which needs cultivation, one of its most interesting characteristics is its adaptability to various types of soil. In countries like the United States and Germany, which have such different historical "soils" and therefore such different theater structures, it follows that audiences and audience reaction (be it positive or negative) will be different as well.

The young America of the early 19th century would not have been carved step by step out of the wilderness if her inhabitants had spent their evenings relaxing at the theater. At the same time across the Atlantic, none of the countless German principalities felt they could exist without their own court theater. The princes have in the meantime disappeared, but the Federal Republic still has the theaters – in every large or medium-sized city – and they still enjoy the princely luxury of being free from economic pressure, due to government subsidy. America's theater system, on the other hand, is constructed along the lines of free enterprise. Theaters are privately financed and are located for the most part in very large cities. They are run as business undertakings – in other words, they must make a profit in order to survive. Thus there are more opportunities for beginners and for experimenters in Germany (where, it is said, there are more regularly performing opera houses than in the rest of the world combined). In America, the emphasis is more on achieving perfection and higher technical standards. One possible disadvantage (or advantage, depending upon the point of view) of the German system is that it does not necessarily have to cater to its public. In America, this is almost a "must".

This picture is of course drastically oversimplified and incomplete, but it does conform for the most part to what is known in the Federal Republic about American theater. Off-Broadway, Off-Off-Broadway and university theater are almost impossible to transplant to foreign soil, with the result that knowledge thereof can only be gained through hearsay or guest performances. "The Living Theatre", which performed almost exclusively in Europe from 1964 until its dissolution in 1970, was especially instrumental in encouraging

Gegenüber: „Viel zu heiß" ist es hier im Münchner Gärtnerplatztheater; Cole Porters „Kiss Me Kate" gehört zu den in Deutschland meistaufgeführten amerikanischen Musicals.

Facing page: Cole Porter's "Kiss Me Kate" is a big favorite in Germany where it is often presented in the opera houses. The photograph shows the number "Too Darn Hot" being performed at the Gärtnerplatz Theater in Munich.

Max Reinhardts biblisches Spektakel „Der Weg der Verheißung", Text von Franz Werfel, 1937 am Broadway.

Franz Werfel's "The Eternal Road", directed by Max Reinhardt on Broadway in 1937.

Dr. Gert von Gontard (Mitte) erhält 1966 aus der Hand des damaligen amerikanischen Generalkonsuls in München, Robert C. Creel, die Columbus-Medaille für seine Verdienste um die deutsch-amerikanische Verständigung. Als Präsident der New Yorker Theatergesellschaft „Deutsches Theater" hatte von Gontard Gastspiele der berühmtesten Theaterensembles aus dem deutschen Sprachraum organisiert und finanziell unterstützt. Links Hermann Proebst, der damalige deutsche Vorsitzende der Columbus-Gesellschaft.

Dr. Gert von Gontard (middle) receives the Columbus Medal from the late American General Consul in Munich, Robert C. Creel, in 1966 as a tribute to his contribution to German-American understanding. As President of the "Deutsches Theater", a New York theater organization, he both organized and financially supported guest tours by established and well known German-speaking theater groups. At left the late Hermann Proebst, then Co-chairman of the Columbus-Society.

durch sein Beispiel deutschen Regisseuren Mut zu unkonventionellen Inszenierungen gemacht. Gemessen am Anspruch der Living-Leute, über das Medium Theater einen neuen Lebensstil und eine neue Form politischer Aktion zu finden, mag dieser Einfluß unerheblich scheinen. Dennoch war er für das deutsche Theater eine Vitaminspritze, wie man sie sich häufiger wünschen möchte.

Überwiegend wird das Bild des amerikanischen Theaters außerhalb der USA nach wie vor vom Broadway geprägt. Unterhaltungsstücke wie die Neil Simons sind auch in der Bundesrepublik erfolgreich: die *Sonny Boys* haben von den Boulevardbühnen aus sogar die Stadt- und Staatstheater erobert. Das Musical, zu dessen Erneuerern der emigrierte deutsche Komponist Kurt Weill (1900–1950) gehört, macht der Operette ihren angestammten Platz in der Publikumsgunst streitig. Nicht nur *My Fair Lady* oder *Anatevka*, sondern auch *West Side Story* und *Hair* haben in der BRD Erfolg gehabt. Gerade dieses publikumswirksame Genre stößt jedoch auf praktische Probleme, da es sich der strikten Unterscheidung nicht fügt, die im deutschen Theatersystem immer noch zwischen Sprech- und Musiktheater gemacht wird. Die Folge: es fehlen Darsteller, die den Anforderungen beider Sparten gleichermaßen gewachsen sind. Andererseits erschwert das Repertoiresystem das Engagement von Musical-Spezialisten oder teuren Stars. Einige der spektakulärsten Erfolge – wie die mehrjährige en-suite-Laufzeit einer kommerziellen Produktion von *My Fair Lady* in Berlin und München – waren dann auch Ausnahmen von der deutschen Theaterregel. In breiterem Rahmen haben sich die Produktionsmethoden des Broadway in der Bundesrepublik nicht durchsetzen können.

Das literarisch anspruchsvolle amerikanische Drama, das in Europa vor allem mit den Namen Eugene O'Neill, Thornton Wilder, Tennessee Williams, Arthur Miller und Edward Albee verbunden wird, fand in Deutschlands Musentempeln natürlich offene Augen und Ohren. Seit den frühen 60er Jahren gehen die Aufführungszahlen dieser „Klassiker der Moderne" jedoch langsam, aber stetig zurück, und für 1975 muß man konstatieren, daß das amerikanische Drama auf deutschen Bühnen weitaus schwächer repräsentiert ist als etwa das englische.

German stage directors to depart from conventional methods. This influence may seem minimal when measured against the group's aims – to find a new life-style and a new form of political activity through the medium of the theater. But it was still a revitalizing shot in the arm for the German theater, and one hopes that it won't be the last.

Outside of the United States, American theater still continues to be associated primarily with Broadway. Broadway comedy of the Neil Simon variety has also been applauded in the Federal Republic. *The Sunshine Boys*, which first played in small commercial theaters, has even conquered the municipal and state theaters. The musical, which numbers the German-born composer Kurt Weill (1900–1950) among its innovators, is threatening to topple the operetta from its accustomed place in the public's favor. Not only *My Fair Lady* and *Fiddler on the Roof* were great successes in the Federal Republic, but also *West Side Story* and *Hair*. But this particular theatrical form runs into practical problems when confronted with the German theater system, which still draws a strict line between spoken drama and musical theater. Musicals don't exactly fit into either category. In Germany, there are few performers who are equally capable in both fields. Another problem is that the repertory system is not geared to the hiring of high-priced stars or of performers who specialize only in musicals. Some of the most spectacular successes, such as the initial continuous long-run of *My Fair Lady* (a commercial production), were exceptions to the German theatrical rule. For the most part, Broadway production methods have not been able to take root in Germany.

American drama of high literary quality (in Europe this brings to mind the names of Eugene O'Neill, Thornton Wilder, Tennessee Williams, Arthur Miller and Edward Albee) has naturally found a receptive audience in Germany. But since the early Sixties, the number of performances of these "Modern Classics" has declined slowly but surely, and in 1975 one cannot overlook the fact that American drama is not nearly as strongly represented on German stages as, for instance, English drama.

Kenneth H. Browns „The Brig" in einer Aufführung des Living Theatre, die auch in der Bundesrepublik zu sehen war.

The Living Theatre was an avant garde American company which made its home for years in Berlin. Here the company's production of Kenneth Brown's "The Brig".

Heidi Brühl spielte Annie Oakley in der deutschen Produktion von Irving Berlins Musical „Annie Get Your Gun".

Heidi Brühl was the star of the German production of Irving Berlin's "Annie Get Your Gun".

Was verdankt nun, in umgekehrter Richtung, das amerikanische Theater deutschen Einflüssen? Keineswegs nur Hildegard Knefs Ninotschka (in Cole Porters *Seidenstrümpfe*, 1955) oder die obskure Wanderbühne des „Hofschauspielers" Mitterwurzer, der von 1884 bis 1891 den Wilden Westen mit einer Aufführung von Schillers *Die Räuber* unsicher machte, in der er die feindlichen Brüder Franz und Karl Moor in Personalunion verkörperte. Deutschsprachige Bühnen waren es auch, die dem amerikanischen Theater im 19. Jahrhundert frühe Anstöße zu künstlerischer Orientierung gaben. Fast ein halbes Jahrhundert vor seiner Musical-Metamorphose wurde Shaws *Pygmalion* erstmals in den USA aufgeführt – in deutscher Sprache! Am „Irving Place Theatre" – einer Bühne, die über ihren begrenzten Zuschauerstamm von Deutsch-Amerikanern hinaus bekannt wurde – versuchte Heinrich Conried (1855–1909) erstmals, literarisch anspruchsvolles Repertoiretheater zu machen. Als Intendant der „Metropolitan Opera" (1903–1908) war Conried es auch, der Gustav Mahler und Enrico Caruso nach Amerika brachte. Die Bemühungen um das Repertoire- und Ensemble-Theater wurden in den 20er Jahren von der New Yorker „Theatre Guild", teilweise unter dem stilistischen Einfluß Max Reinhardts, fortgesetzt. Reinhardt selbst gastierte mit seinem Berliner „Deutschen Theater" 1927 in New York – eben der Stadt, wo er 1943 im Exil starb. Erwin Piscator, der 1934 in die USA emigrierte, gründete an der „New School for Social Research" den berühmten „Dramatic Workshop", aus dem, neben vielen anderen, Elia Kazan, Arthur Miller und Judith Malina vom „Living Theatre" hervorgegangen sind. Bert Brecht, dessen *Dreigroschenoper* auch Off-Broadway erfolgreich war, inszenierte 1947 in Los Angeles eine Neufassung seines *Leben des Galilei* mit Charles Laughton in der Titelrolle. Von den Arbeiten zeitgenössischer Autoren sind Peter Weiss' *Marat/Sade*-Stück oder Günter Grass' *Die Plebejer proben den Aufstand* auch in den Vereinigten Staaten beachtet worden. Quantitativ freilich ist die derzeitige „Exportquote" des deutschen Theaters nicht mit der des Broadway zu vergleichen.

To put the question the other way, what influence has Germany had on the American theater? One could mention Hildegard Knef's portrayal of "Ninotchka" in Cole Porter's *Silk Stockings* (1955), or the obscure road company of one Mr. Franz Mitterwurzer, who between 1884 and 1891 helped to keep the "Wild West" wild with his production of Schiller's *The Robbers*, in which he played both roles of the bitterly hostile brothers, Franz and Karl Moor. Performances in the German language were also a part of the American theatrical scene in the 19th century. Almost fifty years before its musical metamorphosis, Shaw's *Pygmalion* had its United States premiere – in German! The "Irving Place Theatre", which achieved recognition outside of its limited German-American public, was the attempt of Heinrich Conried (1855–1909) to introduce repertory theater of high literary quality to America. It was this same Conried who, as general manager of the Metropolitan Opera, brought Gustav Mahler and Enrico Caruso to America. Attempts at establishing a permanent repertory theater were carried on during the Twenties by the New York Theatre Guild, partly under the influence of Max Reinhardt. He brought his Berlin troupe, the "Deutsches Theater" to New York in 1927 for guest performances. In 1943, he died in exile in this same city. Erwin Piscator, who emigrated to the United States in 1934, founded the famous Dramatic Workshop at the New School for Social Research. Famous graduated include Elia Kazan, Arthur Miller, and Judith Malina (Living Theatre). Bertolt Brecht staged a new version of his *Life of Galileo* in Los Angeles in 1947 with Charles Laughton in the title role. One of his older works, *The Threepenny Opera*, was revived Off-Broadway in 1952 and became one of its all-time successes. Among the works of contemporary German authors which have found recognition in the United States are Peter Weiss' *Marat/Sade* and Guenter Grass' *The Plebeians Rehearse The Uprising*. Quantitatively speaking, of course, the number of current German theatrical "exports" is not to be compared with that of Broadway.

„My Fair Lady", komponiert von dem in Wien geborenen Frederick Loewe, ist seit der Berliner Erstaufführung 1961 das beliebteste Musical in Deutschland.

"My Fair Lady", with a score by Viennese-born Frederick Loewe, had its German premiere in Berlin in 1961 and is still the most popular musical among Germans.

Das Lebensgefühl einer ganzen Generation fand seinen Niederschlag in dem Rock-Musical „Hair", das auch in Deutschland Gegenstand leidenschaftlicher Kontroversen war.

"Hair" caused as much controversy in Germany as in its original production off-Broadway. It is still being played throughout the country.

Ballett und Tanz

Das klassische Ballett des 19. Jahrhunderts war die unbestrittene Domäne von Frankreich und Rußland; weder Deutschland noch Amerika spielten eine andere Rolle als die des Zuschauers, der den Gastspielen berühmter Ballerinen begeistert applaudierte: Bei Fanny Elsslers Besuch in den Vereinigten Staaten im Jahre 1842 unterbrach das Repräsentantenhaus sogar eine wichtige Sitzung, um an einem Staatsempfang zu Ehren der berühmtesten Tänzerin der Pariser Oper teilnehmen zu können.

Erst mit der Tanzrevolution, die um die Jahrhundertwende die Alleinherrschaft des klassischen Balletts beendete, beginnt der gemeinsame Beitrag der beiden Außenseiternationen zur Geschichte des modernen Tanzes. Die Amerikanerin Loie Fuller, einer der Superstars im internationalen Show-Business der 90er Jahre, entdeckte in aller künstlerischen Unschuld die Fortsetzung des Tanzes mit textilen Mitteln: Ihre Technik, Körperbewegungen mit flatternden Schals und weiten Gewändern zu verlängern, weist bereits auf einige Stilmittel des Ausdruckstanzes voraus, den Isadora Duncan und Ruth St. Denis nach altgriechischen und orientalischen Vorbildern schufen. Beide traten bald auch in Europa auf – Isadora schon 1902 in Berlin – und ernteten vor allem in Deutschland begeisterte Zustimmung und Nachahmung; kein Geringerer als Hugo von Hofmannsthal widmete St. Denis 1906 einen begeisterten Essay, und bald hatte die expressive Tanzsucht der schönen Seelen auf deutschen Bühnen ihre zweite Hochburg. Eine Ironie der Ballettgeschichte will, daß der Ausdruckstanz in den USA lange als „German Dance" bezeichnet wurde – in Wirklichkeit kam die Initialzündung aus Amerika. Freilich hat die deutsche Tanzbewegung diese Schuld mit Zinsen zurückgezahlt: Mary Wigman, die ihren Namen (Marie Wiegmann) bewußt amerikanisiert hat, Yvonne Georgi, Kurt Joos und Harald Kreutzberg traten Ende der 20er Jahre mit großem Erfolg auch in den Vereinigten Staaten auf: in New York wurde eine Tanzschule gegründet, deren Leiterin 1931 Wigmans Assistentin Hanya Holm wurde – dieselbe, die zweieinhalb Jahrzehnte später die Tanzszenen von *Kiss Me Kate* und *My Fair Lady* choreographierte. Eine solche Spannweite der künstlerischen Produktion, die von *Tragic Exodus*, einem Ballett über die Emigration aus Hitlerdeutschland, bis zum Broadway reicht, ist in Deutschland schwer denkbar – in den USA

Ballet and Modern Dance

Classical ballet of the 19th century was the exclusive domain of France and Russia. The only role played by Germany and America was that of the spectator, frenetically applauding the famous ballerinas at their guest performances. For example, when Fanny Elssler visited the United States in 1842, the House of Representatives interrupted an important session because the members were so eager to attend a state reception in honor of the most famous dancer of the Paris Opera.

At the turn of the century, a dance revolution ended the absolute supremacy of classical ballet; then the United States and Germany began to contribute to the history of modern dance. The American Loie Fuller, an international show business star of the 1890's, discovered in all artistic innocence that fluttering scarves and flowing robes could extend and accentuate body movements. This technique was to become Art as an element of expressionistic dance, a style created along ancient Greek and oriental lines by Isadora Duncan and Ruth St. Denis. Both artists soon appeared in Europe (Isadora as early as 1902 in Berlin), where they were enthusiastically received and imitated, especially in Germany. No less a personage than Hugo von Hofmannsthal dedicated a rapturous essay to St. Denis in 1906, and it wasn't long before the German stage also fell completely under the spell of "beautiful spirits" expressing themselves in dance. An irony of ballet history is that expressionistic dance was for a long time known as "German Dance" in the United States, whereas in reality, the initial impetus came from America. However, the German dance movement has since repaid this debt with interest: Marie Wiegmann, who changed her name to Mary Wigman, Kurt Joos, and Harald Kreutzberg also appeared with great success in the United States in the late 1920's; the Wigman School was founded in New York, and in 1931, Mary Wigman's assistant, Hanya Holm, became its director – the same Hanya Holm who years later became famous as the choreographer of *Kiss Me Kate* and *My Fair Lady*. Such a span of artistic activity, ranging from *Tragic Exodus*, a ballet about emigration from Nazi Germany, to Broadway is hard to imagine in Germany, but it is not uncommon in the United States. This open-minded approach to light entertainment on the part of "serious" American artists has given the Broadway musical and the classic Hollywood film-musical their own unmistakable dance styles.

Szene aus Isadora Duncans Schule in Berlin (1904).
A Berlin school of dance in 1904, founded by Isadora Duncan.

Mary Wigman Schule in Berlin: Bewegungsskizze mit Lilian Espenak.

Mary Wigman School – the German choreographer carried forward many of Duncan's ideas of interpretive modern dance.

Loie Fuller und Harald Kreutzberg: Showtanz und Ausdruckstanz mit ähnlichen technischen Mitteln und grundverschiedenen Absichten.

Loie Fuller und Harald Kreutzberg: Showtanz und Ausdruckstanz mit ähnlichen technischen Mitteln und grundverschiedenen Absichten.

Loie Fuller, an American showgirl, first did the veil dance in the Paris music halls in the 1890s. It was later picked up and perfected into an art form by such modern dancers/choreographers as Harald Kreutzberg.

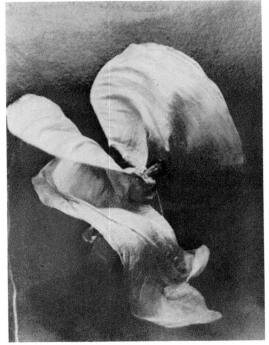

Alfred Austerlitz – bekannter unter seinem Künstlernamen Fred Astaire – stammt von Österreichischen Einwanderern ab. Das Foto zeigt ihn in dem Film ,,Top Hat'', 1935.

Alfred Austerlitz, better known by his stage name of Fred Astaire, shown here in the film "Top Hat" (1935). This son of Austrian immigrants has been a popular favorite on both sides of the ocean.

jedoch keine Ausnahme. Dieser Vorurteilslosigkeit, mit der amerikanische Künstler des ,ernsten Faches' Unterhaltung machen, verdanken das Musical und auch der klassische Revuefilm Hollywoods ihre publikumsnahe und doch völlig eigenständige Tanzkultur.

Das ,,Dritte Reich'' beendete die Hochblüte des Ausdruckstanzes in Deutschland; in den USA konnte er sich als ,Modern Dance' durchsetzen und weiterentwickeln. Auf dem Sektor des klassischen Balletts hatte George Balanchine, seit 1933 Choreograph von Lincoln Kirsteins ,,American Ballett'', inzwischen den tänzerischen Neoklassizismus begründet. In den 40er und 50er Jahren vollzog sich in Amerika eine allmähliche Verschmelzung von Elementen des ,Modern Dance' und solchen des klassischen Spitzentanzes zu jenem Idiom, das heute die internationale, überall verstandene Sprache der modernen Tanzkunst ist. Fast alle amerikanischen Exponenten dieser Entwicklung, wie Martha Graham, ihre Schüler Alvin Ailey und Merce Cunningham, oder Alwin Nikolais, sind mit ihren Kompanien auch in der Bundesrepublik aufgetreten. Nikolais choreographierte auch das vielbeachtete Multi-Media-Experiment ,,Kyldex 1'', das 1973 in der Hamburger Staatsoper aufgeführt wurde; in der Hauptrolle: die amerikanische Tänzerin Carolyn Carlson.

Angesichts dieser beiden Entwicklungen – der unterbrochenen Kontinuität der deutschen Tanzgeschichte einerseits, dem Integrationsprozeß im amerikanischen Ballett andererseits – ist es verständlich, daß New York heute als das wichtigste Tanzzentrum gilt, während die Bundesrepublik erst seit wenig mehr als einem Jahrzehnt wieder international mitreden kann. Der endgültige Durchbruch war das New Yorker Debut des Balletts der Württembergischen Staatstheater Stuttgart im Juni 1969: die amerikanische Kritik bescheinigte dem damals von dem großen John Cranko geleiteten Ensemble einmütig die Zuge-

While the "Third Reich" cut short its development in Germany, expressionistic dance continued to thrive in the United States as "Modern Dance". The neo-classical style in ballet had meanwhile been founded by George Balanchine, who had been the choreographer for Lincoln Kirstein's American Ballet since 1933. In America in the 1940's and 1950's, there was a gradual intermingling of modern dance elements with those of classical ballet, producing an idiom which became today's international and universally understood dance language. Most of the American exponents of this style, artists like Martha Graham, her students Alvin Ailey and Merce Cunningham, or Alwin Nikolais, have also performed with their companies in the Federal Republic. Nikolais was also the choreographer of the much acclaimed multi-media experiment "Kyldex 1", which was presented at the Hamburg State Opera in 1973, with the American dancer Carolyn Carlson in the leading role.

In view of both these developments – the break in the historical continuity of German dance on the one hand, and the integration process in American ballet on the other, it is understandable that New York is today the world's most important dance center. The Federal Republic only reappeared on the international dance scene in the course of the last decade. The final breakthrough came with the New York debut of the Stuttgart State Opera Ballet in June of 1969: The American critics were unanimous in granting the ensemble, then under the direction of the brilliant choreographer John Cranko, elite status in the dance world – the 'German ballet wonder' had been born. The American public was especially impressed by the diversity of the repertoire, the like of which had only been seen from the New York City Ballet – there were the representative, full-length ballets with a plot, such as *The Taming of the Shrew*, and shorter works of distinctly experimental character, such as *Présence*. The smaller, non-subsidized com-

Gegenüber: Das Stuttgarter Ballett mit Marcia Haydée und Birgit Keil in Glen Tetleys „Voluntaries" nach Musik von Francis Poulenc. Das Werk wurde 1975 auch in New York mit großem Erfolg gezeigt.

Facing page: The Stuttgart Ballet's production of Glen Tetley's "Voluntaries" to a score by Francis Poulenc. It was also performed with great success in New York in a guest performance of the company in 1975. The leading dancers were Marcia Haydée and Birgit Keil.

Fred Howard und Persephone Samaropoulo in John Neumeiers Gluck-Choreographie „Don Juan", Frankfurt, 1972.

American John Neumeier is a popular choreographer in Germany. The picture shows his production of "Don Juan" featuring Fred Howard and Persephone Samaropoulo. The ballet was first performed in Frankfurt in 1972.

Die Seele als Käfig, Menschen wie Insekten: 1951 wurde Jerome Robbins' „The Cage", nach Musik von Strawinski, als schockierend empfunden. Nora Kaye, Nicholas Magellanes und das New York City Ballet.

Jerome Robbins' ballet "The Cage", first produced in 1951, was a scandal in its day. This photograph shows Nicholas Magellanes and Nora Kaye in the world première of the work.

Robbins' Bach-Choreographie „Goldberg Variations" wurde während der Olympischen Spiele 1972 in München aufgeführt; Gelsey Kirkland und John Clifford vom New York City Ballet.

In 1972 the New York City Ballet visited Munich during the Olympic Games, when John Clifford and Gelsey Kirkland appeared in Robbins' "Goldberg Variations".

hörigkeit zur Weltelite – das ‚deutsche Ballettwunder' war geboren. Vor allem das Nebeneinander repräsentativer, abendfüllender Handlungsballette wie Der Widerspenstigen Zähmung und kurzer, entschieden experimenteller Arbeiten wie Présence beeindruckte das amerikanische Publikum, das dergleichen nur vom New York City Ballet gewohnt war. Die nicht subventionierten kleineren Kompanien in den USA können ähnliche Vielfalt und Kontinuität in ihren Produktionen schwer verwirklichen, da ihre wirtschaftliche Lage oft zu unsicher ist – Auswirkungen der unterschiedlichen Theaterstrukturen beider Länder.

Nach dem tragischen Tod John Crankos auf dem Rückflug des Stuttgarter Balletts von seiner zweiten Amerikatournee 1973 wurde der Amerikaner Glen Tetley – auch er Graham-Schüler – zum Leiter des Ensembles berufen. Mit dem aus Crankos Kompanie hervorgegangenen, 1942 in Milwaukee geborenen John Neumeier, zur Zeit Ballettdirektor in Hamburg, sind nunmehr zwei der wichtigsten Positionen in der deutschen Ballettlandschaft von Amerikanern besetzt – ein deutliches Zeichen, welches Land heute in der Tanzkunst den Ton angibt.

Bedürfte diese Vorrangstellung noch eines Beweises, so hat ihn das Gastspiel des New York City Ballet 1972 in München erbracht. Nicht nur Karin von Aroldingen – eine deutsche Ballerina des NYCB – sondern vor allem Jerome Robbins' Goldberg Variations wurden als Augenweide und Höhepunkt des olympischen Kulturprogramms empfunden: Die „Wachablösung" der klassischen europäischen Ballettnationen hat sich endgültig vollzogen.

panies in the United States can hardly hope to achieve such variety and such a consistently high artistic level because of their insecure financial situation – one of the consequences of the different theater structures of Germany and America.

After John Cranko's tragic death during the return flight of the Stuttgart Ballet from its second American tour in 1973, the American Glen Tetley (also a Graham student) was chosen to take charge of the ensemble. A former member of Cranko's company, John Neumeier (born in 1942 in Milwaukee), is at present director and head choreographer of the Hamburg State Opera's ballet company, which means that two of the most important positions in German ballet are held by Americans – a clear sign as to who is "leading the dance".

If any further proof of this fact was needed, it was supplied by the guest appearance of the New York City Ballet in Munich in 1972. Jerome Robbins' Goldberg Variations (the cast of which included the German ballerina Karin von Aroldingen) was considered a feast for the eye and the high point of the Olympic year's cultural program. So as far as the dance is concerned, America and Germany have definitely ceased to be mere spectators.

Das totale Tanztheater des Alwin Nikolais wurde auf mehreren Tourneen auch vom deutschen Publikum bestaunt. Eine Szene aus „Imago", aufgeführt auf der Gastspielreise 1966.

A guest performance of the Alwin Nikolais Dance Theatre on one of the company's tours of Germany. The work is "Imago".

Oper und Konzert

Die Musik, auf Worte wenig angewiesen, überwindet Sprachbarrieren am mühelosesten: so war sie von Anfang an prädestiniert, in den kulturellen Beziehungen zwischen den Vereinigten Staaten und Deutschland eine prominente Rolle zu spielen. Die Einwanderer des frühen 19. Jahrhunderts konnten Volksmusik und Kirchengesang auch in ihrer neuen Heimat weiter pflegen und leisteten damit – fast unbewußt – einen wichtigen Beitrag zur Überwindung des puritanischen Lebensgefühls. Vor allem der Chorgesang, institutionalisiert in der urdeutschen Form des „Gesangvereins", wurde im 19. Jahrhundert zu einer musikalischen Massenbewegung, die in der Gründung der New Yorker Oratoriengesellschaft durch Leopold Damrosch 1873 Höhepunkt und künstlerische Rechtfertigung fand. Schon früher – und dies sollte das bequeme Klischee vom Gesangverein als dem geheimen Zentrum deutscher Kultur in Frage stellen – hatten sich vor allem Immigranten aus Deutschland um die Verbreitung der europäischen Kunstmusik in ihrem Gastland verdient gemacht. So soll der Pennsylvanien-Deutsche Johann Conrad Beissel (1690–1768) der erste Komponist in Amerika gewesen sein – eine Tatsache, die ihm allerdings weit weniger zu historischer Unsterblichkeit verholfen hat, als die Rolle, die er in Thomas Manns Roman Dr. Faustus spielt. 1815 wurde in Boston eine „Händel-Haydn-Society" gegründet, fast gleichzeitig entstanden erste Orchester, die deutsche Komponisten spielten und aktiv Nikolaus Lenaus Diktum von Amerika als dem „Land ohne Nachtigall" widerlegen wollten. Zahlreiche Dirigenten in jenem frühen Stadium waren entweder deutschstämmig, oder zumindest in Deutschland, dem klassischen „Land der Musik", ausgebildet. Ähnliches galt für die Komponisten, die, genau wie das Publikum, dem um 1870 spürbar werdenden Einfluß Richard Wagners (1813–1883) bereitwillig erlagen. Bis weit in unser Jahrhundert hinein läßt sich diese prägende Einwirkung spätromantischer deutscher Musik auf amerikanische Komponisten nachweisen. Einzig der ‚Vater der amerikanischen Musik', Charles Ives (1874 bis 1954), vermochte sich ihr zu widersetzen.

Opera and Concert

Music, essentially independent of words, is the art which most easily transcends language barriers. As such, it was predestined to play a prominent role in German-American cultural relations from the very start. The immigrants of the early 19th century brought their folk songs and psalms with them, and this provided – if only subconsciously – a certain lightening of the puritan way of life. Particularly the typical German institution of the "Gesangverein" (semi-professional choirs) grew in popularity in the 19th century, and led to the founding of the New York Oratorio Society by Leopold Damrosch in 1873. Even earlier, German immigrants did a great deal to help acquaint their new homeland with European art music. (And that should help take the edge off the old cliché about the "Gesangverein" being the "secret center of German culture".) In fact, the German Johann Conrad Beissel (1690–1768), of the "Pennsylvania Dutch" colony, was supposedly the first composer in America – although his claim to immortality might derive more from the role he plays in Thomas Mann's novel Dr. Faustus. The first instrumental group which one could call an "orchestra" was put together in Boston in 1798 by Gottlieb Graupner, a German who had played in Haydn's orchestra in London. In 1810 he formed a "Philharmonic Society" which played Haydn's symphonies. In 1815 a "Handel-Haydn Society" was also founded in Boston. This already tends to discredit Nikolaus Lenau's conception of America as "a land without nightingales". Many of the first conductors in America were either of German descent, or had been trained in Germany, the classical "land of music". The same can be said about the composers, who, like the audiences, began to come under the influence of Richard Wagner (1813–1883), starting around 1870. The strong influence of late German Romanticism on American composers was felt well into the twentieth century. Only Charles Ives (1874–1954), the "father of American music", was able to break away from that influence.

Der in Posen geborene Leopold Damrosch (1832–1885), der in New York die „Oratorio Society" und die „New York Symphony Society" gründete.

German-born Leopold Damrosch (1832–1885), founder of the "Oratorio Society" and the "New York Symphony Society".

Damrosch – am Fenster im Hochparterre – dirigiert einen Massenchor, wie er Ende des 19. Jahrhunderts beliebt war.

Huge street choruses were a popular entertainment in the New York of the 1890s. Here Damrosch conducts a choral presentation from his perch in a second story window.

Charleston, das Tanzfieber aus South Carolina, eroberte auch die deutschen Tanzböden.

South Carolina's dance craze the Charleston swept German dance floors as well.

Ella und Louis auf Deutschlandtournee – für viele Deutsche der Inbegriff des Jazz.

Ella Fitzgerald and the late Louis Armstrong toured Germany with great success for years.

Von links: Bruno Walter, Thomas Mann und Arturo Toscanini. Es gibt wohl kein bedeutendes Amerikanisches Orchester, daß Walter nicht dirigiert hätte.

Bruno Walter (left) is shown here with Thomas Mann and Arturo Toscanini. The Berlin-born Walter conducted virtually every major symphony orchestra and opera company in the United States.

Otto Klemperer, vor 1933 Chef der Berliner Krolloper, dirigierte im Exil die „Los Angeles Philharmonic".

Otto Klemperer, born in Hamburg, conducted the Los Angeles Philharmonic throughout the war, returning to Europe to become a major international conductor thereafter.

Weihnachts- und Neujahrsglückwünsche von Paul und Gertrude Hindemith, die 1940 bis 1953 in den USA lebten.

A Christmas and New Year's card from Paul and Gertrude Hindemith, sent out during their residence in the United States which lasted from 1940 to 1953.

Benny Goodman, der ‚König des Swing', in Hamburg. Zu seinem Repertoire gehörte auch Mozarts Klarinettenkonzert.

The King of Swing, Benny Goodman, shown here in a performance in Hamburg. Equally versed in classical music, he was also featured here in a performance of the Mozart clarinet concerto.

Etwa zur selben Zeit beginnt Amerika jedoch, dem Import europäischer Kunstmusik die Ausfuhr seiner ureigensten Musikgattungen entgegenzusetzen. Schon im wilhelminischen Deutschland wurde der Ragtime populär, wenig später begannen Cakewalk, Onestep und Twostep auf den deutschen Tanzböden den Takt anzugeben. Nach dem ersten Weltkrieg traten die verschiedensten Formen des Jazz, auch sie damals in erster Linie Tanzmusik, ihren Siegeszug im Deutschland der ‚roaring Twenties' an: Jeder Musikstil – Dixieland, Swing, Be-bop – und jede Tanzmode – Shimmy, Charleston – wurde vom vergnügungswütigen Publikum der Nachkriegs- und Inflationszeit sofort begeistert aufgenommen. Amerikanische Musiker, wie der deutschstämmige Trompeter Leon Bismarck („Bix") Beiderbecke, wurden zu Idolen; Paul Whiteman (1926) und Louis Armstrong (1932) gastierten, andere konnten ihren Einfluß über das neue Medium der Schallplatte ausüben. Der Jazz geigende (!) Neger, den Ernst Krenek (geb. 1900) zum Titelhelden seiner Oper *Jonny spielt auf* machte, wurde der Berliner Theatererfolg von 1927. Selbst die Jazzfeindlichkeit des Dritten Reiches konnte die Beliebtheit dieser neuen Unterhaltungsmusik nicht verringern: je heimlicher man die kostbar gewordenen Platten abspielen mußte, desto begeisterter hörte man sie.

Nach dem zweiten Weltkrieg trug das enge Zusammenleben mit amerikanischen Soldaten in der Bundesrepublik – nicht zuletzt ihr Rundfunksender AFN – zu einer Vertiefung des Interesses bei. Neben Jazz wurde nun auch Country-and-Western, Rock'n Roll und schließlich die zeitgenössische Popmusik bekannt, und, vor allem bei der Jugend, beliebt. So beliebt, daß die Popmusik-Szene in Deutschland sich heute kaum von der der USA unterscheidet.

Doch auch in der ernsten Musik setzte sich im 20. Jahrhundert der Austausch zwischen beiden Ländern fort. Werke von Charles Ives wurden schon in den 20er und 30er Jahren in Deutschland aufgeführt – als ihr Komponist in Amerika noch fast unbekannt war. Arnold Schönberg (1874–1951), der sich für Ives eingesetzt hat, Paul Hindemith (1895–1963) und zahlreiche andere moderne Komponisten, aber auch Interpreten wie Bruno Walter wurden von Hitler ins amerikanische Exil getrieben, wo sie ihre Arbeit als Kompositionslehrer und Dirigenten unbehindert fortsetzen konnten. Gerade dem bedeutendsten

However, besides importing European music, America also began exporting some of its own musical creations. At an early date, ragtime became popular in Germany, and soon German dance floors felt the rhythms of the cakewalk, the one-step, and the two-step. After the First World War and in the "Roaring Twenties", jazz-influenced American dance music swept through Germany, from the shimmy to the charleston. American musicians, like the trumpeter Leon Bismarck 'Bix' Beiderbecke (of German descent), could be heard by means of the new medium of phonograph-recordings. Others even played in Europe, like Paul Whiteman (in 1926) and Louis Armstrong (in 1932). The sensation of the 1927 theater season in Berlin was the opera "Johnny Strikes up the Band" by Ernst Krenek (b. 1900), with its Black jazz-violinist as the hero of the title. Not even the official condemnation of jazz by the "Third Reich" could completely suppress it: the more secretly one had to play the records, the more precious they became.

A factor in the increasing popularity of American popular music in Germany after the Second World War is the very presence of American troops in the country: at least as many Germans as American soldiers listen to music on the American Forces Network (AFN). Particularly the generation of young Germans has become acquainted with Rock music and Country-&-Western, in addition to jazz. In fact, the music in a German discotheque today hardly differs from what is heard in America.

German-American culture exchange in the twentieth century applies to concert music as well. Works by Charles Ives were already being played in Germany in the 20's and 30's, at a time when the composer was still almost unknown in America. Arnold Schönberg (1874–1951), who was an advocate of Ives, Paul Hindemith (1895–1963), and many other modern composers, as well as interpreters like Bruno Walter, were driven into exile in America by Hitler. There, they were freely able to carry on their work as professors of composition and as conductors or performers. And it was none other than an American pupil of Schönberg, John Cage (b. 1912), who gave the avant-garde composers of the Federal Republic quite a healthy shock when he appeared at the Darmstadt Festival of Contemporary Music in 1958. He showed them for the first time how procedures based on chance can produce the same

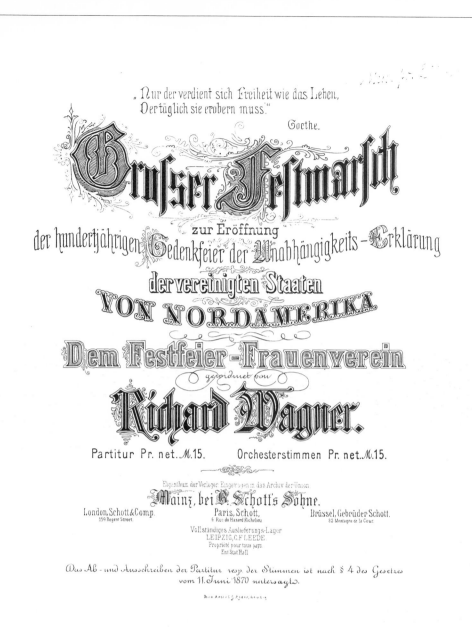

Für die amerikanischen Freunde Richard Wagners fällt
die Zweihundertjahrfeier der Vereinigten Staaten mit dem
hundertjährigen Jubiläum der Bayreuther Festspiele und
des „Rings" zusammen. 1876 gratulierte Wagner den
USA mit einem Festmarsch. Heute gehören amerikanische
Sänger in Bayreuth zu den umjubelten Stars. Auf dem
Farbbild gegenüber Jean Cox 1974 im dritten Akt des
„Siegfried".

Wagner composed a Grand Festival March to commem-
orate the hundredth anniversary of American Independence in 1876 – the same year he opened the Bayreuth
Festival. Thus the American Bicentennial coincides with
the Centennial of Bayreuth. In today's Bayreuth Siegfried
is sung by Alabama-born Jean Cox – opposite page.

Wieland Wagner (1917–1966), Enkel Richard Wagners und Leiter der Bayreuther Festspiele, gratuliert der
amerikanischen Mezzo-Sopranistin Grace Bumbry und
dem deutschen Tenor Wolfgang Windgassen nach der
Bayreuther Tannhäuser-Premiere 1961.

Wieland Wagner (1917–1966), grandson of the composer, and director of the Bayreuth Festival, congratulates
German tenor Wolfgang Windgassen and Missouri
mezzo-sporano Grace Bumbry after their appearance in
Tannhäuser which opened the 1961 Festival.

amerikanischen Schüler Schönbergs, John Cage (geb. 1912), war es vorbehalten, den avantgardistischen Komponisten in der Bundesrepublik Deutschland einen heilsamen Schock zu versetzen: Bei seinem Auftritt in Darmstadt 1958 wurde erstmals offenbar, daß man mit Zufallsmanipulationen zu dem selben klanglichen Resultat kommen konnte wie mit komplizierten Kompositionsverfahren – eine Erkenntnis, die nicht nur die Musik, sondern auch die modernen Künste allgemein revolutioniert hat.

Weit offensichtlicher als solche ästhetischen Einflüsse sind freilich die engen Verflechtungen zwischen deutschem und amerikanischem Musikleben geworden. Der Emigrantengeneration – zu der neben Walter auch William Steinberg oder Otto Klemperer zu zählen sind – folgten jüngere Dirigenten nach: Rafael Kubelik, Chefdirigent des Münchner Rundfunksymphonieorchesters, war gleichzeitig auch Chefdirigent der Metropolitan Opera, wo Günther Rennert zu den gerngesehenen Gastregisseuren gehört. Amerikaner singen in Bayreuth, und Europatourneen der New York Philharmonic oder der Symphonieorchester aus Boston, Philadelphia, Chicago und Cleveland gehören zu den regelmäßig mit Spannung erwarteten Höhepunkten der deutschen Konzertsaison. In den Gastspielen dieser, teilweise im 19. Jahrhundert von Deutschen mitbegründeten Orchester macht sich lebendige Geschichte ebenso bezahlt wie für die jungen amerikanischen Opernsänger, die heute in die Bundesrepublik kommen, um die Chancen zu nutzen, die ihnen das dezentralisierte Musikleben der Alten Welt bietet.

kinds of sound patterns which they were getting by means of complicated compositional methods. This insight produced revolutionary results not only in music, but in other arts as well.

The interweaving between the German and American music scenes is more obvious on a level other than that of aesthetic influence. The generation of immigrants, which included not only Bruno Walter but also William Steinberg and Otto Klemperer, was followed by a generation of younger conductors. Rafael Kubelik, head conductor of the Bavarian Radio Symphony Orchestra in Munich, was concurrently also head conductor of the Metropolitan Opera, where Günther Rennert of the Munich State Opera is also a popular stage-director. Americans appear in Bayreuth; and European tours of the New York Philharmonic, as well as the symphony orchestras of Boston, Philadelphia, Chicago, and Cleveland, all regularly appear as highlights of the German concert season. The guest performances of these orchestras, many of whose founding members were originally from Germany, are the fruition of cultural exchange, an exchange that was never more lively than today, when many young American opera singers and instrumentalists come to the Federal Republic to take advantage of the opportunities which the decentralized musical life of the "Old World" has to offer.

Oft in den USA auf Gastspielreise: Die Regensburger Domspatzen, hier mit der Sopranistin Ingeborg Hallstein.

The "Regensburg Cathedral Sparrows" are a boy's choir with a centuries old tradition. They often visit America. They are shown here with soprano Ingeborg Hallstein.

Im Rahmen der Feierlichkeiten zum zweihundertjährigen Bestehen der USA besuchte das Philadelphia Orchestra unter Eugene Ormandy (oben) 1975 die Bundesrepublik. 1976 werden die Berliner Philharmoniker unter Herbert von Karajan (unten) in den Vereinigten Staaten gastieren.

In a gala Bicentennial Exchange, the Philadelphia Orchestra visited Germany with its musical director, Eugene Ormandy, in 1975. Their visit will be reciprocated by a tour of the Berlin Philharmonic under Herbert von Karajan (bottom picture) in the Bicentennial Year 1976.

Vier Szenen aus Fritz Langs Film „Die Frau im Mond" (1929). Die Montagehalle und die Rampen, auf denen die Rakete an den Start gerollt wird, haben erstaunliche Ähnlichkeit mit dem Cape Canaveral von heute – der Mond weniger.

This "moonscape" was photographed on a sound stage in 1929 Berlin during shooting of the motion picture "The Woman in the Moon" directed by Fritz Lang. The similarity to the real thing at Cape Canaveral is striking.

Bewegliche Bilder: Film und Fernsehen

Motion Pictures and Television

Der Countdown, wie wir ihn kennen, 10-9-8-usw., wurde 1929 von Fritz Lang für den UFA-Film *Die Frau im Mond* erfunden. Er sollte die Spannung vor dem Start erhöhen. Fritz Lang: „Es war ein Schuß ins Schwarze".

Thomas Pynchon, Filmfan und Romanschreiber, schildert so (in *Gravity's Rainbow*) die Erfindung jenes dramaturgischen Geniestreichs, den man den nüchternen Technikern von Peenemünde in der Tat kaum zugetraut hätte. Fritz Lang (geb. 1890) als Ghostwriter der Raketenstarts von Cape Canaveral, den kostspieligsten Fernsehinszenierungen der 60er Jahre: Eine besondere Pointe in der 50jährigen Geschichte des amerikanisch-deutschen Film- und Fernsehgeschäfts.

Immer noch sind es Leinwand und Bildschirm, von denen man in Deutschland erfährt, wie es in Amerika eigentlich aussieht und angeblich zugeht. Fast jeder Deutsche hat die rotbraunen Felstürme des „Monument Valley" einmal in einem Western gesehen, die Highways von Los Angeles aus TV-Krimiserien kennengelernt oder vom „Krümelmonster" aus der *Sesame Street* etwas über die amerikanische Umweltproblematik gehört. Umgekehrt: zahllose Amerikaner haben in *Cabaret* das in Schauplatz und Stimmung hervorragend erfaßte Berlin der 30er Jahre erlebt oder in Langs *Metropolis*, dem aufwendigsten deutschen Stummfilm, die Vision einer inhumanen Großstadtwelt hautnah erfahren.

Nie wieder waren die Filmbeziehungen zwischen den USA und Deutschland so intensiv und fruchtbar, wie in den 20er- und 30er Jahren. Die besten deutschen Regisseure – Ernst Lubitsch, F. W. Murnau, Otto Preminger, Douglas Sirk, Fritz Lang, Joseph von Sternberg, Max Reinhardt – und berühmte Schauspieler wie Emil Jannings und Marlene Dietrich lebten und arbeiteten in der amerikanischen Filmmetropole. Sie beeinflußten Regisseure wie D. W. Griffith und Orson Welles, der die Filme Fritz Langs studierte, ehe er sich an seinen Erstling *Citizen Kane* wagte.

The countdown as we know it, 10–9–8–7, etc., was invented by Fritz Lang in 1929 for the UFA-film *Die Frau im Mond*. He put it into the launch scene to heighten the suspense. "It is another of my damned 'touches'," Fritz Lang said.

(Gravity's Rainbow, pg. 753)

That is how Thomas Pynchon, film-fan and novelist, describes the discovery of this brilliant dramatic device, a discovery which would have been quite out of character for the serious-minded technicians from Peenemünde. So one could call Fritz Lang the ghostwriter for the rocket launches at Cape Canaveral, the most expensive "TV spectaculars" of the 1960's – just an interesting footnote from the pages of the fifty year history of American-German film relations.

The film is still a medium through which Germany learns about America – how it looks and, to an extent, how it lives. Almost every German has at some time seen the reddish-brown mountain peaks of Monument Valley in some Western. He has seen the highways of Los Angeles in a detective series, and been made aware of American sociological problems by the Cookie Monster from *Sesame Street*. But Americans have also learned from film. Through *Cabaret*, millions experienced the electric atmosphere of Berlin of the 1930's; in Fritz Lang's *Metropolis*, the most lavish of German silent films, they shuddered at the vision of an inhuman skyscraper-world.

Cinematic relations between America and Germany were never so fruitful as during the 1920's and the 1930's. The best German directors – Ernst Lubitsch, F. W. Murnau, Otto Preminger, Douglas Sirk, Fritz Lang, Joseph von Sternberg, Max Reinhardt – and famous stars like Emil Jannings and Marlene Dietrich all lived and worked in the American film capital. They influenced such directors as D. W. Griffith and Orson Welles (who studied the films of Fritz Lang before attempting his first effort, *Citizen Kane*). Hollywood stars Gloria Swanson, Douglas Fair-

Fritz Lang mit seiner Frau Thea von Harbou, die das Drehbuch zu „Die Frau im Mond" verfaßte. Als Dr. Goebbels Lang die Leitung der Reichsfilmkammer antrug, bat dieser um Bedenkzeit und verließ Berlin mit dem nächsten Zug. Endstation seiner Reise war schließlich Hollywood.

Fritz Lang is shown here with his wife Thea von Harbou who wrote the screenplay to "The Woman in the Moon". When Dr. Goebbels offered to appoint Lang director of the Reich's Film Division; the director asked for some time to think it over, then got on the next train out of Berlin, going subsequently on to Hollywood.

Während der Dreharbeiten zu dem monumentalen deutschen Ausstattungsfilm „Das Weib des Pharao" (1921), der es durchaus mit vergleichbaren Hollywood-Produktionen der Zeit aufnehmen konnte: Der Schauspieler Emil Jannings und der Regisseur Ernst Lubitsch.

Two famous German emigrants of the cinema were director Ernst Lubitsch and actor Emil Jannings, shown here on the set of the film "The Pharao's Wife", part of the same era in cinema that produced the spectacular productions of Cecil B. de Mille in Hollywood.

F. W. Murnau und Emil Jannings bei den Dreharbeiten zu dem Film „Der Fuchs" in Hollywood.

F.W. Murnau and Emil Jannings on the set of "The Fox" in Hollywood.

Marlene Dietrich in Josef von Sternbergs „Der blaue Engel", 1929.

Marlene Dietrich's legs first came into prominence in Josef von Sternberg's film "The Blue Angel", produced in Berlin in 1929.

Fritz Langs Film „M" machten den aus Wien stammenden Schauspieler Peter Lorre berühmt. Lorre und Lang arbeiteten später beide in Hollywood.

Viennese-born Peter Lorre first became famous in Fritz Lang's production of "M", still a favorite with German and American art theater audiences.

Max Reinhardt (ganz links neben Douglas Fairbanks) stattet Hollywood 1928 einen Besuch ab.

Max Reinhardt (extreme left) visits Hollywood in 1928 where, among others, he was greeted by Douglas Fairbanks, directly to his right.

Hollywoods Sterne: Gloria Swanson, Douglas Fairbanks, Clark Gable, Buster Keaton waren in deutschen Kinos ebenso bekannt und beliebt wie in ihrer amerikanischen Heimat. Gary Cooper und Humphrey Bogart wurden beiderseits des Ozeans Leitbilder einer ganzen Generation von „tough guys", während Marlene Dietrich als „blauer Engel" die blonde Vamp-Ära Hollywoods mitprägte.

Im zweiten Weltkrieg kamen weder amerikanische Filme in deutsche Kinos, noch umgekehrt. Dennoch blieb Hollywood Vorbild für die Musikfilme der deutschen UFA, die das Publikum von der Kriegsrealität ablenken sollten. Währenddessen entstanden in den USA zwei geniale Tragikomödien, die, darin ihrer Zeit um Jahrzehnte voraus, Hitler als wildgewordenen Kleinbürger demaskierten: Ernst Lubitschs *Sein oder Nichtsein* und Chaplins *Großer Diktator*. Vor allem Lubitschs analytisches Satyrspiel läßt noch heute dem Zuschauer das Lachen in der Kehle gefrieren.

Obwohl Hollywood durch die frühe Entwicklung des Fernsehens in den USA bald nach dem Krieg in seine schleichende Krise kam, eroberte der amerikanische Film die Kinos der Bundesrepublik Deutschland. Von *High Noon* über *Easy Rider* bis zu den Filmen des Lang-Fans Bogdanovich diskutieren deutsche Cineasten hauptsächlich amerikanische Produktionen. Vergleichbares hatte der deutsche Film in den beiden letzten Jahrzehnten auf dem amerikanischen Markt nicht mehr anzubieten. Nur einzelne Schauspielerinnen und Schauspielern (Elke Sommer, Hardy Krüger, Curd Jürgens) und dem amerikanischen Erfolg der Produktionen Rainer Werner Faßbinders ist es zu verdanken, daß Deutschland als ehedem bedeutende Filmnation nicht völlig ins Off gerät.

Was der deutsche Kinofilm nicht leistet, kann auch das deutsche Fernsehen nicht wettmachen. Hier liegen die Gründe hauptsächlich in der öffentlich-rechtlichen Struktur der deutschen Fernsehanstalten und ihrer daraus resultierenden chronischen Finanznot. Die Folge ist, daß das privatrechtliche, kommerziell orientierte amerikanische Fernsehen, zumindest auf dem Unterhaltungs-

banks, Clark Gable, and Buster Keaton were just as popular in Germany as they were at home. On both sides of the ocean, Gary Cooper and Humphrey Bogart became the idols of a whole generation of "tough guys", while Marlene Dietrich's "blue angel" spread its wings over the Hollywood era of the blonde vamp.

During World War II, there were no American films to be seen in German theatres, and vice versa. But Hollywood was still the model for the musical films of the German UFA, whose purpose was to offer escape from the brutal realities of war. At this time in the United States, two tragicomedies were produced, which, in their treatment of Hitler as a petit bourgeois gone mad, were years ahead of their time: Ernst Lubitsch's *To Be or Not To Be* and Charles Chaplin's *The Great Dictator*. The analytic satire of the former still sends audiences into convulsions of laughter.

Even though Hollywood itself suffered from the early postwar development of television in the United States, American films were king in the Federal Republic. American productions were the main topic of conversation among German filmmakers – from *High Noon* to *Easy Rider*, and now the films of the Fritz Lang fan, Peter Bogdanovich. The German film market did not have nearly as much to offer in the last two decades. The fact that the German film industry did not completely "fade out" was due to individual actors – Elke Sommer, Hardy Krüger, and Curd Jürgens – and, lately, to the American success of the films of Rainer Werner Fassbinder.

German television cannot compensate for what is lacking in German commercial films. The reasons for this are structural – German television is not commercially sponsored, it is not a profit-making organization, which means that money is in short supply. This is why, at least in the sector of light entertainment, there are so many German-dubbed versions of American television programs. It would be hard to imagine the early evening program without *Flipper*, *The Virginian*, or the longtime favorite, *Bonanza*. And when it gets dark in *The Streets of*

„Cabaret" ist schon wenige Jahre nach seiner Entstehung zu einem Klassiker in den Repertoirekinos geworden. Nach Christopher Isherwoods „Berliner Geschichten" gedreht, trug der Film nicht nur Liza Minelli (im Bild mit Michael York) und Regisseur Bob Fosse einen Oskar ein, sondern auch Rolf Zehetbauer, dem Ausstattungschef der Münchner Bavaria, in deren Studios der Film gedreht wurde.

"Cabaret", shot entirely in Germany and based on Christopher Isherwood's "Berlin Stories", featured Liza Minelli and Michael York in a picture that won oscars not only for Miss Minelli and director Bob Fosse but also for German set designer Rolf Zehetbauer.

„Columbo" (mit Peter Falk) und „Flipper" gehören zu den Weitgereisten unter den amerikanischen TV-Serien.

The American series "Columbo" (starring Peter Falk) and "Flipper" are among the many U. S. television products that are well traveled.

sektor, auch die deutschen Programme beeinflußt. So reichhaltig und vielfältig ist das Angebot amerikanischer TV-Serien auf deutschen Mattscheiben, daß *Flipper*, *Die Leute von der Shiloh-Ranch* oder der Dauerbrenner *Bonanza* aus dem Vorabend-Programm nicht mehr wegzudenken sind. Und später, wenn es dunkel wird in den *Straßen von San Francisco*, New York oder Los Angeles, harrt der mehr oder minder erwachsene TV-Zuschauer gespannt der neuen Abenteuer des glatzköpfigen, Lollipop-lutschenden Lieutenant Kojak von der New York Police oder des vertrottelten Fuchses Columbo, der den Donnerstagabend erst richtig spannend macht.

Um die Ehre des deutschen Fernsehens zu retten: es hat auch zur Entstehung des ‚jungen deutschen Films' entscheidende Beiträge geleistet. Als Koproduzent half es manchem Film auf die Leinwand, der, wie Faßbinders *Der amerikanische Soldat*, klassische Hollywood-Genres – hier den Gangsterfilm – zum stilistischen Vorbild hatte. Auch Außenseiter und Experimentalfilmer des New American Cinema, wie Ed Emshwiller, Stan Brakhage oder der berühmtere Andy Warhol, haben in der Bundesrepublik und Österreich Nachahmer und Nachfolger gefunden. Denkbar, daß die gemeinsame Filmtradition der 20er Jahre einmal wieder auflebt.

San Francisco, New York or Los Angeles, viewers of all ages are eagerly awaiting the latest adventures of the lollipop-loving Lieutenant Kojak of the New York Police, or that sly fox, Inspector Columbo, in his "permanent-wrinkle" clothes.
But German television can point with pride to its significant contribution to the new wave of German cinema, for instance the films of Rainer Werner Faßbinder and Volker Schlöndorff. The television industry has acted as co-producer on several important projects sharing the costs and the rights with commercial contributors. The highly individual and experimental filmmakers of the New American Cinema, such as Ed Emshwiller, Stan Brakhage, or the more famous Andy Warhol, have found imitators and successors in the Federal Republic and in Austria. So the mutual film tradition of the 1920's may not be dead after all.

Santa Claus trifft Buffalo Bill: Brauchtum und Lebensfreude

Santa Claus meets Buffalo Bill: Folklore and Humor

Erste Eindrücke von deutscher Wesensart wurden Amerika von den pietistischen Sekten vermittelt, die im 17. und 18. Jahrhundert in die Kolonien einwanderten. Die strikten religiösen Vorschriften, denen diese Gruppen sich unterwarfen, prägten auch ihren Lebensstil: Rustikale Einfachheit, unerschütterliches Gottvertrauen und redlicher Fleiß waren die Charakterzüge, durch die sie sich auszeichneten und die fortan den Deutschen zugeschrieben wurden. Blieben viele nationale Bräuche der Einwanderer ihren neuen Nachbarn auch unverständlich, so fanden doch der Weihnachtsbaum, sein festlicher Schmuck und das dazugehörige leckere Backwerk wie *lebkuche, sprengerle,* Pfeffernüsse und *matzebäume* schnell allgemeinen Beifall und darauffolgend weite Verbreitung. Ebenso der Weihnachtsmann, der aber erhebliche Veränderungen durchmachen mußte, ehe er als „Santa Claus" durch den Zeichenstift des deutschstämmigen Karikaturisten Thomas Nast seine heutige rundliche, pausbäckig-gutmütige Erscheinung erhielt. Daneben schuf Nast, der 1846 emigrierte, das einprägsame Bild des „Uncle Sam" sowie die Symbole der beiden großen Parteien: den Esel der Demokraten und den Elefanten der Republikaner.

„Besonders dem Einfluß der deutschen Einwanderer verdanken wir es", notierte Präsident Kennedy, „daß unser tägliches Leben von dem strengen und ernsten puritanischen Gepräge befreit wurde. Die Deutschen hielten zäh an ihren Vorstellungen vom ‚kontinentalen' Sonntag als einem Tag der Erholung, des Frühstücks im Grünen, des Familienbesuchs, des ruhigen und friedlichen Biertrinkens in einem Gartenlokal fest, bei dem man genüßlich der Musik einer Blaskapelle zuhören konnte." Solche Formen bürgerlicher Geselligkeit lernten die Amerikaner an den deutschen Einwanderern des 19. Jahrhunderts kennen, die darüberhinaus – als weitere Eigenart – ein reges Vereinsleben entfalteten: Überall im Lande be-

America received its first impressions of the German mentality from the members of the pietistic sects who emigrated to the Colonies in the 17th and 18th centuries. The strict religious observances practiced by these groups colored their whole life-style: rustic simplicity, unshakable faith in God, and industriousness were their outstanding characteristics, and these qualities were henceforth known as "German". Many national customs of the immigrants always remained a mystery to their neighbors, but there was one which quickly found acceptance all over – the Christmas tree with its festive decorations, including mouth-watering *lebkuche, sprengerle, pfeffernüsse,* and *matzebäume.* Father Christmas also became very popular, but he had to undergo quite a transformation before emerging from the pen of German-born caricaturist Thomas Nast as Santa Claus, of the round belly and rosy cheeks. Nast, who emigrated in 1846, also created the figure of Uncle Sam as well as the symbols of the two big political parties – the Democratic donkey and the Republican elephant.

President John F. Kennedy made an interesting cultural observation: "To the influence of the German immigrants in particular – although all minority groups contributed – we owe the mellowing of the austere Puritan imprint on our daily lives. The Puritans observed the Sabbath as a day of silence and solemnity. The Germans clung to their concept of the 'continental Sunday' as a day not only of churchgoing, but also of relaxation, of picnics, of visiting, of quiet drinking in beer gardens while listening to the music of a band." Americans learned about this kind of relaxation from the German immigrants of the 19th century. These people were also great 'joiners' – male choruses, athletic clubs, and hunting associations sprang up all over the country. These groups organized competitive events, which also provided the opportunity to get together and have a good

„Gemütlichkeit" in den USA: Deutscher Biergarten in New York im Jahre 1825.

The German Beer Garden in New York – one of many popular New York German eating establishments. The picture is dated 1825.

Ein bayrischer Biergarten wie er im Buche steht auf der Weltausstellung in Seattle 1964/65.

A Bavarian beer garden on the grounds of the Seattle World's Fair in 1964/65.

Kulinarischer Import aus dem Lande der „Krauts": Frankfurter und Bier bei Nathan's auf dem New Yorker Rummelplatz Coney Island.

"From a hot dog to a national habit" – this slogan has designated Nathan's establishment which grew from a simple frankfurter stand over the last fifty years to a huge establishment in New York's Coney Island. In Germany the Frankfurt sausage is protected by law and may not be made in any other city.

Das Bild könnte beim Kölner Karneval gemacht worden sein: ein „Funkenmariechen" bei der alljährlichen Steuben-Parade in New York.

The Steuben Parade takes place every year in New York City's German quarter, Yorktown, on the upper East Side.

Schwesterlich beieinander stehen die Bavaria und die Freiheitsstatue: Festwagen der Vereinigten Bayern von New York bei der Münchner 800-Jahrfeier 1958.

On the occasion of the 800th anniversary of the City of Munich, the United Bavarians of New York were part of the festive parade through downtown Munich. Their float bears mock-ups of both the statue of Bavaria and the Statue of Liberty.

Der aus Landau in der Pfalz eingewanderte Thomas Nast wurde als Zeichner des Familienjournals „Harper's Weekly" bekannt. Seiner spitzen Feder, die ihn zum gefürchtetsten Karikaturisten seiner Zeit machte, entstammen auch versöhnliche Figuren wie „Santa Claus" von 1886.

Santa Claus – a joint creation of poet Clement Clark Moore, who first mentioned the figure in his poem "The Night Before Christmas", and German-born artist Thomas Nast, who is best known for his biting political cartoons in the late 19th century.

Buffalo Bill prägte das Amerikabild der Deutschen nicht nur in Groschenheften, sondern auch durch die Tourneen seiner Wildwest-Show um die Jahrhundertwende. Gekrönte Häupter rechneten es sich zur Ehre an, in seinen nachgestellten Postkutschenüberfällen die Opfer zu spielen.

Buffalo Bill figures importantly in the American image as seen through German eyes. Initially made famous in pulp magazines, his popularity soared when he brought his Wild West Show to Europe at the turn of the century. Crowned heads were only too pleased to play the victims in his simulated stagecoach hold-ups.

gannen Männerchöre, Turnerriegen und Schützengilden Veranstaltungen zu organisieren, bei denen sie ihre Kräfte miteinander messen konnten und die reichlich Gelegenheit zu gemütlichem Treiben boten. Zu dieser Zeit trat auch das Bier, Motivation und Alibi der geselligen Lebensart, von den Zentren deutscher Einwanderung New York, St. Louis und Milwaukee aus seinen Siegeszug durch die ganzen Vereinigten Staaten an.

Neben diesem köstlichen Gerstensaft bereicherte die deutsche Küche den amerikanischen Speiseplan um eine Reihe von Gerichten, wie beispielsweise den Sauerbraten, die Bratwürste und das Sauerkraut, das sogar für den Spitznamen der Deutschen herangezogen wurde („Krauts"). Auch solche Spezialitäten wie der Rollmops, der Pumpernickel und eine spezifische Kuchenform, die *pie*, von der die Pennsylvania Dutch über 40 verschiedene Variationen entwickelten, entstammen deutschen Kochbüchern. Amerika revanchierte sich mit dem Puter – den Feinschmecker als die delikateste Entdeckung der Neuen Welt preisen –, dem knusprigen Mais, den saftigen fingerdicken Steaks und den in jüngster Zeit so allgegenwärtigen Hamburgern und Hot Dogs.

Wie das Deutschlandbild des Amerikaners durch die Romantik eines Alt-Heidelberg, die gesellige Gemütlichkeit eines Bier- oder Weingartens und die Urwüchsigkeit eines bayerischen Mannsbildes in Lederhosen geprägt bleibt, so sind aus dem Amerikabild des Deutschen die Indianer und Cowboys nicht mehr wegzudenken. Die Begeisterung für den „Wilden Westen" hat alle Generationen gleichermaßen erfaßt: Überall in der Bundesrepublik gibt es Vereine zur Pflege dieses Ausschnitts der amerikanischen Folklore. Alljährlich veranstalten sie Zeltlager, wo Väter neben Söhnen im Federschmuck oder in *buckskin* gekleidet zwischen Wigwams um Lagerfeuer herum sitzen und aufmerksam den *tall tales* aus der Zeit der großen Kämpfe lauschen.

time. It was at this time that beer, that close companion of leisure, began its triumphal march from New York, St. Louis, and Milwaukee (cities with large German populations) across the entire United States.

But this delicious 'barley brew' was not the only German contribution to American gastronomic life. To go with the beer there was, for example, sauerbraten or wurst, not to mention sauerkraut ('krauts' later became a nickname for Germans), pumpernickel bread, and for fish fanciers, "rollmops". And one must not forget the pie, of which the ingenious Pennsylvania Dutch concocted more than forty kinds. The Americans countered with the turkey, which gourmets consider the most delicious discovery of the New World; corn on the cob, thick juicy steaks, and the now universal hamburger and hot dog.

When an American thinks of Germany, he still sees, for the most part, romantic Old Heidelberg, sunny beer gardens, and earthy Bavarians in 'lederhosen'. Germans, on the other hand, cannot imagine America without cowboys and Indians. The Wild West appeals to all generations: throughout the Federal Republic, there are German associations working to preserve this chapter of American folklore. Every year they organize camps, where fathers and sons, wearing buckskin or feathered headdresses, sit in front of their 'tepees' around the campfire and listen attentively to tall tales of the great battles of yesteryear.

Rodeo in Nürnberg. US-Soldaten haben für dieses „Reiterspiel" viele deutsche Anhänger gefunden, wenn auch vorwiegend unter den Zuschauern.

Rodeo – this bit of cow punching is being performed for a German-American audience by G. I.s stationed at Nürnberg.

Albert Einstein (1879–1955) veröffentlicht die Relativitätstheorie.	**1905**	Albert Einstein (1879–1955) publishes his Theory of Relativity.
Friedensnobelpreis an Theodore Roosevelt (1858–1919) für die Vermittlung des russisch-japanischen Friedens 1905; Roosevelt besucht den Kaiser in Deutschland. Internationales Nachtarbeitsverbot für Frauen. In Heidelberg und Frankfurt tagt die erste internationale Konferenz für Krebsforschung.	**1906**	Nobel Peace Price to Theodore Roosevelt (1858–1919) for mediating the Russo-Japanese peace of 1905; Roosevelt visits the Kaiser in Germany. International prohibition of night work for women. The first International Conference for Cancer Research in Heidelberg and Frankfurt.
Heinrich Conried (1855–1909), Intendant der Metropolitan Opera, holt Gustav Mahler (1860–1911), den neuen Chefdirigenten der New Yorker Philharmoniker, als Gastdirigenten an die „Met". Gründung der amerikanischen Nachrichtenagentur UP (United Press).	**1907**	Heinrich Conried (1855–1909), head of the Metropolitan Opera, invites Gustav Mahler (1860–1911), the new Musical Director of the New York Philharmonic, to the "Met" as guest conductor. Foundation of North American news agency UP (United Press).
Sigmund Freud (1856–1939): *Charakter und Analerotik*, Beginn der tiefenpsychologischen Charakterlehre.	**1908**	Sigmund Freud (1856–1939): *Character and Anal Eroticism*. Beginning psychoanalytical character analysis.
In Hollywood wird das erste Filmatelier errichtet. Walter Gropius (1883–1969) baut in Alfeld die „Fagus-Fabrik".	**1911**	The first motion picture studio in Hollywood is opened. Walter Gropius (1883–1969) builds the "Fagus Fabrik" in Alfeld.
Thomas Woodrow Wilson (1856–1924) wird zum 28. Präsidenten der Union gewählt. Einführung der progressiven Einkommenssteuer (steigender Steuersatz bei steigendem Einkommen) in den USA. „Armory Show" in New York, Boston und Chicago: eine Ausstellung europäischer Malerei vom Fauvismus bis Kubismus. Hans Bredow (1879–1959) entwickelt in den USA ein Verfahren zur Musikübertragung durch Lautsprecher. Die Uraufführung von Igor Strawinskis (1882–1971) Ballett *Le Sacre du Printemps* löst in Paris einen Skandal aus.	**1913**	Thomas Woodrow Wilson (1856–1924) becomes 28th President of the U.S. Introduction of the progressive income tax (rising tax rate in accordance with rising income) in the U.S. "Armory Show" in New York, Boston and Chicago: an exhibition of European painting from fauvism to cubism. In the U.S., Hans Bredow (1879–1959) develops a method of reproducing music through a loudspeaker. The premiere of Igor Stravinsky's (1882–1971) ballet *Le Sacre du Printemps* causes a scandal in Paris.
Die Ermordung des österreichischen Thronfolgers durch serbische Offiziere wirkt als auslösendes Moment für den Ersten Weltkrieg. Nach Kriegserklärungen Österreichs, Deutschlands und Großbritanniens stehen sich Anfang August gegenüber: die Alliierten (Rußland, Frankreich, England) und die Mittelmächte Deutschland und Österreich. Nach Ablauf des Jahres endet der zunächst erfolgreiche Vorstoß deutscher Truppen nach Frankreich in einem Grabenkrieg. An der Ostfront gelingt es deutschen Truppen, den russischen Angriff auf Ostpreußen zurückzuschlagen. „German-American-Alliance": Massentreffen zur Resolution gegen die Teilnahme Amerikas am Krieg. Gründung des „American Field Service" zur Betreuung Verwundeter. Herbert Hoover (1874–1964) wird Leiter des Kriegsernährungshilfswerks für Europa.	**1914**	The assassination of the Austrian crown prince by a member of a Serbian terrorist society triggers the outbreak of World War I. After the declaration of war, in early August the Allies (Russia, France and England) are confronting the Central Powers, Germany and Austria. By the end of the year, the initially successful thrust of German troops into France has ground to a halt and trench warfare begins. On the Eastern Front, German troops succeed in repelling the Russian attack on East Prussia. "German-American-Alliance": Mass meeting for the purpose of a resolution against American participation in the war. Foundation of "American Field Service" for care of the wounded. Herbert Hoover (1874–1964) becomes head of the European War Relief Program.
Gründung weiterer amerikanischer Organisationen mit dem Ziel, die Neutralität der USA zu unterstützen. Hugo Junkers (1859–1935) konstruiert das erste Ganzmetallflugzeug. David Wark Griffith (1875–1948): *Die Geburt einer Nation*, Film über den amerikanischen Bürgerkrieg.	**1915**	Foundation of additional American organizations dedicated to uphold U.S. neutrality. Hugo Junkers (1859–1935) builds the first all-metal airplane. David Wark Griffith (1875–1948): *The Birth of a Nation*. Motion picture dealing with the American War between the States.
An der Westfront versuchen die Kriegsgegner nach den erfolglosen Offensiven des Vorjahrs einander durch Materialschlachten zu zermürben, doch bringen weder die Kämpfe bei Verdun (700.000 Tote) noch die alliierte Somme-Offensive (eine Million Tote) eine Entscheidung.	**1916**	On the Western Front, after none of the offensives of the preceding year succeeded in ending the stalemate, the adversaries try to wear each other down by massive expenditures of men and materiel. However, neither the fight for Verdun (700,000 dead) nor the Allied offensive on the Somme (one million dead) succeeds in bringing about a decision.
Zu Anfang des Jahres nimmt Deutschland den unbeschränkten U-Boot-Krieg gegen England auf. Daraufhin erklären die USA den Mittelmächten den Krieg. Schon im Sommer des Jahres nehmen die ersten amerikanischen Einheiten an den Offensiven der Alliierten gegen die deutschen Stellungen an der Westfront teil. Es bleibt jedoch beim militärischen Patt. In der russischen Oktoberrevolution gelangen die Bolschewiken unter Führung Lenins an die Macht; Rußland scheidet aus der Entente aus. Max Reinhardt (1873–1943), Hugo von Hofmannsthal (1874–1929) und Richard Strauss (1864–1949) begründen die Salzburger Festspiele.	**1917**	At the beginning of the year, Germany resumes unrestricted submarine warfare against England. The U.S. thereupon declares war against the Central Powers. By summer, the first American units are taking part in Allied attacks on German positions on the Western Front. The military stalemate, however, continues. During the October Revolution in Russia, the Bolsheviks under Lenin come to power. Russia withdraws from the Entente. Max Reinhardt (1873–1943), Hugo von Hofmannsthal (1874–1929) and Richard Strauss (1864–1949) found the Salzburg Festival.
Präsident Wilson gibt sein 14-Punkte-Friedensprogramm bekannt: Öffentlichkeit aller internationalen Vereinbarungen, Freiheit der Meere und des Welthandels, Rüstungsbeschränkungen, Gründung eines Völkerbundes als Garant unparteiischer Gerechtigkeit im Völkerleben. Die neue russische Regierung schließt einen Waffenstillstand mit den Mittelmächten. Im Westen beginnt die große deutsche Frühjahrsoffensive. Sie scheitert an der Materialüberlegenheit der Alliierten und dem Einsatz von amerikanischen Divisionen. Durch den alliierten Gegenangriff werden die deutschen Truppen endgültig in die Verteidigungsstellung gezwungen. Gegen Ende des Jahres ist ihre Lage hoffnungslos. Der deutsche Kaiser dankt ab, die Republik („Weimarer Republik") wird ausgerufen. Alle deutschen Fürsten danken ab. Am 11. November Unterzeichnung des Waffenstillstandes.	**1918**	President Wilson proclaims his 14-point peace program: No secret international agreements; freedom of the seas and of world trade, restrictions on armaments, foundation of a League of Nations as a guarantee of impartial justice in all dealings between nations. The new Russian government concludes an armistice with the Central Powers. In the West, the great German spring offensive starts but fails because of Allied superiority in regard to men (newly-arrived American divisions) and materiel. The Allied counter-attack ends with the Germans definitively on the defensive. Toward the end of the year, their situation is hopeless. The German Kaiser abdicates, the Republic ("Weimar Republic") is proclaimed. All German princes abdicate. On November 11, signing of the armistice.

Unter dem Vorsitz Frankreichs tritt in Versailles die Friedenskonferenz unter Teilnahme von 27 Staaten zusammen, Deutschland bleibt ausgeschlossen. Präsident Wilson kann sein 14-Punkte-Programm nicht zur Grundlage der Verhandlungen machen, einzig die Idee des Völkerbundes als Garant der auszuhandelnden Friedensbestimmungen wird aufgegriffen.

Die Bestimmungen des Versailler Friedens fallen auf Betreiben Frankreichs äußerst hart aus: Deutschland muß große Teile seines ehemaligen Staatsgebietes abtreten, darunter alle Gebiete links des Rheines an die Franzosen; es muß als Urheber des Krieges Reparationen für die Verluste und Schäden der Alliierten und eine Wiedergutmachung in Form von Sachwerten und Geldzahlungen leisten.

In Weimar tritt die Nationalversammlung zusammen und wählt Ebert zum ersten Reichspräsidenten. Die Weimarer Verfassung tritt in Kraft.

Nach dem Rücktritt der ersten Regierung der neuen Republik muß die neue Regierung den Versailler Friedensvertrag bedingungslos unterzeichnen. Die Alliierten hatten Verhandlungen über die Bestimmungen des Vertrags abgelehnt und mit dem Einmarsch in Deutschland gedroht, falls er nicht ratifiziert werde.

Gründung der Deutschen Arbeiterpartei, später NSDAP. In Weimar begründet Walter Gropius (1883–1969) das staatliche „Bauhaus".

Der Völkerbund (mit Sitz in Genf) tritt erstmals zusammen. Der amerikanische Kongreß lehnt den Beitritt mit der Begründung ab, der Bund sei zum Instrument der Siegermächte geworden; darüberhinaus verweigert der Kongreß die Ratifizierung des Versailler Vertrages. Durch den 18. Verfassungszusatz wird die Herstellung und der Vertrieb von Alkohol in den USA verboten (Prohibition), der 19. Zusatz erteilt den Frauen das Stimmrecht.

Auf der Konferenz von London werden die deutschen Reparationsleistungen auf 132 Milliarden Goldmark festgesetzt, zahlbar innerhalb von 37 Jahren: eine unter den gegebenen wirtschaftlichen Verhältnissen unrealistische und unerfüllbare Forderung, die primär durch Frankreichs Revanche-Gefühle diktiert wurde. Die Reparationen bleiben daher für die nächsten 10 Jahre das schmerzhafteste innenwie außenpolitische Problem der Weimarer Republik. Der Unmut, der sich bei weiten Teilen der Bevölkerung über die ständigen wirtschaftlichen Schwierigkeiten infolge der Reparationszahlungen ansammelt, richtet sich zunehmend gegen die Politiker, die das Versailler „Friedensdiktat" erfüllen müssen, und in der Folge auch generell gegen die Demokratie als Staatsform.

Die Vereinigten Staaten schließen einen separaten Friedensvertrag mit Deutschland.

In London wird der P.E.N. Club, eine internationale Schriftstellervereinigung, gegründet.

Eugene O'Neill (1888–1953): *Kaiser Jones*, wird uraufgeführt.

Richard Strauss dirigiert in New York eigene Werke.

Die 1911 gegründete Carl-Schurz-Austauschprofessur wird erneuert: der Kernphysiker Arnold Sommerfeld (1868–1951) lehrt in den USA; im kommenden Jahr folgen ihm viele amerikanische Physiker zum Studium nach München.

Die drahtlose Bildübertragung von Europa nach Amerika gelingt.

Hermann Hesse (1877–1962): *Siddharta*.

T. S. Eliot (1888–1965): *Das wüste Land*.

Sinclair Lewis (1885–1951): *Babbitt*.

Thomas Mann (1875–1955) hält in Berlin seine Rede *Von deutscher Republik*.

Friedrich Wilhelm Murnau (1899–1931) führt Regie bei *Nosferatu*.

Französische Truppen besetzen das Ruhrgebiet, Zentrum der deutschen Industrie, da Deutschland die Reparationszahlungen nicht in vollem Umfang leisten kann.

Arnold Schönberg (1874–1951) beginnt, die Zwölftontechnik systematisch anzuwenden.

Gründung der Carl-Duisberg-Gesellschaft.

Ministerialdirigent Dr. h. c. Edmund F. Dräcker (geboren 1888) heiratet Kate Barbara Silverworth-Smith, geschiedene Gräfin Itzenplitz-Kippenburg.

Der Dawes-Plan tritt in Kraft. Unter dem Vorsitz des amerikanischen Finanzmannes Charles Dawes (1865–1951) hat eine unabhängige Kommission die jährlichen Reparationsraten auf erträgliche 2,5 Milliarden Goldmark festgesetzt.

1919

Presided over by France, the peace conference starts at Versailles. 27 countries participate, Germany remains excluded. President Wilson does not succeed in making his 14-point program the basis of negotiations. Only the idea of a League of Nations which is to guarantee the peace to be negotiated is accepted.

France sees to it that the conditions of the Versailles Peace Treaty are extremely harsh: Germany has to cede large sections of its former territory, including all areas west of the Rhine, which are annexed by France; being held responsible for starting the war, Germany must also make reparations for losses and damages suffered by the Allies, payable in cash or in goods.

The National Assembly meets in Weimar and elects Ebert the first President of the Reich. The Weimar Constitution goes into effect.

After the first government of the Weimar Republic has resigned, the new government is obliged to sign the Versailles Peace Treaty unconditionally. The Allies had refused all negotiations in regard to the conditions of the treaty and threatened to invade Germany if it was not ratified.

Foundation of the German Workers' Party, later NSDAP.

In Weimar Walter Gropius (1883–1969) founds the state-supported "Bauhaus".

1920

The League of Nations (with headquarters in Geneva) meets for the first time. The Congress of the United States declines to join on the ground that the League had become an instrument of the victorious powers. Moreover, Congress refuses to ratify the Versailles Treaty.

By means of the 18th Amendment, the manufacture and sale of alcoholic beverages is prohibited in the U.S. (Prohibition), the 19th Amendment grants women the vote.

1921

During the London Conference, German reparations are fixed at 132 billion Gold Marks payable within 37 years, a demand both unrealistic and unfulfillable under existing economic conditions, and one which had been dictated primarily by France's desire for revenge. Thus the reparations remain for the next ten years the most painful foreign as well as domestic problem of the Weimar Republic. The resentment growing within the population because of the constant economic difficulties caused by the reparation payments is increasingly directed against the politicians who are obliged to fulfill the Versailles "peace dictates", and later against the democratic form of government itself.

The United States concludes a separate peace treaty with Germany.

In London, the P.E.N. Club, an international writers' association, is founded.

Premiere of *The Emperor Jones* by Eugene O'Neill (1888–1953).

Richard Strauss conducts his own compositions in New York.

The Carl Schurz exchange professorship, founded in 1911, is renewed: the nuclear physicist Arnold Sommerfeld (1868–1951) teaches in the U.S. The following year, numerous American physicists follow him to Germany to study in Munich.

1922

Successful wireless picture transmission from Europe to America.

Hermann Hesse (1877–1962): *Siddharta*.

T. S. Eliot (1888–1965): *The Waste Land*.

Sinclair Lewis (1885–1951): *Babbitt*.

Thomas Mann (1875–1955) makes his speech *Of the German Republic* in Berlin.

Friedrich Wilhelm Murnau (1899–1931) directs *Nosferatu*.

1923

French troops occupy the Ruhr, center of German industry, because Germany cannot make the reparation payments in full.

Arnold Schönberg (1874–1951) begins his systematic use of the twelve-tone technique.

Foundation of the Carl Duisberg Society.

Ministerialdirigent Dr. h. c. Edmund F. Dräcker (born 1888) marries Kate Barbara Silverworth-Smith, divorced Countess Itzenplitz-Kippenburg.

1924

The Dawes Plan comes into force. Presided over by the American financier Charles Dawes (1865–1951) an independent commission has set yearly reparation installments at a bearable 2.5 billion Gold Marks.

Nachdem Deutschland den Dawes-Plan anerkannt hat, räumen die Franzosen das Ruhrgebiet. Im Locarno-Vertrag verpflichten sich Frankreich und Deutschland, ihre seit 1919 bestehenden gemeinsamen Grenzen zu achten. *Goldrausch* von und mit Charlie Chaplin (geb. 1889). Das Bauhaus wird nach Dessau verlegt. F. Scott Fitzgerald (1896–1940): *Der große Gatsby*, bekanntester Roman des Jazz-Age. Franz Kafkas (1883–1924) *Der Prozeß* erscheint posthum, 2 Jahre später folgt der Roman *Amerika*. Der deutsche Dirigent und Komponist Wilhelm Furtwängler (1886–1954) ist während der Wintersaison Gastdirigent beim „New York Philharmonic Orchestra".	**1925**	After Germany has recognized the Dawes Plan, the French troops withdraw from the Ruhr. In the Treaty of Locarno, France and Germany pledge themselves to respect their common borders existing since 1919. *The Gold Rush* by and with Charlie Chaplin (b. 1889). The Bauhaus is moved to Dessau. *The Great Gatsby*, the best-known novel of the Jazz Age, by F. Scott Fitzgerald (1896–1940). *The Trial* by Franz Kafka (1883–1924) appears posthumously; two years later the novel *Amerika* follows. During the winter season, the German conductor and composer Wilhelm Furtwängler (1886–1954) is guest conductor of the New York Philharmonic Orchestra.
Aufnahme Deutschlands in den Völkerbund, bewirkt durch Gustav Stresemann (1878–1929). Gründung der Deutschen Lufthansa. Ernest Hemingway (1899–1961): *Fiesta*. Paul Whiteman gastiert in Deutschland.	**1926**	Germany joins the League of Nations, thanks to the efforts of Gustav Stresemann (1878–1929). Incorporation of the Deutsche Lufthansa. *The Sun Also Rises* by Ernest Hemingway (1899–1961). Paul Whiteman makes guest appearances in Germany.
Die Weltwirtschaftskonferenz in Genf empfiehlt die Liberalisierung der Weltwirtschaft. Erste überseeische Funksprechverbindungen. Charles A. Lindbergh (1902–1975) überquert im Alleinflug den Atlantik von New York nach Paris. Hermann Hesse: *Der Steppenwolf*; dieser Roman erlebt fast 40 Jahre später seine ‚Renaissance' in der amerikanischen Hippie-Bewegung. ‚Tarzan' Johnny Weißmüller schwimmt den Freistilweltrekord. Ernst Kreneks (geb. 1900) Jazz-Oper *Jonny spielt auf* wird in Leipzig uraufgeführt. Max Reinhardts „Deutsches Theater" gastiert in New York.	**1927**	The World Economics Conference in Geneva recommends liberalizing the world economy. First transatlantic radio telephone communications. Charles A. Lindbergh (1902–1975) crosses the Atlantic from New York to Paris in a solo flight. *Der Steppenwolf* by Hermann Hesse. Almost 40 years later, this novel experiences a renaissance through the American hippie movement. "Tarzan" Johnny Weissmuller sets a world record in free-style swimming. First performance in Leipzig of *Johnny Strikes up the Band*, Jazz Opera by Ernst Krenek (b. 1900). Guest appearance in New York of Max Reinhardt's "Deutsches Theater".
Der vom amerikanischen Außenminister Frank Kellogg (1856–1937) angeregte und nach ihm benannte Pakt wird von insgesamt 54 Staaten (bis Ende 1929) unterzeichnet. Er sieht die Ächtung des Krieges als Mittel internationaler Politik vor. General Motors übernimmt die Opel-Werke als AG.	**1928**	The Pact suggested by and named after the American Secretary of State Frank Kellogg (1856–1937) is signed by a total of 54 States (by the end of 1929). Its purpose is to outlaw war as a means of settling international differences. General Motors takes over the Opel Company.
Der Dawes-Plan wird durch den Young-Plan abgelöst. Unter dem Vorsitz des Amerikaners Owen Young (1874–1962) werden die jährlichen Reparationszahlungen auf 600 Millionen Mark festgesetzt. An der New Yorker Börse kommt es zum „Schwarzen Freitag": Der Zusammenbruch der Kurse eröffnet die Wirtschaftskrise in den USA; allgemeine Geldknappheit und als Folge Massenarbeitslosigkeit. Durch Vernachlässigung ihrer internationalen Zahlungsverpflichtungen durch die USA greift die Krise auf Europa über. Erich Maria Remarques (1898–1970) Kriegsroman *Im Westen nichts Neues* erscheint und ist bereits im selben Jahr Bestseller Nr. 1 in den USA. Der Tonfilm setzt sich allgemein durch.	**1929**	The Dawes Plan is superseded by the Young Plan. Under the chairmanship of the American Owen Young (1874–1962) the yearly reparation payments are fixed at 600 million Marks. "Black Friday" at the New York stock exchange. The collapse of the market touches off the Depression in the U.S.: An overall shortage of money and widespread unemployment prevail. Because of American balance of payment difficulties the crisis spreads to Europe. Erich Maria Remarque's (1898–1970) war novel *All Quiet on the Western Front* appears and becomes the year's best seller in the U.S. "Talkies" conquer the motion picture industry.
Die Wirtschaftsdepression trifft Deutschland mit aller Härte: viereinhalb Millionen Arbeitslose. Die Krise bringt den Nationalsozialisten unter Adolf Hitler einen großen Wahlerfolg. Frankreich zieht die letzten Besatzungstruppen aus dem Rheinland und Saargebiet ab. Befreiungsfeiern in diesen Gebieten. Gründung der Carl-Schurz-Gesellschaft in den USA.	**1930**	The Depression hits Germany hard: four and a half million unemployed. Due to the economic crisis, the National Socialists under Hitler do very well in the election. France pulls her last troops out of the Rhineland and the Saar; freedom celebrations in those areas. Foundation of the Carl Schurz Society in the U.S.
Bau des Empire State Buildings. Die Do X nimmt den Passagierverkehr auf und befördert 70 Personen nach New York. Georg Wilhelm Pabst (1885–1967) verfilmt die *Dreigroschenoper* von Bert Brecht (1898–1956) und Kurt Weill (1900–1950).	**1931**	The Empire State Building is completed and dedicated. The "Do X" starts passenger service and flies 70 persons to New York. Georg Wilhelm Pabst (1885–1967) makes a motion picture of the *Threepenny Opera* by Bert Brecht (1898–1956) and Kurt Weill (1900–1950).
Durch die Abmachungen der Konferenz von Lausanne wird das Problem der Reparationen endgültig aus der Welt geschafft: Deutschland zahlt eine abschließende Summe von 3 Milliarden Mark. Die Wirtschaftskrise hält unvermindert an. Erneuter Wahlsieg der Nationalsozialisten. Louis Armstrong gastiert in Deutschland. William Faulkner (1897–1962): *Licht im August*, Roman. Gründung des ersten Goethe Instituts in München.	**1932**	By means of agreements made during the Conference of Lausanne, the matter of reparations is finally settled: Germany makes a final payment of 3 billion Marks. The Depression continues. The National Socialists once more are successful at the polls. Louis Armstrong makes guest appearances in Germany. *Light in August*, a novel by William Faulkner (1897–1962). Foundation of the first Goethe Institute, Munich.

Adolf Hitler (1889–1945) wird Reichskanzler. Der Reichstagsbrand dient ihm zum Vorwand, kommunistische Politiker zu verhaften und die sozialistische Presse zu verbieten. Bei den Reichstagswahlen erhält Hitlers Partei wieder die meisten Stimmen und erringt in Koalition mit den Deutschnationalen die absolute Mehrheit im Parlament. Gegen die Stimmen der Sozialdemokraten verabschiedet der Reichstag das Ermächtigungsgesetz, das die gesetzgebende und -ausführende Gewalt in Hitlers Händen vereinigt. Ende der parlamentarischen Republik. Verbot und Auflösung der Parteien, stattdessen Einheitsstaat mit Einheitspartei. Ausschluß aller „Nicht-Arier" aus dem öffentlichen Dienst. Einrichtung von Konzentrationslagern für Gegner des Regimes. Auch in der Außenpolitik bahnt sich eine entscheidende Wende an: Deutschland verläßt die internationale Abrüstungskonferenz und tritt aus dem Völkerbund aus. Durch ihre Beschäftigung im Rahmen staatlicher Großprojekte (Bau von Repräsentativgebäuden und der Autobahnen) sinkt die Zahl der Arbeitslosen von 6 auf 4 Millionen. Ende der Wirtschaftskrise in Deutschland, die sich jedoch in den USA verschärft.

Franklin Delano Roosevelt (1882–1945) wird zum 32. Präsidenten der USA gewählt (Wiederwahl in den Jahren 1936, 1940, 1944). Er verkündet den nationalen Notstand und beginnt die Politik des „New Deal". Ziel ist die Schaffung einer stabilen sozialen Ordnung durch Weckung eines neuen Gemeinschaftsgefühls. Roosevelt sammelt einen kompetenten Beraterstab („brain trust") um sich. Glänzende Zusammenarbeit mit dem Kongreß bei Verabschiedung der Gesetze, die die Wirtschaftsdepression beenden sollen. Roosevelt führt bewußt Elemente staatlicher Wirtschaftsplanung ein: öffentliche Arbeitsbeschaffung, Aufsicht über die Banken, Produktionskontrollen in der Landwirtschaft. Im Zuge dieser Maßnahmen wird auch das gigantische Projekt zur Eindämmung des Tennessee River in Angriff genommen, das weite Teile der USA mit billigem Strom versorgen soll. Die Prohibition wird aufgehoben.

Beginn der Emigration deutscher Künstler und Intellektueller in die Vereinigten Staaten.

Fritz Langs (geb. 1890) Spielfilm *Das Testament des Dr. Mabuse* wird in Deutschland verboten.

Otto Klemperer wird Dirigent des philharmonischen Orchesters von Los Angeles.

Abwertung des Dollars um 40 % als weiterer Schritt zur Stabilisierung der Wirtschaft.

Nach dem Tod des Reichspräsidenten Hindenburg übernimmt Hitler auch dieses Amt.

In den USA wird John Dillinger vom FBI zur Strecke gebracht.

Henry Miller (geb. 1891): *Wendekreis des Krebses.*

Nürnberger Gesetze: Mischehen zwischen „Ariern" und Juden werden verboten, den Juden das Bürgerrecht genommen. Gesetz über den Aufbau einer Wehrmacht: Einführung der allgemeinen Wehrpflicht; Beginn der planmäßigen Aufrüstung.

Präsident Roosevelt verkündet sein 2. „New Deal"-Programm mit vornehmlich sozialen Reformen: Koalitionsrecht der Gewerkschaften und kollektive Lohnverhandlungen, Sozialversicherung und -fürsorge, Arbeitslosenunterstützung. Dazu kommt die Schaffung neuer Arbeitsplätze im Rahmen weiterer staatlicher Projekte.

In seiner Außenpolitik hatte sich Roosevelt bereits im Vorjahr um engere Zusammenarbeit mit den übrigen amerikanischen Staaten und um neutrale Haltung im Streit zwischen Bolivien und Paraguay bemüht. Dem folgt nun ein selbstauferlegtes Verbot der Waffenlieferung an kriegsführende Staaten und der Wirtschaftsboykott gegen sie. Roosevelt strebt Neutralität der USA in allen internationalen Konflikten an.

Olympische Spiele in Berlin.

Kündigung des Locarno-Paktes: deutsche Truppen besetzen das Rheinland.

Margaret Mitchell (1900–1949): *Vom Winde verweht.*

Verbot des „Deutschen Künstlerbundes"; Ausstellung „Entartete Kunst", eine nationalsozialistische Diffamierung moderner, vor allem abstrakter Kunstwerke und -strömungen.

Max Schmeling (geb. 1905) schlägt Joe Louis (geb. 1914) k.o.; Louis revanchiert sich 2 Jahre später.

Das im nationalsozialistischen Deutschland verbotene Bauhaus wird in Chicago unter der Leitung von Laszlo Moholy-Nagy (1895–1946) als „New Bauhaus" weitergeführt.

Carl Orff (geb. 1895): *Carmina Burana,* szenische Kantate nach mittelalterlichen Gedichten.

1933

Adolf Hitler (1889–1945) becomes Chancellor. The Reichstag Fire provides him with a pretext for arresting Communist politicians and prohibiting the publication of Socialist newspapers. Hitler's party again captures more votes than any other, and by means of a coalition with the German Nationalists attains the absolute majority in Parliament. Overriding the votes of the Social Democrats, the Reichstag passes the Enabling Act, which places the power of making as well as carrying out the laws in Hitler's hands: end of the parliamentary Republic; all parties dissolved and prohibited, in their place one party within one state; exclusion of all "non-Aryans" from Government posts; building of concentration camps for all enemies of the regime. In the field of foreign policy there are radical changes: Germany withdraws from the International Disarmament Conference and resigns from the League of Nations. Because of jobs created by large-scale, state-supported building projects (public buildings and autobahns), the number of unemployed is reduced from 6 million to 4 million. End of the Depression in Germany, which continues and worsens in the U.S.

Franklin Delano Roosevelt (1882–1945) becomes 32nd President of the U.S. (re-elected in 1936, 1940 and 1944). He declares a national emergency and introduces the "New Deal". His goal is to create a stable social order and awaken a new community spirit. Roosevelt calls upon competent counsellors ("the Brain Trust"). Excellent cooperation with Congress in passing laws which are to end the depression. He consciously introduces elements of economic planning by the state – creation of jobs, supervision of the banks, production controls in agriculture. Among the projects is the damming of the Tennessee River to bring inexpensive electric power to large parts of the U.S. Prohibition is repealed.

Start of the emigration of German artists and intellectuals to the U.S.

Fritz Lang's (b. 1890) motion picture *The Last Will of Dr. Mabuse* is banned in Germany.

Otto Klemperer becomes the conductor of the Los Angeles Philharmonic.

1934

Devaluation of the dollar by 40 per cent as a further step in stabilizing the economy.

After the death of President Hindenburg, Hitler takes over this office as well.

In the U.S., the FBI kills John Dillinger.

Tropic of Cancer by Henry Miller (b. 1891).

1935

Nuremberg Laws: Marriage between "Aryans" and Jews is prohibited, and Jews are deprived of their civil rights. A law referring to the formation of an army is passed: compulsory military service and methodical rearmament start.

President Roosevelt announces his second "New Deal" program which consists mainly of social reforms including coalition right and collective bargaining for unions, social security and insurance, and unemployment insurance. More new jobs are created by state-sponsored projects. In regard to foreign policy, Roosevelt has already worked toward closer cooperation with other American countries during the previous year and has maintained a neutral stance in the dispute between Bolivia and Paraguay.

This is now followed by a self-imposed embargo on the sale of arms to belligerent states and an economic boycott. Roosevelt's goal is to maintain the neutrality of the U.S. in all international conflicts.

1936

Olympic Games in Berlin.

Renunciation of the Locarno Pact: German troops occupy the Rhineland.

Gone with the Wind by Margaret Mitchell (1900–1949).

Prohibition of the German Society of Artists. Exhibition of "Degenerate Art", a national-socialist defamation of modern, primarily abstract trends and works of art.

1937

Max Schmeling (b. 1905) knocks out Joe Louis (b. 1914). Louis retaliates two years later.

The Bauhaus, prohibited in National Socialist Germany, is carried on in Chicago as the "New Bauhaus" under the guidance of Laszlo Moholy-Nagy (1895–1946).

Carmina Burana, a scenic cantata by Carl Orff (b. 1895), based on medieval poems.

Einmarsch der deutschen Wehrmacht in Österreich, das an das Deutsche Reich angeschlossen wird. Auf der Münchner Konferenz, zu der sich die Vertreter Deutschlands, Italiens, Frankreichs und Englands treffen, wird die Abtretung des Sudetenlands geregelt.
9. November: Beginn der offenen Judenverfolgung in Deutschland (sogenannte „Reichskristallnacht").
Die USA beginnen mit einer vorsorglichen Aufrüstung.
Otto Hahn (1879–1968) und Fritz Straßmann (geb. 1902) entdecken die Kernspaltung.

Einmarsch deutscher Truppen in Böhmen und Mähren. Das Gebiet wird Reichsprotektorat. Premierminister Chamberlain, der an den Münchner Verhandlungen teilnahm, erklärt das Ende der englischen Stillhalte-Politik. In fast allen europäischen Staaten werden Kriegsvorbereitungen getroffen. Militärbündnis zwischen Deutschland und Italien. Englische und französische Garantien für Polen. Nicht-Angriffspakt zwischen Rußland und Deutschland.
1. September: Deutsche Truppen dringen in Polen ein.
England und Frankreich erklären am 3. September den Krieg. Nach der Kapitulation Warschaus wird der größte Teil Polens deutsches Generalgouvernement.
Amerika gibt seine Neutralität auf und verkauft Waffen an England. Mißglücktes Bombenattentat auf Hitler im Münchner Bürgerbräukeller.
Ernst Heinkel (1888–1958) entwickelt das Düsenflugzeug.
John Steinbeck (1902–1968): *Früchte des Zorns*, im folgenden Jahr von John Ford (1895–1973) verfilmt.

Deutschland besetzt Norwegen und Dänemark, Belgien und Holland. Angriff auf Frankreich. Italien tritt auf der Seite Deutschlands in den Krieg ein. Nach siegreichem Vordringen in Nordfrankreich kampflose Besetzung von Paris. Waffenstillstand mit Frankreich. Beginn der deutschen Bombardierung Englands. Deutschland und Italien verbünden sich mit Japan im Dreimächtepakt. In Amerika nimmt der „Nationale Verteidigungsrat" seine Arbeit auf: Beschleunigung des Aufrüstungsprogramms.
Thomas Wolfe (1900–1938): *Es führt kein Weg zurück*, Schilderung seiner Eindrücke aus dem nationalsozialistischen Deutschland bei den olympischen Spielen 1936, erscheint posthum.
Der große Diktator: Hitlerpersiflage von und mit Charlie Chaplin.
Fantasia von Walt Disney (1901–1966), amerikanischer Zeichentrickfilm nach klassischer Musik.

Deutsche Truppen fallen am 22. Juni in Rußland ein. Deutschland führt einen Zweifrontenkrieg. Militärpakt zwischen Rußland und England.
Das Leih- und Pachtgesetz ermächtigt den amerikanischen Präsidenten, auswärtige Staaten nach eigenem Ermessen mit Kriegsgütern zu unterstützen. Rußland erhält den ersten Milliardenkredit.
Die Japaner greifen Pearl Harbor am 7. Dezember an und vernichten amerikanische Kriegsschiffe. Die USA erklären Japan den Krieg, daraufhin erfolgt am 11. Dezember die Kriegserklärung von Deutschland und Italien an die USA.
Das deutsche Soldatenlied „Lily Marleen" wird populär.
Orson Welles (geb. 1915) dreht *Citizen Kane*.
Roosevelt und Churchill verkünden die „Atlantik-Charta": Meinungs- und Religionsfreiheit, Freiheit von Not und Furcht, Selbstbestimmung aller Völker, gleicher Zugang zu den Rohstoffquellen und dauernder Friede werden als Kriegsziele definiert.
2. 12. 1942, 15.30 Chicagoer Zeit: Enrico Fermi (1901–1954) macht die fortlaufende Erzeugung von Atomenergie durch Kettenreaktion der Uranspaltung möglich: Beginn des Atomzeitalters.
Durch die Niederlage in der Schlacht um Stalingrad am 31. Januar gerät die deutsche Ostfront in Bedrängnis. Sie weicht vor der russischen Gegenoffensive immer weiter nach Westen zurück. In Teheran beschließen Roosevelt, Stalin und Churchill die Errichtung einer neuen Front in Frankreich.
Casablanca, Konferenz zwischen Roosevelt und Churchill: Forderung der bedingungslosen Übergabe Deutschlands. Verstärkte Luftoffensive der Alliierten gegen Deutschland und seine Verbündeten.

1938	The German army marches into Austria, which is incorporated into the German Reich. At Munich, where representatives of Germany, Italy, France and England meet, the surrender of the Sudetenland is agreed upon. November 9: Start of open persecution of the Jews in Germany (so-called "Reichskristallnacht", "Crystal Night"). The U.S. begins precautionary rearmament. Otto Hahn (1879–1968) and Fritz Strassmann (b. 1902) discover nuclear fission.
1939	German troops march into Bohemia and Moravia which are declared protectorates of the Reich. Prime Minister Chamberlain, who had attended the negotiations in Munich, proclaims the end of England's appeasement policy. Preparation for war begins in nearly all European states. Military alliance between Germany and Italy. British and French guarantees on behalf of Poland. Non-aggression pact between Russia and Germany. September 1: German troops march into Poland. England and France declare war on September 3. After the capitulation of Warsaw, the larger part of Poland is administrated by the German General Staff. America abandons its neutrality and openly sells arms to Britain. Failure of an attempt to assassinate Hitler by means of a bomb in the Bürgerbräu-Keller in Munich. Ernst Heinkel (1888–1958) develops the jet plane. *Grapes of Wrath* by John Steinbeck (1902–1968). Made into a motion picture the following year by John Ford (1895–1973).
1940	Germany occupies Norway and Denmark, Belgium and Holland. Invasion of France. Italy enters the war on the side of Germany. After a victorious advance in Northern France, Paris is occupied without resistance. Start of the German air raids on England. Germany and Italy ally themselves with Japan in the Three Power Pact. In America, the "National Defense Council" starts its work: acceleration of the rearmament program. *You Can't Go Home Again* by Thomas Wolfe (1900–1938): His impressions of Nazi Germany on occasion of the Olympic Games in 1936 are published posthumously. *The Great Dictator*, a spoof on Hitler by and with Charlie Chaplin. *Fantasia* by Walt Disney (1901–1966). American cartoon feature as an accompaniment to classical music.
1941	German troops invade Russia on June 22. Germany is now fighting on two fronts. Military alliance between England and Russia. The Lend-Lease Act empowers the president of the U.S. to aid foreign states by supplying them with arms. Russia is granted its first one-billion dollars in credit. The Japanese attack Pearl Harbor on December 7, destroying American battleships. The U.S. declares war on Japan, whereupon Germany and Italy declare war on the U.S. on December 11. The German soldiers' song "Lili Marleen" becomes popular. Orson Welles (b. 1915) creates *Citizen Kane*. Roosevelt and Churchill proclaim the "Atlantic Charter": freedom of speech and of religion, freedom from want, and freedom from fear. Self-determination for all peoples, equal access to raw materials and lasting peace are declared to be the goal of the war.
1942	December 2, 1942, 3:30 P.M. Chicago time. Enrico Fermi (1901–1954) succeeds in generating continuous atomic energy through chain reaction: Beginning of the Atomic Age.
1943	After the defeat at the Battle of Stalingrad, January 31, the German Eastern Front is imperiled. It continues its retreat to the West before the Russian counter-offensive. In Teheran, Roosevelt, Stalin and Churchill decide on the establishment of another front in France. Casablanca: Roosevelt and Churchill confer. Demand of unconditional surrender on the part of Germany. Allied air raids on Germany and its allies are stepped up.

6. Juni: Nach planmäßiger Konzentration von Material und Truppen beginnen die Alliierten die Invasion in der Normandie. Innerhalb von drei Monaten gelingt es ihnen, unter dem Schutz von 10.000 Flugzeugen und mit intensiver Unterstützung durch Marineeinheiten mehr als 2,5 Millionen Soldaten und 4 Millionen Tonnen Kriegsmaterial an Land zu bringen. Die deutschen Truppen weichen zurück.
20. Juli: Ein Bombenattentat deutscher Offiziere auf Hitler mißlingt. Erster Einsatz der V-Waffen: V 1 am 14. 6., V 2 am 6. 9.
Franz Werfels (1890–1945) *Jakobowski und der Oberst* wird in New York uraufgeführt.

Während russische Verbände die Weichsel überschreiten, erreichen amerikanische Einheiten den Rhein. Sowjetische Truppen erobern Berlin (2. Mai). Hitler begeht Selbstmord. Bei Torgau an der Elbe treffen sich die vorgeschobenen Armeespitzen der Russen und Amerikaner.
Generaloberst Alfred Jodl unterzeichnet die bedingungslose Kapitulation am 7. Mai in Reims im Hauptquartier des amerikanischen Oberkommandierenden General Eisenhower.
Zur Sicherung des Weltfriedens gründen in San Francisco 51 Staaten die UNO.
Nach dem Abwurf von amerikanischen Atombomben über Hiroshima und Nagasaki (6. und 9. August) kapituliert auch die japanische Armee.
In Potsdam bei Berlin setzen die Regierungschefs der Siegermächte (Truman als Nachfolger des im April verstorbenen Präsidenten Roosevelt, Stalin, Churchill) ihre Verhandlungen über die zukünftige Deutschlandpolitik fort, die sie auf der Konferenz von Jalta im Frühjahr begonnen hatten. Sie beschließen die Entwaffnung und Entmilitarisierung Deutschlands, planmäßige Entnazifizierung, Prozesse gegen Kriegsverbrecher, Einrichtung demokratischer Selbstverwaltung. Zunächst wird Deutschland jedoch in 4 Besatzungszonen aufgeteilt und durch einen alliierten Kontrollrat verwaltet.
Beginn der Nürnberger Kriegsverbrecherprozesse gegen 21 ehemals hohe Regierungsbeamte des Naziregimes und Generäle der Wehrmacht.
Die *Frankfurter Rundschau* wird als erste große deutsche Nachkriegszeitung lizensiert.

In den Besatzungszonen finden die ersten Wahlen statt. Parlamentarische Vertretungen arbeiten Länderverfassungen aus und wählen Regierungen.
Umfangreiche humanitäre Hilfe setzt ein: Gründung der CARE-Organisation: Versendung von Geschenkpaketen an bedürftige Familien.
Gründung der Fulbright-Commission.
Die Serienproduktion des Volkswagens wird aufgenommen.
Carl Zuckmayer (geb. 1896): *Des Teufels General*, Drama über die Problematik des Widerstandes im Krieg.

Außenministerkonferenz in Moskau. Uneinigkeit der Siegermächte in der Frage deutscher Reparationen. Rußland fordert Zahlungen in Höhe von 10 Milliarden Dollar. Die Westmächte wollen auf solche Leistungen verzichten, damit Deutschland möglichst bald von wirtschaftlicher Hilfe unabhängig wird. Der amerikanische Außenminister Marshall legt den nach ihm benannten Plan einer Wirtschaftshilfe für Europa vor; die Sowjetunion lehnt ihn ab.
Doppelzonenabkommen zwischen der amerikanischen und der britischen Zone in Deutschland.
Thomas Mann (1875–1955) veröffentlicht *Dr. Faustus*.
Bert Brecht inszeniert in Los Angeles eine Neufassung von *Leben des Galilei* mit Charles Laughton (1899–1962) in der Hauptrolle.
Im Horizontalflug wird erstmals die Überschallgeschwindigkeit erreicht.

Der Marshall-Plan (eigentl. „European Recovery Program") wird durch den amerikanischen Kongreß verabschiedet: für einen Zeitraum von vier Jahren erhalten 16 westeuropäische Staaten Warenlieferungen, Geldanleihen und Schenkungen, um ihre Produktion anzukurbeln und sie wieder zu wirtschaftlicher Selbständigkeit zu führen. Auf Druck Moskaus treten die Staaten Osteuropas dem Programm nicht bei. Die Spannungen zwischen Moskau und Washington nehmen ständig zu. Beginn der Ära des „Kalten Krieges": Berlin-Blockade durch sowjetische Truppen. Berlin wird durch die alliierte Luftbrücke versorgt. In Bonn tritt der parlamentarische Rat mit der Aufgabe zusammen, eine Verfassung auszuarbeiten.

1944

June 6. After months of preparation, the Allies invade Normandy. Within three months, under cover of 10,000 planes and supported by the Navy, more than 2.5 million men and 4 million tons of materiel are landed. The German troops fall back.
July 20. Failure of a bomb plot against Hitler by German officers.
First use of the V weapons: V1 on June 14, V2 on September 6.
Jacobowsky and the Colonel by Franz Werfel (1890–1945) is first performed in New York.

1945

While Russian troops cross the Vistula, the Americans reach the Rhine. Soviet troops take Berlin (May 2). Suicide of Hitler. Advance guards of the Russian and American armies meet at Torgau, on the Elbe.
General Alfred Jodl signs the Unconditional Surrender in Reims on May 7, at the headquarters of the American Commander-in-Chief, General Eisenhower.
In order to safeguard world peace, 51 states join in founding the UNO in San Francisco.
After atom bombs have been dropped on Hiroshima and Nagasaki (August 6 and 9), the Japanese army also surrenders.
At Potsdam near Berlin, the Heads of Government of the victorious allies (Truman as successor of Roosevelt, who had died in April, Stalin, Churchill) continue their negotiations on the future of Germany, which had begun at Yalta in the spring. They decide on the disarmament and demilitarization of Germany, methodical denazification, trial of war criminals, establishment of democratic self-government. For the time being, however, Germany is divided into 4 zones of occupation and administrated by an Allied Control Council.
Beginning of the Nuremberg War Criminal Trials of 21 former high officials of the Nazi regime and generals of the German army.
The *Frankfurter Rundschau* is licensed as the first major German postwar newspaper.

1946

The first elections take place in the occupied zones. Parliamentary representatives draft constitutions and elect governments.
Extensive humanitarian aid begins: Founding of the CARE organization. Sending of gift packages to needy families.
Founding of the Fulbright Commission.
Mass production of the Volkswagen begins.
The Devil's General by Carl Zuckmayer (b. 1896), a play on the problems of the Resistance during the war.

1947

Conference of foreign ministers in Moscow. Disagreement of the victorious allies as to the question of German reparations. Russia demands payments amounting to 10 billion dollars. The western powers are willing to renounce all such claims in order to make Germany independent of economic aid. The American Secretary of State, Marshall, submits his plan for economic aid to Europe; the plan (known as the "Marshall Plan" after its creator) is turned down by the Soviet Union.
Bizonal agreements between the British and American zones in Germany.
Publication of *Dr. Faustus* by Thomas Mann (1875–1955).
Bert Brecht directs a new version of the *Life of Galileo* in Los Angeles. In the title role: Charles Laughton (1899–1962).
First breaking of the sound barrier during horizontal flight.

1948

The Marshall Plan (officially the "European Recovery Program") is ratified by Congress. During a period of four years, 16 Western European countries will receive shipments of merchandise, loans and gifts in order to stimulate their production and assist them in becoming economically independent. Due to pressure on the part of Moscow, the Eastern European states do not take part in the program. Increased tension between Moscow and Washington. Start of the era of the Cold War.
Blockade of Berlin by Soviet troops. Berlin is supplied by the Allied "Big Lift".
In Bonn, the Parliamentary Council meets for the purpose of drafting a constitution.

Währungsreform als Auftakt des wirtschaftlichen Wiederaufbaus.
Freie Universität Berlin aus studentischer Initiative mit amerikanischen Geldern gegründet.
Norman Mailer (geb. 1923): *Die Nackten und die Toten*, amerikanischer Kriegsroman.
In München eröffnet die „American Library".

Im Zuge der militärischen Sicherung Westeuropas gegen einen möglichen Angriff der Sowjetunion gründen die USA, Kanada und 10 europäische Staaten das Nordatlantische Verteidigungsbündnis (NATO): Die USA sichern jedem Teilnehmer individuelle Rüstungshilfe zu. Durch die Verabschiedung des Grundgesetzes durch die Länderparlamente entsteht aus der amerikanischen, englischen und französischen Besatzungszone die Bundesrepublik Deutschland als freiheitlich-demokratischer Rechtsstaat mit der Hauptstadt Bonn. Aus der russischen Besatzungszone geht die Deutsche Demokratische Republik als sozialistische Volksdemokratie hervor.
Nach den ersten freien Wahlen zum Bonner Bundestag wird Konrad Adenauer (1876–1967) 1. Bundeskanzler. Als ersten völkerrechtlichen Akt schließt die Bundesrepublik einen Vertrag mit den USA über den Beitritt zum Marshall-Plan ab.
Die Vereinigten Staaten unterstützen im Rahmen der UNO Südkorea gegen die militärische Invasion aus Nordkorea.
Theodor Heuss (1884–1963) wird erster Bundespräsident der BRD.
In Frankfurt findet die erste Buchmesse nach dem Krieg statt.
Die Universität Maryland nimmt ihren Lehrbetrieb in Europa auf.
Arthur Miller (geb. 1915): *Tod eines Handlungsreisenden*.

Aufhebung der Lebensmittelrationierung in der BRD.
Das Ballett *Das Zeitalter der Angst* von Leonard Bernstein (geb. 1918) und Jerome Robbins (geb. 1918) nach W. H. Auden (1907–1974) wird in New York uraufgeführt.

Die Westmächte beenden offiziell den Kriegszustand mit Deutschland.
Rußland gibt eine solche Erklärung erst 1955 ab.
Aufnahme der BRD in den Europarat und in die Europäische Gemeinschaft für Kohle und Stahl.

Die Westmächte schließen mit der Bundesrepublik den Deutschland- oder Generalvertrag ab: er sieht die Integration Westdeutschlands als gleichberechtigten Partner in die Europäische Gemeinschaft vor.
Die letzten Produktionsbeschränkungen für die deutsche Wirtschaft aus dem Besatzungsstatut werden hinfällig. Wiedergutmachungsvertrag mit Israel: Die Bundesrepublik zahlt 14,5 Milliarden Mark an den Staat Israel und die jüdischen Weltverbände.
Wiederbegründung des Goethe Instituts.
Fred Zinnemann (geb. 1907) dreht *Zwölf Uhr mittags (High Noon)*.

Der Koreakrieg endet durch Verhandlungsfrieden.

Ellis Island, seit 1892 Durchgangslager der amerikanischen Immigranten, wird geschlossen: Zeichen für das Ende der Masseneinwanderung.

Die Bundesrepublik tritt der NATO bei. Die Westmächte stimmen einer Wiederbewaffnung Westdeutschlands zu. Damit ist die Souveränität der Bundesrepublik in vollem Umfang hergestellt. Aufnahme diplomatischer Beziehungen zwischen der Sowjetunion und der BRD.
Bau des UNESCO-Gebäudes in Paris.
Uraufführung von Charles Ives (1874–1954) *IV. Symphonie*, geschrieben zwischen 1910 und 1916.
Die Mitgliedsstaaten der Montanunion (Deutschland, Frankreich, Italien und die Benelux-Länder) gründen in Rom die Europäische Wirtschaftsgemeinschaft (EWG) mit Sitz in Brüssel. Sie ist gedacht als erster Schritt zu einer wirtschaftlichen und politischen Einheit Europas.
Durch Einsatz von Bundestruppen erzwingt Präsident Eisenhower die Einschulung von Negerkindern in Little Rock/Arkansas und damit Erfüllung einer Entscheidung des Obersten Gerichtshofes zur Integration des Schulsystems. Beginn der Bürgerrechtsbewegung um die Gleichstellung der Schwarzen in der amerikanischen Gesellschaft.
Start von Sputnik 1.
West Side Story, Musical von Leonard Bernstein, in New York uraufgeführt.

1949

Currency reform as the first step toward German economic reconstruction. The Free University at Berlin is founded through the initiative of students, the necessary money supplied by the U.S.
The Naked and the Dead, American war novel by Norman Mailer (b. 1923).
Opening of the "American Library" in Munich.

In order to create a military safeguard to protect Western Europe against possible agression on the part of the Soviet Union, the U.S., Canada and 10 European States found the North Atlantic Treaty Organization (NATO). The U.S. guarantees each partner individual aid for rearmament. By means of the ratification of the Basic Law (Grundgesetz) by the parliaments of the individual states, the American, British and French zones of occupation are joined together to form the Federal Republic of Germany, a free and democratic constitutional state with Bonn as its capital. The Russian zone of occupation becomes the German Democratic Republic, a socialist people's republic.
As a result of the first free elections of the Bundestag in Bonn, Konrad Adenauer (1876–1967) becomes the first chancellor of the new federation. The Federal Republic's first action as an independent nation is the signing of a treaty with the U.S. by which it joins the Marshall Plan.
According to the statutes of the United Nations, the United States supports South Korea against the military invasion of North Korea.
Theodor Heuss (1884–1963) becomes the first President of the FRG.
The first postwar Book Fair in Frankfurt a. M.
The University of Maryland starts its European teaching program.
Death of a Salesman by Arthur Miller (b. 1915).

1950

End of food rationing in the FRG.
The ballet "The Age of Anxiety" by Leonard Bernstein (b. 1918) and Jerome Robbins (b. 1918), based on W. H. Auden (1907–1974), is first performed in New York.

1951

The Western Powers officially terminate the State of War with Germany. Russia does not make any such proclamation until 1955.
The FRG is admitted to the European Council and the European Association for Coal and Steel.

1952

The Western Powers and the FRG conclude the German or General Agreement: it provides for the acceptance of Germany as a full partner in the European community. The last restrictions on German production based on the statutes of occupation expire. Restitution Agreement with Israel: the FRG pays 14.5 billion Marks to the State of Israel and to the world-wide Jewish agencies.
Re-establishment of the Goethe Institute.
Fred Zinnemann (b. 1907) directs *High Noon*.

1953

Over two years of peace talks lead to the end of the Korean War.

1954

Ellis Island, American Immigration Center since 1892, is closed, marking the end of the period of mass immigration to the United States.

1955

The Federal Republic of Germany formally becomes a member of NATO. The western powers permit rearmament of West Germany, which is the last step in restoring full sovereignty to the FRG. Establishment of diplomatic relations between the FRG and the USSR.

1956

Construction of the UNESCO Building in Paris.
Charles Ives (1874–1954): Premiere of the *Fourth Symphony*, written between 1910 and 1916.

1957

In Rome, the member nations of the Montan-Union (France, Italy, West Germany, and the Benelux Countries) found the European Economic Community (EEC) with headquarters in Brussels. It is meant as a first step toward an economically and politically united Europe.

To enforce the decision of the Supreme Court to insure integration of the school system, President Eisenhower dispatches federal troops to Little Rock, Arkansas. Beginning of the modern civil rights movement for racial equality.
Launching of Sputnik I.
Premiere of *West Side Story* by Leonard Bernstein.

John Cage (geb. 1912) bei den Darmstädter Ferienkursen für Neue Musik.

Günter Grass (geb. 1927): *Die Blechtrommel*.

documenta II in Kassel; im Zentrum der Ausstellung stehen die Werke der neuen amerikanischen Malerei: „action painting" (Jackson Pollock, Robert Motherwell, Franz Kline); „color field painting" (Mark Rothko, Barnet Newman); „pop art" (Robert Rauschenberg, Jasper Johns).

John F. Kennedy (1917–1963) wird 35. amerikanischer Präsident. Nach dem Vorbild Präsident F. D. Roosevelts umgibt er sich mit einer Gruppe intellektueller Berater. Er verkündet ein Programm der „Neuen Grenzen": Erhöhung des Bildungsetats, Schaffung eines Ministeriums für Städtefragen, Steuerreform. Der Kongreß verhindert die Verabschiedung der Gesetzesvorlagen.
Höhepunkt der seit 1958 andauernden Berlinkrise. Am 13. August Bau der Mauer.
Erste Erdumkreisung eines amerikanischen Astronauten (John H. Glenn).
Beginn regelmäßiger Devisenausgleichsabkommen zwischen den Vereinigten Staaten und der Bundesrepublik Deutschland.

My Fair Lady, Musical von Lerner und Loewe, 1956 in New York uraufgeführt, steht in der BRD an erster Stelle in der Aufführungsstatistik musikalischer Werke.

Atomteststopp-Abkommen zwischen Amerika, England und Rußland: Verbot von Atomversuchen über der Erde und unter Wasser. Damit erstmals nach Kriegsende wieder direkte Ostwestverhandlungen. Beendigung des „Kalten Krieges". Die Ära der Entspannungspolitik zwischen Ost und West beginnt.
Bei seinem Deutschlandbesuch triumphaler Empfang für Präsident Kennedy in Berlin.
22. November: Ermordung Kennedys in Dallas/Texas. Vizepräsident Lyndon B. Johnson (1908–1973) wird sein Nachfolger.
Konrad Adenauer tritt vom Kanzleramt zurück, das er seit 1949 ohne Unterbrechung bekleidet hatte.
Aaron Copland (geb. 1900) komponiert ein Auftragsballett für die Eröffnungswoche des Münchner Nationaltheaters.

Präsident Johnson, durch seinen überwältigenden Wahlerfolg im Amt bestätigt, führt die Politik seines Vorgängers erfolgreich weiter: Verabschiedung des Bürgerrechtsgesetzes, das die Registrierung von schwarzen Wählern vereinfacht. Höhepunkt der Bürgerrechtsbewegung. „Krieg gegen die Armut": unter diesem Programm werden große Summen zur Verbesserung der Lage unterprivilegierter Schichten bereitgestellt. Erhöhung des Bildungsetats. Der Präsident nimmt den Zwischenfall in der Bucht von Tonkin zum Anlaß, die amerikanische Truppenstärke in Vietnam drastisch zu erhöhen.

Jahrestagung der „Gruppe 47" in Princeton.

Präsident Johnson kommt zu Adenauers Begräbnis nach Deutschland.
Der farbige Bürgerrechtskämpfer Martin Luther King (geb. 1929) wird in Memphis/Tennessee erschossen, Robert Kennedy (geb. 1925) ereilt im Wahlkampf in Los Angeles das gleiche Schicksal. Infolge des wachsenden Widerstandes gegen seine Vietnam-Politik verzichtet Präsident Johnson auf die Bewerbung um seine Wiederwahl.
Peter Weiss (geb. 1916): *Vietnam-Diskurs* in Deutschland uraufgeführt.
documenta IV in Kassel: Pop-Art und „New Abstraction". Unter anderen stellen Andy Warhol (geb. 1928) und Roy Lichtenstein (geb. 1923) aus.

Der neue amerikanische Präsident Richard M. Nixon (geb. 1913) beginnt seine Amtszeit mit einem Programm der Ostwestentspannung („Ära der Verhandlungen"): Sein Besuch in Rumänien ist die erste Visite eines amerikanischen Präsidenten in einem kommunistisch-regierten Land seit 1945.
Die Bundestagswahl bringt eine entscheidende Wende in der deutschen Nachkriegsgeschichte: Die CDU, die 20 Jahre lang die Regierungsverantwortung getragen hatte, wird von einer Koalition aus SPD und FDP abgelöst. Mit Willy Brandt (geb. 1913) wird seit 1930 erstmals wieder ein Sozialdemokrat Regierungschef. Er bemüht sich vorrangig um eine Verständigung mit den Staaten Osteuropas („Bonner Ostpolitik").

1958 John Cage (b. 1912) participates in the festival of contemporary music at Darmstadt.

1959 Günter Grass (b. 1927): *The Tin Drum*.
Exhibited in the "documenta II" in Kassel are: Robert Motherwell, Franz Kline, Jackson Pollock ("action painting"); Barnet Newman, Mark Rothko ("color field painting"); and Jasper Johns, Robert Rauschenberg ("pop art") among others.

1961 John F. Kennedy (1917–1963) becomes 35th President of the United States. Following the example of President F. D. Roosevelt, he assembles a group of outstanding advisors. He proposes his "New Frontier" to increase funds for education, to create a department for urban problems and to implement tax reforms. Congress blocks passage of the bills.
The crisis in Berlin since 1958 reaches a climax on August 13, when East Germany begins construction of the Berlin Wall.
Beginning of the German-American Offset-Agreement to share in the costs of stationing U.S. troops in Germany.
John H. Glenn, the first U.S. astronaut to orbit earth in a space capsule.

1962 The 1956 musical *My Fair Lady* by Lerner and Loewe is the most performed musical stage work in West Germany.

1963 Treaty to ban underwater and atmospheric nuclear testing signed by the U.S., Great Britain and the Soviet Union. First direct East-West negotiations since the end of World War II. Termination of the Cold War. Relaxation of tensions between East and West.
President Kennedy's trip to Germany: triumphant reception in Berlin.
November 22: President Kennedy assassinated in Dallas. He is succeeded by Vice President Lyndon B. Johnson (1908–1973).
Konrad Adenauer leaves the office he had held uninterruptedly since 1949.
Premiere of a ballet by Aaron Copland (b. 1900), commissioned for the festival week of the reopening of the National Theater in Munich.

1964 After his landslide election, President Johnson successfully carries on the policies of his predecessor. Passage of civil rights legislation facilitating registration of Black voters. Highpoint of the Civil Rights Movement. The "War on Poverty": the mobilizing of funds to improve the situation of the underprivileged. Increase of the federal budget for education.
The Tonkin Gulf incident: the alleged North Vietnamese attack on an American destroyer in international waters leads to a drastic increase in American troop strength in Vietnam.

1966 The German organization of authors "Gruppe 47" holds its annual meeting in Princeton.

1967 President Johnson comes to Germany to attend Adenauer's funeral.

1968 The Black civil rights leader Martin Luther King (b. 1929) is assassinated in Memphis, Tennessee. Robert Kennedy (b. 1925) is shot while campaigning in Los Angeles.
President Johnson decides not to seek reelection, in light of the general resistance to his policies in Vietnam.
Premiere of *Vietnam Discourse* in Germany, by Peter Weiss (b. 1916). "documenta IV" in Kassel: Pop-Art and "New Abstraction". The exhibition includes works by Andy Warhol (b. 1928) and Roy Lichtenstein (b. 1923).

1969 The new American President, Richard M. Nixon (b. 1913), begins his term of office with a program to relax East-West tensions. His trip to Rumania is the first visit since 1945 of an American president to a communist-ruled country.
The election in the Bundestag marks a decisive change in postwar German history; the CDU, which had held power for 20 years, is displaced by a coalition of SPD and FDP. Willy Brandt (b. 1913) becomes the first Social Democratic Head of Government since 1930. He primarily attempts to reach an understanding with the states of Eastern Europe ("Bonner Ostpolitik").